The Home Fronts
of Iowa, 1939–1945

THE HOME FRONTS

of Iowa, 1939–1945

Lisa L. Ossian

UNIVERSITY OF MISSOURI PRESS
COLUMBIA

University of Missouri Press, Columbia, Missouri 65211
Printed and bound in the United States of America

First paperback printing, 2018

ISBN 978–0–8262–2176–6 (paperback : alk. paper)

Library of Congress Cataloging-in-Publication Data

Ossian, Lisa L., 1962–
The home fronts of Iowa, 1939–1945 / Lisa L. Ossian.
p. cm.
Includes bibliographical references and index.
ISBN 978–0–8262–1856–8 (hardcover : alk. paper)
1. World War, 1939–1945—Iowa. 2. World War, 1939–1945—Social aspects—Iowa. 3. Iowa—History—20th century. 4. Iowa—Social conditions—20th century. I. Title.
D769.85.I8O86 2009
977.7'032—dc22
2009028085

∞™ This paper meets the requirements of the American National Standard for Permanence of Paper for Printed Library Materials, Z39.48, 1984.

Jacket design: Kristie Lee
Page design and composition: Jennifer Cropp
Typefaces: Minion, Mona Lisa, and Bickham Script

The University of Missouri Press gratefully acknowledges the support of The State Historical Society, Inc., of Iowa City, Iowa, in the publication of this book.

To my own home fronts—

my daughters Bailey, Nellie & Brita

Contents

Preface

The war changed everything except human needs and desires.

—William O'Neill, *A Democracy at War* (1993)

How does one begin to write about the complexities surrounding World War II? This war, as John Keegan so succinctly states in the foreword to his extensive study of it, is the largest single event in human history. The war involved six of seven continents and all the oceans; it killed fifty million people and wounded countless others. Historians have examined numerous pieces of the puzzle within this massive event, but not the state of Iowa and its citizens' reactions and contributions. Iowa, as one small piece of the world, experienced much of the drama and heartache of this war despite the state's physical distance from the areas of combat and destruction.

Most American World War II histories of domestic involvement have focused on paid industrial work and have been organized chronologically or by topics such as patriotism and discrimination, and an unequal depiction of the home-front activities has often resulted. In my attempt to produce a more broad-ranging account, my research of the Iowa home front branched into an analysis of four separate fronts: farm, production, community, and kitchen. All were historic terms used throughout the war years.

This divided examination of the home front provides a clearer picture of the nonmilitary work as well as the rhetoric surrounding American citizens' involvement in the war effort as deemed necessary by the federal government. Through this analysis, I have attempted to answer the following question: how did Iowans so quickly transform their relatively isolationist perspective regarding involvement in this threatening world conflict into an overwhelmingly enthusiastic attitude, which they sustained throughout the war effort? In other words, how did Iowans so swiftly convert from reluctant, skeptical citizens to very energetic soldiers? By answering this question, I hope to gain a different perspective concerning another, more general historical question: why has World War II been so consistently remembered as "the good war"?

In essence, American citizens became soldiers in this total world-war effort. The concept of a soldier sometimes involves combat, but it also encompasses the ideas of service, sacrifice, risk, and duty. Every American (every man, woman, and child) was encouraged to remember, at all times, the war effort because every citizen as soldier played a necessary part. America as a nation ill prepared for war needed drastic and dramatic contributions from its citizens in war production, yet it also needed to cling to its democratic ideals.

Citizens became soldiers fighting on one or more of the four home fronts to support the war effort. Their work, whether paid or volunteer, needed to be organized with effective leadership, but, above all, it had to be a voluntary commitment, since America had to fight differently than did the fascist nations. Otherwise, this second world war, another war based on democracy but now framed by President Franklin Roosevelt's "Four Freedoms," would be only a wasteful sham, with its sacrifices made in vain.

Iowa serves as an interesting place to study this transformation from citizen to soldier for two reasons. First, since it is located in the center of the United States, the state was removed from the possibly threatened coasts, and second, like other residents of this supposed isolationist region, many Iowans resisted another involvement in European wars. Iowa was also historically Republican. Though Iowa as a state cast its electoral votes for Franklin Roosevelt in 1932 and 1936, it turned away from the president in 1940 and 1944. In short, Iowa hardly seemed like a potentially enthusiastic or committed area for supporting this conflict against the Axis powers. If Iowans transformed into energetic soldiers for the war effort, other states surely would as well.

My study has necessarily taken a less traditional route. I have relied for factual and numerical information on standard primary sources such as census records, state publications, agricultural yearbooks, and industrial reports, along with newspaper accounts, but I have also paid particular attention to the advertisements, speeches, editorials, advice columns, oral histories, travelogues, poems, paintings, photographs, posters, songs, recipes, letters, diaries, radio broadcasts, movies, novels, short stories, cartoons, scrapbooks, yearbooks, memorials, and memoirs from this era. From the information in this variety of sources, I have tried to condense the rhetoric and emotion of the war effort in Iowa. In trying to capture this emotional content from historical sources, I have striven to better understand why Iowans so overwhelmingly supported this war effort. People's actions are so often based on their feelings surrounding an event; World War II would be no different, despite its complexity.

Acknowledgments

"I hate war" is one quotation engraved on a wall at the Franklin Delano Roosevelt Memorial in Washington, D.C. I read those words just days before this book was completed, reminding me of poignant and powerful phrases. Sometimes it is the simplest words that are the most necessary, capturing the strongest and deepest of meanings. At the end of this book's process, it now seems to me that the most necessary phrases from those closest to me can best capture my deepest thanks and praise.

My parents, Susan and Roger Ossian, have been both the rock and the pressure needed to create my education. Mom always provided the constancy—supper at six and weekly library visits—that children need to create and explore, and she never let us complain too much about anything. "Buck up," she still says, and that phrase has carried me through many a tough academic day. Dad has always been very good with the needed words "You can do it." He first took me to the Iowa State University Library when I was eight and remembers my wanting, at the age of ten, to write "big books." Also, whenever things in life have gone slightly or dramatically off course, another motivating statement from Dad has been "Turn it to your advantage."

My brothers, Daniel and Roger Jr., have been my constant companions. As kids, we spent many hours outside exploring and often playing war. Perhaps my interest in military history began there—with the army jackets and canteens slung over our young frames as we ran and waded through the fields. My brothers' encouraging words were often "Let's go . . ."

My three daughters—Bailey, Nellie, and Brita (their births spanning a twelve-year range) have kept me reasonably busy, somewhat sane, and always grounded in the present. Motherhood's constant duties of meals and laundry and school only renewed my sympathy for all the World War II mothers who had to function under much more difficult circumstances. My daughters have sacrificed as well for my work; my oldest daughter still reminds me of the dot-matrix printer's shriek in our living room as it churned out yet another draft. Sometimes they've asked, "Why do you have to write a book?" but at other times I've heard them telling their friends, "My mom is writing a book." Over the years, the most urgent call from my daughters has always reminded me of what is truly important—varying in its intensity by the added number of syllables: "M-o-m."

A very big thank you certainly goes to Dr. Dorothy Schwieder, my major professor for the dissertation that became this book. In fact, she was the one to suggest the topic of Iowa during the Second World War. "No one has explored it," she said. But mostly Dorothy (took me a long time to finally call her by her first name) kept after me with her gently persistent, dedicated belief that I must complete the work. I still remember her saying, "I'll get you through this."

Another big thank you goes to my professor and friend Dr. Kathleen Hickok. I first enrolled in her women's literature course when I was only nineteen years old, and she remembers my telling her later in the semester that I wanted "to do what she does." Kathy has always, somehow, believed in my potential—even when I was not a very promising student who didn't talk or write very much. Her patient smile, kind words—especially her often-repeated phrase "You're good at that," and numerous recommendation letters have carried me through.

I received research support in the form of two dissertation grants from the private State Historical Society, Inc., at the beginning of this process. Their wonderful phrase contained within two acceptance letters was "the enclosed check" (certainly a lovely encouragement for a beginning historian).

I must mention the public library and the coffee shop (Espresso Yourself) at Winterset where I found the needed resources and refuge to work. Every librarian at the small town library—particularly Sally Morris—was always very polite at receiving yet another request for an interlibrary loan, simply answering with the phrase "I'll get this right in." And Rita Drysdale, previous owner of the coffee shop, always knew a cup of coffee with cream and a quiet table at which to work was "my usual."

Michael Vogt, my friend and curator at the Iowa Gold Star Military Museum, never once tired of talking about the Second World War or suggesting yet another source. Not only does he always provide a "yes" to a conversation, but he has never said "no" when I've asked him several times (along with his wonderful wife, Maggie Harlow-Vogt) to help me move, a mark of true friendship. He simply begins yet another long history talk with the phrase "You know . . ."

And at the end, I need to especially thank Mike Pearson, who shared my exciting news when the University of Missouri Press accepted my book for publication. As I tried to explain the long process to my new friend, he simply summed it all up: "Determined indeed." And when I needed the final fact-checking library visits or just the plain emotional encouragement to complete the work, what meant the world was Mike's smile, along with "you bet" or "sounds good."

And so to all my other family, friends, and colleagues who have helped and encouraged me along the way, after all these hours and days researching and writing, the words can be condensed to one simple but necessary phrase: "thank you."

The Home Fronts
of Iowa, 1939–1945

Introduction

Her heart turned over: how could there be this ridiculous talk of war when little boys in all countries collected stones, dodged cleaning their teeth, and hated cauliflower?

—Jan Struther, *Mrs. Miniver* (1940)

"Iowa," a journalist wrote in early 1940, "is in a piece of pie at the potluck dinner given by the Ladies' Aid Society at Pleasant Hill Methodist Church." Iowans liked to describe themselves in such simple terms, as fair, helpful, democratic, generous, simple, almost quaint. The writer continued, "There's plenty to eat at the Pleasant Hill Potluck Dinners. There are more than 60 people at the dinner this noon. They take their loaded trays, with a cup of dark and steaming coffee, and sit around the room beneath the temperance posters."[1] This was Iowa at its typical best before the war, consisting of comfort, caring, and consensus.

Phil Stong, in a widely read "state biography" published in 1940 titled *Hawkeyes,* also described the state's citizens in terms of food, as "good, rich, Iowa mayonnaise." Stong believed Iowans belonged to "a good and practical land" and that they had settled in "an integrated and sympathetic society."[2] These popular images of the greatest food-producing spot in the world illustrated an idealized Iowa, yet Iowa was much more than a potluck.

The years before the war were certainly confusing ones for Iowa's citizens, as they were for the rest of the world. In many ways, 1940 was "the catch year." Farmers were caught within increasing government involvement and their dependence on it, along with added mechanization, yet they still embraced an agrarianism of the past. Laborers were caught within a fear of losing status and control in a mechanized world short on resources yet yearned for respectability, stable jobs, and strong unions. Merchants were caught within enlarging marketing areas and specialization yet longed for the power and simplicity of the Main Street of the past. Employed women and housewives were caught within increasing responsibilities and independence along with expanding paid and volunteer work roles yet were unsure of their futures because, as historian Susan M. Hartmann describes, the perceived role for women was still as wives and mothers, and married women remained responsible for the physical and psychological maintenance of the home. Hartmann calls this emphasis on the sanctity of the home "the unshaken claim of the family."[3]

Iowa's people before the war seemed to be caught within their social and economic circles; they were not yet able to move forward to the complex modern world brought on by the approaching total and technological war, nor were they able to move back in time, thought, or action to their pleasant ideological pasts. "What lay ahead was not simply another war," historian Richard Ketchum notes. "It was a global revolution, and when it was over—no matter how it turned out—the possibility existed that there would be no turning back to the tried and true, to the good old days we had known before the Depression." Iowan Henry A. Wallace had also concluded in 1940, "The good old days are not coming back. We are going on into a new world with a determined will to make it a better one."[4]

Families would serve in this new world in large numbers, both before and during the Second World War. By November 1940, six brothers from the Patten family of Odebolt, Iowa, were serving on the battleship *Nevada* in the same section, the boiler division. Gilbert, Allen, Ray, Clarence, Marvin, and Bruce Patten received assignments to the same ship after obtaining special permission, and before their volunteer enlistment they playfully posed for a photo spelling their last name in semaphore figures. Two other Patten boys, Ted and Bick, were still waiting to pass the age requirements for enlistment at that time. In late 1940, George and Frank Sullivan of Waterloo, from another large family, approached the end of four years of duty in the navy and were stationed on a destroyer in Pearl Harbor.[5]

The Pattens and the Sullivans were just two of the many American families filled with worries, wishes, and fears that these young men would need much more than luck in this volatile world fast approaching what would be the most devastating war ever.

Prelude to War ~ 1939

The storm clouds of war rumbled and roared, threatened and thundered during the later years of the 1930s. The tension of possible turmoil proved to be an almost intolerable prelude. When and where would war begin? At the end of August 1939, the *Des Moines Register* editors posed this question: "But if war does come, what should our purpose be?" The editors suggested three major precepts—to stay out of the fighting, to preserve our free institutions, and to avoid a war boom. The editorial noted that "the horribleness of slaughter" should be reason enough to stay out of the European entanglement, but in addition, American isolation or elevation above the conflict "might contribute a powerful mediating force." Mostly, the dread of another Great War with its disturbing destruction and death as well as economic and political collapse caused what was arguably a pretense of belief in neutrality. "Once we got in, we should lose our balance like the others," reminded the *Register.* "We did the last time."[6]

On September 1, 1939, the Nazi blitzkrieg blasted Poland, with German planes bombing and tanks invading that land. War had once again exploded within the world on possibly a massive scale. What now? How would citizens from the United States respond? Americans, in answer to a public-opinion poll that very day, sided with Poland. And former president Herbert Hoover, the only president born in Iowa, declared that day to be "one of the saddest days that has come to humanity in 100 years." Hoover, the humanitarian who had saved millions of lives through his international famine-relief efforts after World War I, deeply understood war's horrors. "A senseless war seems inevitably forced upon hundreds of millions of people," Hoover warned fellow Americans. "It means the killing of millions of the best and most courageous of men who might contribute to human progress. It means the killing and starvation of millions of women and children." Other Iowans also worried about the world's children. Conrad Lander from the small town of Briston listened long to the radio that fateful first day of blitzkrieg, saying that he "felt sorry for the common people." "If we just now could be wise enough and little enough in God's sight," Lander thought, "how blessed for us and our children."[7]

That September day *Des Moines Register* employees posted bulletins of the dreaded fighting outside their building. "It's a damn shame to have to do the whole thing over again," one passerby commented. "If they had cleaned it up right the last time, we wouldn't have to go through it now." Most female pedestrians kept on walking past the city building, not stopping to read the glaring headline "WAR!" Some Iowans simply felt compelled to reminisce about the tragedies of the last world war. An elevator operator described the general mood of workers that day: "People ain't takin' it too happy but there ain't anything they can do about it. They're gonna have to go on with it just the same." A stenographer also seemed to sum up the feelings of the day, commenting, "It makes me shudder. I can remember the last one too well."[8]

Although public opinion sided with Poland, Americans still remained evenly divided about whether to enter this war; only the South polled 60 percent in favor of war. The Midwest, despite later myths of it as an isolationist center, did not distinguish itself with a larger percentage of isolationist opinion at the beginning of Europe's war, nor even by the Pearl Harbor attack. Midwestern residents, as did all Americans, expressed various concerns as they wondered what to do in this war and which side to take, if any. "This nation will remain a neutral nation," President Franklin D. Roosevelt declared in his Fireside Chat shortly after the Nazi invasion. "But, I cannot ask that every American remain neutral in thought as well. . . . Even a neutral cannot be asked to close his mind or close his conscience."[9]

During the next week, one journalist gathered several poetic statements of Iowans' varied reactions to the beginning of distant war:

> "War in Europe is reverberating in the peaceful cities and towns and cornlands of Iowa."
>
> "Farm wives turn the magneto crank on the telephone and talk to their neighbors of war."
>
> "Men in overalls, sitting around the general store, speculate on death in Poland."

"The price of sugar is up. A Communist meeting in Des Moines is broken up. . . . Europe is at war."[10]

Other Iowans reacted with far less reflection, like the pranksters who hung from a Mississippi River bridge an effigy labeled "Hitler the Rat." Emotions stayed up, moods stayed down. War seemed both distant and immediate. By October, only 5 percent of Americans believed the United States should declare war on Germany. What to do? Praying and working seemed possible answers to this burning question. During a Columbus Day peace rally, a thousand Catholic children attended peace rites and offered prayers. One woman emphatically noted that mothers should remember the Great War and those soldiers who had not come home. "Don't be timid," Alice Omans advised, "but let your tears stream over your faces as you work as we did in those terrible years."[11]

Precepts of Isolationism—1940

During the confusing summer of 1940, two actors costumed as Nazis received thirty cents an hour to promote a movie titled *I Married a Nazi,* and the pair almost caused a riot in downtown Des Moines. Playing the fascist roles perfectly, the muscular young men theatrically clicked the heels of their black leather boots as they marched from Walnut to Locust Street. Some girls giggled at the sight, and one drunken man thought they were police officers and tried to ask directions, but several other men and women started to gather on the street with "blood in their eyes." "It's a pretty bum gag," one man muttered. Another yelled out his threat: "If you walk two blocks more in those uniforms, I'll take 'em off." A Nazi invasion, while highly unlikely in the Midwest, still seemed faintly plausible as a few Iowans' extreme fears emerged on that moody, humid August afternoon. Iowans could not escape depictions of approaching war (real or imagined), and even the Iowa State Fair displayed a large pictorial exhibit of the European War that summer to show "the horrors of present war."[12]

Most Americans still remembered the last world war all too well and did not want to enter this brewing conflict if at all possible—but this resistance to war did not necessarily equal a simple isolationism. The myth of midwestern isolationism has persisted throughout the sixty years since the end of the Second World War along with a general misperception of isolationism—that it was merely a cowardly, stubborn refusal to face the cold hard facts of world war. Rather, isolationism can be defined in several ways. Some historians have explained that isolationism, at times, represented a consideration of world tensions rather than just a reflexive avoidance of conflict. Qualms concerning the Great War's destruction, worries regarding the Great Depression's ramifications, and questions about Great Britain's vulnerabilities colored the context of the complex concept of isolationism. In other words, isolationists expressed legitimate concerns about the last world war and its futility as well as the present-day economic depression and its dilemmas. Isolationism, at times, presented very tangible and logical, as well as emotional, reasons to avoid participation in a global conflict that would almost certainly prove very costly in money and especially in lives. Isolationists in all parts of the country continued to ask whether anything could possibly be gained from voluntary entry into another world war.

Historian David Kennedy captures within a single sentence this complex essence of isolationism and much of its nuance. "Isolationism may have been more pronounced in the landlocked Midwest," Kennedy maintains, "but Americans of both sexes, of all ages, religions, and political persuasions, from all ethnic groups and all regions, shared in the postwar years of feeling apathy toward Europe, not to mention the rest of the wretchedly quarrelsome world, that bordered on disgust."[13] Isolationism was an overwhelming desire to stay out—to save time, money, grief, and lives. But fears, responsibilities, and commitments continued to billow and rage in the stormy winds as the escalating tension began to bludgeon Americans. War talk transformed eventually over the fateful years 1940 and 1941 into action as the march of violent and invasive global events continued, drawing and coercing the United States and its citizens more and more into the Second World War.

The ideas contained within isolationism, as historian Manfred Jonas outlines, remained credible. "What set isolationists apart from other Americans," Jonas explains, "was not fear of war per se—since that was to some degree a universal fear—nor unwillingness to tackle the major political and economic problems that were troublesome here and abroad." Jonas theorizes that isolationism, though not a fully developed political philosophy, did not base itself on "ignorance and folly" but rather became "a considered response of the small town residents and farmers who often had a distrust of Europe along with a fear of the big city and the big corporation." Jonas also maintains that isolationists, even though the United States no longer benefited from the geographic protection of two oceans because of military and technological advances, still wanted to work out world problems independently.[14]

When the Nazis invaded Denmark and Norway in April 1940, and then the Netherlands and Belgium in May, and France in June, the severe course of world events began to seriously rock the isolationist base. Americans' defensive instincts sharply increased as Paris dramatically fell. The Committee to Defend America by Aiding the Allies organized its initial membership that month and, despite its roundabout mission, formed over three hundred chapters by the end of the year, with chapters in every state except North Dakota (where the nation's leading isolationist, Senator Gerald Nye, resided). William Allen White, as committee chair and a Kansas newspaper editor, insisted that his organization run a full-page advertisement in newspapers across the country, and an ad appeared in both the *Des Moines Register* and the *Des Moines Tribune* with the screaming headline "STOP HITLER NOW!" The copy explained the committee's position: "We can help—if we will act now—before it is forever too late. We can help by sending planes, guns, munitions, food. We can help to end the fear that American boys will fight and die in another Flanders, closer to home."[15]

Paranoia also surfaced in a small Iowa town the month that France surrendered to the Nazis when a German music professor at Luther College received a large painted swastika and question mark on his front door, dripping blood red. Other Iowa commentary, far more thoughtful though still expressive of fears, emerged in texts such as Paul Lichtenstein's brief letter to the editor of the *Des Moines Register.* "Christianity is the foundation of peace and contentment," Lichtenstein argued. "War is hell. Let's keep out of it." And some Iowans worried about social issues, such as a continued racism in their own country. Would black soldiers, for example, also be fighting for a new world at home? "When they come back from another war," Iowan Laurence Lobbins wondered, "will they still be denied the right to vote, the right to jobs and the right to freedom in the land of the free?"[16]

Six prominent Iowans decided to take action against what they considered a pretense of legitimate isolationism by sending a telegram to

President Roosevelt on Thursday, June 13, "urging that the United States Navy go to the aid of the Allies, even if that step means a declaration of war by this nation." These internationalist Iowans also sent telegram copies to Roosevelt's cabinet, Iowa's congressmen, and the Committee to Aid France and England. As former Iowa attorney general George Cosson declared when he signed his name to the telegram, "This is the most important time in history in the last 2,000 years."[17]

A year after the invasion of Poland, the deeply isolationist America First Committee formed on September 4, 1940, with Chicago as its headquarters. America First eventually enlisted 800,000 members and cited these four guiding principles: rearm the country as Fortress America, consider no foreign invasion a possibility, believe in the essence of American democracy, and continue to contend that the president's policies weaken America's defense. "This is the policy of the America First Committee today," the group's most famous spokesman, Colonel Charles Lindbergh, explained. "It is a policy not of isolation, but of independence; not of defeat, but of courage."[18]

And on September 16, 1940, the first peacetime conscription in the history of the United States (under the Burke-Wadsworth Act) began its bureaucratic business. Across the country more than sixteen million men registered for the draft, including 375,000 of Iowa's men, of whom 281,456 were ultimately eligible to be drafted. During the national draft-number drawing near the end of October, tense excitement filled the autumnal air as corn huskers stopped work to gather near radios and young businessmen surrounded bulletin-board postings to learn their fate. The president drew the first number: 158. Only two of the seven Polk County men who held that draft number were unmarried and therefore eligible for the military's initial role call, barring any physical problems. Military officials continued to call draft numbers throughout the day as this federal attempt to create order out of chaos began. From October 1940 to March 1941, approximately 2,680 Iowa men received the draft selection letter with its traditional salutation, "Greetings."[19]

War edged closer. Older Iowa mothers reflected on their sons' possible sacrifices, hoping the United States would be better prepared by establishing its armed forces early. "It's the only thing to do," a woman who gave her name as Mrs. Lawrence Fulke told the *Des Moines Tribune*, "to build up a defense, a powerful defense which will keep us out of war." Another mother, Sophie Rissman, offered her opinion: "I believe all mothers should be against conscription. We don't want war. We have had one—and yet I'm afraid there are many boys who would want to fight." And younger women wondered aloud as well. "I wouldn't vote for war now," answered Ruth Olmstead, a twenty-eight-year-old secretary, "but it might be a good thing if we went to war against Hitler today." And Alee Earl, a twenty-year-old stenographer, remarked, "I think the draft will keep us out of war, though, and we want to keep out."[20]

"We may go into the valley of death—we may lose this democracy," wrote the president of the Iowa Parent-Teacher Organization, Millicent Lincoln. "We have sent our sons to register for the draft, to prepare our country's defense. Shall we not consecrate ourselves to a democratic way of life at home?" Overall, U.S. voters favored conscription two to one, even during this presidential-election year, and 58 percent of Iowans approved the draft measure. In fact, a majority of every state's citizens favored conscription.[21] War now seemed not only possible but probable.

Another group formed in September 1940—the Iowa Industrial and Defense Commission—with powerful members from Iowa labor unions and coal mines as well as from the Farm Bureau and the Grange, along with John Deere Company administrators and members of the Manufacturers' Association. This diverse collection of representatives gathered in Governor George Wilson's office one fall morning, and he outlined their mission: "The fundamental precept must be based upon one of national cooperation." The governor also noted that the commission would "continue all deliberations upon a plan of unselfishness and working toward the welfare of both the state and the nation." The commission faithfully met monthly until shortly after Pearl Harbor with a varied agenda of action on corn-alcohol production, emergency medical services, tire rationing, and Civilian Defense Committees.[22]

The 1940 presidential-election campaign alleviated some of the war tension with the idea that the country's democratic institutions would carry on despite exterior circumstances, but of course, war talk dominated election politics. By October, Wendell Willkie's Republican supporters across the country had prioritized the reasons for their political support. Most Republican voters and some Democrats opposed a third term for Roosevelt based simply on principle and past practice, that is, they believed presidents should not serve more than two terms. Others believed the country desperately needed a change. A third reason was voters' negative reactions to New Deal legislation and its perceived excess spending. Willkie was a successful businessman, many Republican voters believed, who could lead this country more efficiently. But the biggest reason was the belief that President Roosevelt would get the country into war. "My vote goes to Willkie for the one promise he gives us," declared Davenport resident E. Marxen, "to keep our boys out of the shambles of the European wars. I would rather be poor than live high on our boys' blood money."[23]

The presidential election in November 1940 certainly stirred up more dust amidst these storm clouds of war. Although a majority of Iowa voters had selected Franklin Roosevelt in 1932 and again in 1936, which way would this historically Republican state go in 1940? For some Iowans, the last eight years of the New Deal had proven too much—a boondoggle of too much excess government and too much wasted money, but in this election Roosevelt had Henry Wallace as his running mate. Wallace had been editor of the popular family farm journal *Wallaces' Farmer* before serving as secretary of agriculture for the first two terms of Roosevelt's tenure. In addition to the prospect of having Wallace as vice president, some Iowans favored Roosevelt because they thought the Agricultural Adjustment Act (AAA) had saved many Iowa farmers from a terrible crisis, but the economic talk eventually turned to war. Could Roosevelt keep us out? Would he lead us through? Or was he directing this country to ruin?

Dallas County rural residents, typical of other Iowans, answered these questions in various ways. A seventeen-year-old farm boy named Howard Bell admitted that his family did not discuss politics at his house but still believed he would cast his vote for Willkie because Roosevelt did not deserve a third term and would only get the country into the war. Roy Meadows, a forty-six-year-old farmer, answered the political question more decisively, "I'm for Roosevelt because I'm a farmer and I think he has helped the farmer." Although Meadows acknowledged that he had been a Republican all his life, he concluded, "I vote for the man, not the ticket." Tom Mash, a farmer in his mid-forties, believed the two candidates did not offer enough of a difference in those difficult times, but his wife believed strongly that it was a poor time to change presidents. As she stated, "In ordinary times, two terms would be enough for any man." And then she concluded her independent statement by pointing out, "You can see my husband doesn't influence me."[24]

The issue of war remained paramount, and changing presidents even during an approaching war seemed risky and unnecessary. Farmers, never a terribly unified political group, certainly remained individualistic that fall. When a reporter polled Dallas County farmers, one seventy-three-year-old farmer named A. Copeland gave a sharp retort: "I don't give a blank who we get for president. I say this, though, we were in a blank of a shape when we had Hoover." Some thought Roosevelt had remedied the farm depression; as one put it, "I'll vote for Roosevelt for a third term, but I don't think he'll get it again. . . . Roosevelt has helped the farmer a lot through the AAA and the corn sealing." And Oscar Danielson, perhaps playing up the farmer role, answered with the folksy response "I'm satisfied with the horse we've got hitched up now."[25]

Knoxville businessmen seemed no more united in political perspective than the farmers. A local drugstore owner, E. O. Osborn, prescribed the party line: "I'm a dyed in the wool Republican. I will vote for Willkie because he indorses [*sic*] the idea that work is the salvation of life; that any country continuing the practice of taxing the thrifty to provide for those willing to be kept is doomed." T. L. Crawford, the pool hall owner, gave a different perspective: "This war business is mighty serious right now. I think we'll be into war in spite of everything before long. Did I vote for Roosevelt in 1936? You bet I did." Iowans' notoriously stubborn stance of independence showed up in shoe repairman Ernest Safris's response: "I haven't made up my mind yet between Roosevelt and Willkie. I want to wait and see how this war situation comes along." And Knoxville's seventy-two-year-old baker, George Spears, raised a more fundamental issue: "I think that that square-jawed Roosevelt would be a good war president if it wasn't for the third term."[26]

On election day, Americans decided not to change their president, especially with war clouds looming, but Iowa was not in the majority. Only ten of the forty-eight states voted Republican: Vermont, Maine, and eight midwestern states, including Iowa, where Wendell Willkie earned a 53,570-vote lead.[27] But did the vote represent isolationist sentiment? Or did the numbers repudiate New Deal measures—along with FDR's liberal vice president, Wallace, even though he was Iowa's native son and had previously served as secretary of agriculture? No one was entirely sure, but Iowa farmer Martin Paardekooper pulled no political punches regarding the election results. "Of all the states benefited by the New Deal farm program," Paardekooper explained, "Iowa is among the most favored, yet our misled and backbiting farm vote turned down Roosevelt and Wallace for Wailing Wendell. . . . You can't pick plums under a persimmon tree. If you guessed wrong, pucker up your lips, take your medicine, and quit bellyachin.' Or move to Missouri."[28]

Although few Iowans actually planned to move to Missouri, a number of proposed wartime projects such as a hospital at Ft. Des Moines, an army troop training center, and two aircraft plants did venture south. The industrial plums of wartime production often went to loyal and cooperative states, and Iowa's defense dreams began fading fast after its Republican record was reestablished, with only the proposed $8 million ordnance plant at Burlington remaining.[29]

When the No Foreign Wars Committee organized its national membership in December 1940 with Verne Marshall, a newspaper editor from Cedar Rapids, at the lead, the group's purpose was vague. Some citizens interpreted the committee's mission as "genuine anti-war agitation," while other Iowans, familiar with the chairman's self-promotion tactics, believed the group would accomplish nothing more than simply to "boost Verne Marshall." The editor of the *Bellevue Herald* labeled the group embarrassing: "It is to be regretted that an Iowan heads the group; we are just a bit ashamed of it." A woman from Marshall's hometown commented on the situation with a bit more perspective. "I agree with most of their ideas and our not sending our boys over there to fight," Mrs. C. A. Sponar acknowledged, "but I do not believe that there can ever be a just peace in the world with Adolf Hitler or a Nazi Germany ruling the European continent. For it would not be long before they would try to dominate our continent also."[30]

Pretense of Neutrality ~ 1941

Over the first sixteen months of European war, isolationists had hoped to sway Americans to their point of view by presenting a number of very strong personal and political points, and 39 percent of Americans in early 1941 did still believe that entering the war was a mistake. Some citizens remained undecided, but almost 25 percent now favored war, compared to only 5 percent during the initial Nazi invasion. The Gallup Poll continued to label the Midwest as "the center of U.S. isolationists," mostly because "the war spirit" remained concentrated in the South. Despite the labels, the percentage difference was not that significant: the central states claimed 45 percent as isolationist, but the United States as a whole remained 40 percent against entry into the war.[31]

The level of involvement mattered. The Lend-Lease debate (whether to provide arms, munitions, and food to Great Britain without formal payment) lasted from Roosevelt's "Arsenal of Democracy" speech in December 1940 until the congressional vote in March 1941, when it passed with a huge majority in the House (317 to 71) but not in the Senate (60 to 31). Questions remained about continuing neutrality: Did Great Britain truly need our aid? How could ships be protected during transport? Would our provision of convoys or escorts inevitably draw the United States into the war?

In January 1941, isolationists continued to present scenarios with strong emotional overtones for remaining neutral. Isolationist Senator Burton Wheeler of Montana portrayed the darkest image of all during the Lend-Lease debate when he predicted that every fourth boy would be plowed under in death by the unnecessary European war. (This "fourth boy" quotation was a grim analogy of war deaths to the New Deal and the federal government's order at the beginning of the AAA to plow under a quarter of the cotton plants to increase market prices later.) Wheeler's rant became even darker. "Our boys will be returned," he gloweringly threatened, "returned in caskets, maybe; returned with bodies maimed; returned with minds warped and twisted by sights of horrors and the scream and shriek of high-powered shells." President Roosevelt rebuked Wheeler, calling his words "dastardly, rotten, and unpatriotic." Unlike Wheeler, an Iowa man, Franklin Bruggeman from Arcadia, drew a rather calm AAA analogy, suggesting that the government should "seal our American boys" for the next three years (just as corn had been sealed in storage for better market values). Iowan Harry McCarthy's proclamation to a *Des Moines Register* reporter, however, had a far more ringing resonation: "Never again should we send our American youth to Europe to fight Europe's battles."[32]

Young and even old men, despite opposing rhetoric, began to prepare for military service during these official years of neutrality. A "bewhiskered"

Fred Omans, age seventy-two, answered the call when Polk County began its official registration in February 1941 for "a home guard." Though leaning on his cane, he assured officials that he could "handle with a great deal of authority anything if the occasion arose." Like him, many Iowans of all ages, though they did not want overseas involvement, finally began to prepare for war.[33]

After the Nazi invasion of Russia in the summer of 1941, Iowans began to articulate their private beliefs with even stronger voices. An earlier presidential executive order had created civilian defense areas, and New York City's mayor, F. H. LaGuardia, directed this volunteer effort, encouraging each governor to write to every mayor and head county supervisor to ask them to form county defense councils. Governor Wilson of Iowa sent a recruiting letter to local leaders on August 18, 1941, that began, "Reposing special confidence in your patriotism, and knowing of your capacity for getting things done, I am asking that you accept appointment to the county defense council . . ." The governor received hundreds of letters, accepting or declining the committee work, as well as a variety of Iowans' personal comments regarding the war; the comments centered on three major concerns: the Great War, the Great Depression, and Great Britain.[34]

Iowa leaders mostly offered their support toward any state or national defense effort, using such words of emphasis as *cooperation, service, patriotism, duty, obligation, faith, confidence, honor, loyalty,* and *responsibility.* "I am glad to serve my country at this crucial time," Mrs. Gail Martin from Oskaloosa declared. Another woman, Mrs. Fred Benson, simply stated, "I consider it a patriotic duty." A few leaders worried about their available time and commitments to other organizations. Gertrude Flickinger, president of the Mount Pleasant Business and Professional Women's Club, replied, "I have hesitated about accepting as the functions and duties are still somewhat vague. However, I shall accept the commission as my patriotic duty in this time of stress."[35]

Other Iowans declined the defense council request by giving such reasons as health concerns, family issues, business pressures, lack of employees, lack of time, involvement with other committees, or commissions in the military. Thomas Murphy, president of his Red Oak company, lived periodically in Los Angeles because of his hay fever and asthma, but he still volunteered for the Montgomery County chairmanship, though at a distance. "Defense is going on at a pace out here," Murphy described the activity in his coastal setting; "many nights a week I can hear the big planes tuning up at the Douglas plant, although I suppose we are ten or twelve miles from the factory." Because of the overwhelming war tension, Murphy promised to do whatever he could, even from California.[36]

The *Oelwein Daily Register* editor, R. V. Lucas, considered himself "as patriotic as any Iowan" but wrote that he did not possess the necessary time for his local defense council, but the publisher of the *Cherokee Daily Times,* Justin Barry, although "pretty loaded up with jobs," felt that this was one duty he could not "shirk" and therefore promised "conscientious service." Waverly's mayor, I. H. McDaniel, despite all his other pressures, strongly asserted his commitment: "To refuse to serve on this Council would be cowardly, and to serve on the same will be considered a privilege of an American Citizen." Most leaders seemed eager, despite stresses or skepticism, as the threatening war friction frightened them. Clare Dougherty from Allerton offered this morale booster: "This war must be won and I feel that this can be accomplished only through the united effort of all of us."[37]

Even if local leaders did not personally support President Roosevelt or the New Deal, the approaching war caused too much local concern for them to withhold their support for it. Insurance agent Hugh Jackson honestly noted, "I am exceedingly bitter towards the New Deal. It has been difficult for me to be even part way fair to any set up 'from Washington.'" Still, he understood that the war warranted far more concern than petty political power plays, so he continued, "I am patriotic and I am willing and ready at all times to serve my country and to help in good causes."[38]

Part of the isolationist pattern consisted of concerns about Great Britain, but citizens tended to swing to one or the other extreme regarding English citizens. Partly through their awareness of charities such as Knittin' for Britain and Bundles for Britain, and partly through their seeing news reports and photographs of English war scenes, 68 percent of Americans by January 1941 believed their own country's future safety depended upon England's winning the war. That still left a third of Americans who did not, and this third questioned the supposed vulnerabilities of Great Britain as well as the continued strategic importance of this alliance. Some Iowans lumped any perceived war support for England into their own collective term: *pro-British propaganda.*[39]

During this crucial prelude, political talk in Iowa contained a mixture of emotions but not a simple isolationism regarding either the European war or Japanese aggression in China. After reading the August edition of *Fortune,* W. N. Finch wrote to Governor Wilson: "I am convinced that we are into this thing up to our necks and will have to fight our way out. I know democracies are slow about going to war. . . . A few weeks or months ago I took a little poll as to the sentiment among our republican [*sic*] friends. . . . Most of them said it was Roosevelt's war. But I am telling you it is our war. So I am thinking just now about saving Iowa, which is all quite incidental to the defeat of Hitler and saving what is left of our American system of government. For the time being we must adjourn peanut politics and 'quit ourselves like men.'"[40]

In another personal letter to the governor, J. F. Loughlin, an attorney from Cherokee, wrote, "My dear George: This letter is for your scrap pile. I am very glad to cooperate, and I realized that someone must take a part in community activities. We are going through a period where billions and billions are being wasted, and yet [we citizens must lend] a service that we are called upon to render as our patriotic duty." Loughlin simply wanted a little expense money for his efforts and ended his letter, "I realize that you are powerless to correct this situation, and it is because of the situation and realizing its extent, that I am willing to cooperate. However, George, a fellow gets a little sour sometimes in doing all of this work for nothing. Please forgive this outburst, George, and let it go."[41]

Another letter to the governor, from William Anderson, a funeral director in West Branch, also described cautious local moods. "The sentiment for War in this part of State is decidedly at a very low ebb and as a result of this the defense sentiment lags," Anderson began. "This I think is quite natural because of the fear that a definite move for the defense will be misinterpreted as a move in favor of war and I find that our people here are moving cautiously. However, we will attempt to handle this in such a way as to cause no embarrassment to you or the good State of Iowa."[42]

Iowa, though historically Republican and once again with a Republican governor, did elect two Democratic senators in the late 1930s, though not ones considered "New Dealers." Senator Guy Gillette, in fact, had been targeted by Roosevelt's special election committee for defeat in Iowa's 1938 primary because of his independent stance on New Deal legislation. Still, Gillette won not only the primary but also his Senate seat and continued serving in prominent positions such as the Senate Foreign Relations Committee, where his vote in June 1939 allowed further neutrality legislation to remain in effect until the next congressional session in 1940.[43]

Senator Clyde Herring, Iowa's other Democratic senator, expressed his neutral standpoint a day after the 1939 Nazi blitzkrieg: "I am against the entry of the United States in any foreign conflict." But Herring dropped his stance of neutrality during the following two years before American entry into war and voted for repeal of the arms embargoes to Great Britain, France, and Russia; for the peacetime selective-service law and the later extension of service; and for the first $7 billion of the Lend-Lease Program. Herring also worked to bring to Iowa the two major ordnance plants, which were constructed throughout 1941.[44]

While 60 percent of U.S. citizens had favored entry into the war at the beginning of 1941, by October the Gallup Poll showed that 70 percent favored war or had "decided that it is more important to defeat Hitler than to keep out of the war." Still, the Brigadier General Robert Elkington Wood stared out from an October cover of *Time* asking Americans, "What price war and what price peace?"[45]

At the end of November 1941, President Roosevelt carved the Thanksgiving turkey at his polio center in Warm Springs, Georgia, but he cut his vacation short on Monday and headed back to Washington, DC. The Japanese crisis had escalated to the breaking point, and the Philippines appeared to be the likely target of an attack. The U.S. military thus prepared for immediate war that early December as citizens prepared for Christmas.[46]

War tension had quickly grown intensely thick. When a local reporter fired the Japanese question at two farmers from Decatur, the first, Donald Price, a forty-six-year-old veteran, still remembered the last war all too well. "I've had a little experience with overseas operations," Price reflected. "I was with the Rainbow division in the first war. I lost a lung in France. I'm bitterly opposed to an expeditionary force unless it's positively necessary." A younger farmer, who could not remember the Great War, still hesitated at any question of war. "No one wants to see war," B. D. Hullinger began. "If we have to fight to protect our national interests, then we'll have to. But I'd have to know it was that." On December 2, the

Des Moines Register's front-page headline begged the crucial question: "War with Japan?"[47]

On the evening of Friday, December 5, over three thousand Iowa men and women gathered in Des Moines to hear Carrell Binder, head of the *Chicago Daily News* foreign service, speak about "the worldwide war situation." Observing an attentive audience asking pertinent questions, the *Des Moines Register* reporter covering the event declared that this group did not reflect the stereotypical "isolationism of middle western folk" who are "reachable only through emotion and prejudice." This reporter believed that, rather than being knee-jerk isolationists, the men and women of Iowa displayed "practical, realistic 'horse sense.'" They were, in the words of historians Keith McFarland and David Roll, developing "a broad geopolitical view of national security," or advancing beyond "hemispherism."[48]

Two days later, war struck at Pearl Harbor, and all but two of Iowa's congressional representatives declared themselves ready for the war vote. "Of course a resolution declaring a state of war to exist will pass," asserted Senator Herring, "and, of course, I shall vote for it. I think it will pass unanimously." Herring also expressed his rancor toward the legislators who had remained isolationist until this final hour: "I hope people will now realize what a fine situation we would be in had we followed the advice of the Lindberghs, the Nyes and the Wheelers, and I wish they would vote against a declaration of war so the country could continue to see them in their true colors." Senator Gillette responded more positively, adding the diplomatic comment, "This is not the time to look backward but to look forward. It is a time to put all our power into action to force this thing to a conclusion." Representative Thomas Martin from Iowa City hesitated a bit before the actual congressional vote. "My first reaction," noted Martin, "is that we are doing the ultimate in a hysterical approach to a hasty declaration of war. I am determined to keep my mind open until things become clearer." But Representative Ben Jensen seemed to express Iowans' feelings best. "I have to vote for a declaration of war," emphasized Jensen. "It is not a question of whether or not we want war, any longer. We are compelled to fight." The vote was 82–0 in the Senate in favor of the war resolution and 388 to 1 in the House.[49]

The prelude of tensions ended suddenly. War had begun.

Rush to War ~ December 1941

For many months, war had edged closer yet in most ways had still seemed unreal. Japan's attack on Pearl Harbor brought the stark reality of global war to Iowa's communities far from its edge. Suddenly radio announcements shattered the Sabbath calm with the news that the Japanese had attacked the Hawaiian Islands. That Sunday, December 7, isolationism became a moot issue. As a writer for Iowa's history journal, *The Palimpsest,* noted, Pearl Harbor had "rocked the very foundations of isolationism in the Hawkeye State."[50]

Davenport's residents, typical of other communities, gathered around the radio for the latest war news. This ordinary Sunday had transformed Iowans' and Americans' thinking from shock to disbelief to worry, partly because the attack on Pearl Harbor occurred during that almost Christmastime of the year, a time that should be filled with presents and peace. But within that single day, America's communities transformed from being in a period of hesitant hope to one of war.[51]

That Sunday also brought a sadness to many families with the thought that raising the army had not been a symbolic gesture. This attack and its resulting shock brought national unity to America and its communities, which now strongly encouraged the war effort. As Gladys Holmes, a nurse stationed in Honolulu, wrote to her aunt in Winterset, "If you people back home had seen what I saw, you would go to work with all your energy devoted to winning this war."[52]

Local newspapers reacted swiftly with extreme anger toward the Japanese. A short editorial in the *Winterset News* declared this an "unworthy war": "Those unfortunate peoples of Japan, whether they be descendants of monkeys or bundles from heaven," the editor screamed, "they'll pay for their unworthy war on this nation. Pay with their lives, their lands, and their dried up leaders who believe in Hitler." This was the entire editorial. Weeks later, only one public response from this small town seemed not quite so angry; rather, this high school girl's word-play poster message to wartime knitters punned itself as rather calm and quietly determined: "Remember, Purl Harder." This knitting poster gained statewide attention.[53]

The next day began a new era. At 11:30 a.m. Iowa time, President Roosevelt addressed Congress with his infamous war message referring to "a day that will live in infamy." That same day, more than a hundred navy applicants kept the Davenport recruiting office open until three in the morning. Years later, one of the people Archie Satterfield interviewed for his book *The Home Front* distinctly remembered his drive through the Midwest the day after Pearl Harbor. "We left home on Monday, December 8th," he recalled, "and in every town we went through we saw these lines of young boys waiting in front of the courthouse or recruiting office to join up and fight. It was very moving, very reassuring to know we were unified." In Tuesday's radio talk, the president further defined American involvement: "We are all in it together, all the way. Every single man, woman, and child is a partner, in the most tremendous undertaking of our American history."[54]

This patriotic urge continued, and exactly six months later on the steps of the Iowa Statehouse (again on a Sunday afternoon, June 7, 1942, at 1:25 p.m.), 58 volunteer "Pearl Harbor Avengers" swore their military oath. At the same moment, 267 other Iowa men elsewhere in the state and 12,326 young men across the nation also participated in the Pearl Harbor Anniversary Ceremony, pledging to serve their country.[55]

Chapter 1

Soldiers of the Soil ~ The Farm Front

Bacon is a bullet against Hitler. Lard is a bomb against Japan.

—*Wallaces' Farmer* (July 11, 1942)

Food is an important weapon of war. During World War I, Food Administrator Herbert Hoover had stressed that food would win the war. Before the United States entered World War II, Secretary of Agriculture Claude Wickard declared in his Indiana twang that again food would "win the war and write the peace." The farmer would be the soldier of the soil, fighting on the farm front, producing the food needed to nourish the ravenous, greedy monster that was modern, total war. As Wickard warned, "War is a hearty eater."[1]

Food for Freedom became the urgent, patriotic agricultural campaign to develop and maintain all-out production, and Iowa's farmers, representing a leading agricultural state, played a significant role in this national battle. The Food for Freedom campaign urged all farmers to grow less of the five basic crops of wheat, corn, cotton, rice, and tobacco, and instead to concentrate their efforts on producing more pork, beef, eggs, dairy products, fruits, and vegetables. These agricultural products could then be canned or preserved to fill the dietary needs of the armed services and of America's allies, creating the best-fed army and alliance in the world. On December 9, 1941, the American Farm Bureau pledged its dedication to the federal Food for Freedom campaign: "Agriculture's part in this war is to supply food for victory—food for victorious armies—our own and those of our allies."[2]

Throughout the war, the motivation for Iowa farm families' participation in this campaign remained "the boys." The *1943 Iowa Year Book of Agriculture* actually introduced its detailed but dull reports with this rather emotional message: "Boys, who be-grimed and hungry after a long day at hay-making or other field work, and often let the screen door slam as they called out, 'Hey, Mom, what do we have to eat,' were now among the islands of the South Pacific, or were in Africa, Sicily, Italy, Alaska, and in all parts of the world; but the old call of 'what do we have to eat' echoed back to the Iowa farm." This was the motivation: feeding "the boys." Iowa's *Year Book of Agriculture* concluded, "Though it was but an echo, 'Mom and Pop' saw to producing enough food that not one of those boys would go hungry."[3]

The farm front started preparing itself very early in the war. *Life* magazine informed the nation, even before Pearl Harbor, that ten million American workers had begun "quietly laboring to produce the munitions which might have more to do with winning the war than any bomb or shell." The war workers were farmers; the munitions, food. Farm families would be contributing an added wartime effort as agriculture would need to break all previous production records for this war. Because of predicted labor and machinery shortages, farmers would work longer hours, farm women would play an even more significant role, and boys and girls would attempt to accomplish "the work of grown men," especially in the midwestern production of soybeans, hogs, corn, and milk. American farmers planned to support the best-fed army in the world along with the added industrial war workers. As *Prairie Farmer* proclaimed, "Food means victory. And victory means freedom."[4]

The first Iowa farmer to file his Food for Freedom goals was Clarence Howell, owner and operator of a 129-acre farm in northwest Madison County. He would not stand alone; *Wallaces' Farmer* described the future work demanded of each farmer by the federal government: "The Food-for-Freedom program called for every farmer to put every acre of land, every hour of labor, every bit of farm machinery, fertilizer, and other supplies to the use that would best serve the nation's wartime needs."

Since less than 15 percent of the nation's men were farmers in the early 1940s, Food for Freedom became "a job for Atlas himself."[5]

From Pearl Harbor on, war and only war would be everyone's focus, and agricultural production seemed to have no bounds. Even the weather cooperated. Although Depression-era farmers had eagerly awaited the opportunity to produce and perhaps prosper, all-out production under wartime conditions came with the risks of surpluses, inflation, and waste. The Food for Freedom farm-front fight needed to coordinate its battles. Some government regulation would be needed to coordinate agricultural production goals by determining the number of increased acres to be put into production and the proportion of newly introduced crops to old ones, and farmers as soldiers of the soil needed to follow these orders for a victorious farm front. But all-out production and profit were weighted with a concern that this profit would come at someone else's expense.

Writer David Hinshaw in his 1943 book, *The Home Front,* drew a farm analogy to illustrate the deliberate, all-out efforts needed after Pearl Harbor despite previous midwestern isolationist politics. He explained the new focus, "Men brought up on farms know how to make a balking horse pull his load without beating or cursing him. The simple, never-failing way is to spread a handful of dirt over his tongue, get back in the wagon while the horse is indignantly trying to spit the dirt out, and tell him to 'get-up.' He does. And in a hurry." Hinshaw believed in this elemental approach because a horse can think of only one thing at a time, just like most people, farmers included. The attack on Pearl Harbor had simply and dramatically provided the much-needed dirt in the mouth. Hinshaw concluded, "Dirt in his mouth, an unexpected attack from an unsuspected source, switches his mind from balking to his new troubles."[6] The only focus now for American farmers was Food for Freedom.

Tractors as Tanks

The farm-front effort officially began in the spring of 1942, and *Life* dedicated a late May issue to "spring planting" with the comment that "this year must bear the richest harvest in the world's troubled history." The magazine offered descriptions of Iowa's beauty and strength, which would be needed in this production effort: "At the beginning of May, in Iowa, the world's most bountiful soil was rolled over in long black ribbons by tractors that throbbed against its weight, then harrowed smooth for planting by countermarching teams of horses." Iowa's agricultural prosperity rested on its history of "a stabilizing diversity": general farming or a combination of animals and plants set on rich land. "The Iowa landscape has always reflected prosperity," the *Life* article continued. "An airplane view shows long, straight roads following the section lines, punctuated at neat intervals by the windbreak of trees that shelters the white farmhouse, the capacious red barn and tall silo."[7]

Iowa's rural landscape began to change, however, with the loss of its horses and silos and the corresponding addition of more tractors and steel machine sheds. The key element of wartime farm production would be increased mechanization, as advertisers continually tried to point out. And *Prairie Farmer* warned its readers of the increasing government demands upon farmers: "Farmers must do a better job of farming than ever before—and that means they must make full use of every bit of labor-saving machinery at their command."[8] To fuel this drive for greater production, farmers increasingly turned to "power farming"—the use of gas-engine tractors and implements.

Horses still plodded and plowed with a rather constant presence on Iowa farms, especially on smaller units, which could not risk the considerable financial commitment for new equipment along with the constant energy and maintenance bills that went with it. With horses, farmers could literally grow the fuel they needed. Horses and mules labored importantly on Iowa's farms during the wartime emergency, with its gas rationing and machinery shortages, but horses started dying in increasing numbers from what was commonly known as sleeping sickness; Iowa veterinarians initiated a vaccination campaign in 1942 and 1943 against this disease, equine encephalitis. In 1944, Iowa still claimed the title of leading horse state, with 612,000 head, and 45 percent of Iowa farms remained entirely dependent on animal power.[9]

Many farmers did not want to give up their horses for emotional reasons. One *Iowa Veterinarian* editor noted the sentiment farmers still felt for the horse despite "the efforts of certain machinery manufacturers and star-gazing editors who seem intent to eliminate all horses from the work and recreation of our country." This editor was referring to such industrialists as Henry Ford, whose tractor advertisements depicted a matched pair of workhorses labeled as "14,000,000 Beloved Culprits." Ford emphatically called the horse "a waster of land and time, the primary wealth of the farmer." Other tractor ads continued to attack the use of horses throughout the war as misguided, unprofitable, and simply romantic.[10]

By the middle of World War II, despite a steel shortage and rationing of machinery, farmers adopted mechanization to the point where Iowa farmers averaged one tractor for every 218 acres.[11] All-out production demanded a faster pace than any horse could ever provide. Three distinct advertising messages about agricultural mechanization explained this need for power during the war: tractors ranked as a necessary weapon for total warfare, Americans had developed a long and successful history of using machines, and machines provided a better quality of life on the farm, along with a promised future of freedom.[12]

The slogans proclaimed by tractor advertisements undeniably made the connection between the war and the farm, the soldier and the farmer, the battle and the harvest, as the following lines from advertisements suggest:

> "1942/The Year of the Tractor as well as the Tank—PRODUCE and WIN!"
> "This, too, is mechanized warfare!"
> "He drives a Weapon . . . and the FARMALL fights for *food!*"
> "The Man Behind the Plow Backs the Man Behind the Gun!"
> "Battle Lines of the Food Front"
> "Plowshares are Swords"
> "Farm Commando—Ready to Roll!"

The design of the military tank used in the Great War had replicated an early tractor model with crawler wheels, and images showing comparisons of tanks and tractors, synthesized as symbols of American defense, continued to be used throughout the Second World War. The farmer may not literally have been on the fighting front, but at home he was fighting to produce with a much-needed weapon. When Iowa farmer Robert Leichliter of Ogden fell ill, his neighbors lined up all their tractors across his cornfield in what the *Des Moines Register* called "Zero Hour for Attack on Homefront, not Battlefront." The reporter described the zealous lineup as if it were an actual battlefront: "The roar of the 34 tractors as they charged across the fields might be compared with a string of army tanks charging across the countryside."[13]

The second message from popular farm journals compared the strength and imagination of early Americans to present-day farmers with historic symbols of men fighting against the odds. Symbols such as Paul Revere, westering pioneers, or citizens fighting in the Revolutionary War developed this theme of American ingenuity and technological competence. Albert Loveland, chairman of the Iowa Agricultural Adjustment Act Committee, enhanced the image of the founding fathers when he compared the battle on the farm front to the Minute Men of the American Revolution. The *Iowa Agriculturist* issued a similar message to its readers (mostly young male agricultural students at Iowa State College): "The whole life and training of generations of Americans fit us to excel in mechanized warfare," the Iowa State College article began. "From pioneer days we have been an ingenious people. Starting in a vast, undeveloped country, we have had the inventive skill and the resolution to shorten distances and lighten toil with machinery." The tractor as tank seemed no exception, but rather was a further elaboration of a long and proud tradition of American ingenuity.[14]

The third message, especially from tractor advertisements, was often delivered with very emotional promises along with sharply contrasting military messages because the war was proving to be a war of engines with an optimistic belief in their strength. Power farming meant freedom and better living not only for one's family but for the world, and many ads claimed that mechanization would create a farm to which sons and daughters would enthusiastically return after war's end, increasing the longevity of the family farm. In a study of wartime advertising, Frank Fox called this Madison Avenue message "the illusion of omnipotence: an abiding faith that the world's problems could be solved by machines."[15] The government and corporations were telling Iowa farmers that tractors could potentially solve their two largest problems—the overwhelming physical demands of all-out production and the difficulty of maintaining the family farm. In 1946, 40 percent of the state's farmers, according to an Iowa Poll (conducted by the *Des Moines Register*), felt "handicapped" by not being able to buy sufficient farm equipment. Tractors topped the list for necessary mechanical purchases.[16]

A British traveler writing after the war noted of the midwestern mechanical speed-up that "the most mechanized agriculture in the world has been mechanized more rapidly than ever before." Later, many agriculturalists concluded positively that a mechanized farm offered a better lifestyle, while others, especially smaller-scale farmers, perceived the changes negatively, believing that using machinery rather than horses separated farmers from the earth they worked.[17] But during the Second World War, no choice could be considered—mechanization must be adopted. All-out production mattered desperately, and machines just might fulfill their advertised promises.

The promise also brought peril. The physical dangers of mutilation or even death from accidents involving farm machinery posed a severe drawback to mechanized agriculture, which became the most dangerous industry in America during the war years. In 1945, President Harry Truman declared a National Farm Safety Week, July 22 through 28, because more than 20,000 people on farms had died in accidents, including fires, in 1943 alone.[18]

Iowa farmers were utilizing a large number of the three machines that caused the greatest number of farm accidents—tractors, combines, and corn pickers. One out of every ten agricultural accidents in Iowa resulted from corn pickers, including the following two incidents involving Kossuth County farmers during November harvests. George Wempen mangled his leg in a new corn picker when his new Unionall pants became caught in a power take-off with no safety cover. And Milton Bebo had been working alone when his belt caught in the machine—neighbors found him over an hour later, pinned to the machine.[19] Both men survived their accidents, but others were not so lucky.

Accidents multiplied not only from mechanization, but from wartime conditions as well. Iowa State College Extension underlined the safety point that most farmers knew the necessary precautions but hurried and ignored safety measures, whereas farmers should be remembering to exercise extreme caution, care, and responsibility—always. *Prairie Farmer* best summarized the cautionary tale: "With inexperience and insufficient help, longer hours with accompanying fatigue, and use of patched up machinery, American farmers have greater need than ever before to adopt safe practices."[20]

When farmers neglected safety precautions, accidents resulted, such as the particularly tragic one that *Wallaces' Farmer* described like this:

"No telegram to announce the death of her son came to Mrs. Arthur Ovren, Buena Vista county, Iowa. She stood at her kitchen window and saw her son thrown to the ground and killed instantly. . . . Russell's clothing caught on a lever on the spreader, he lost his balance, was thrown to the ground, run over, and dragged for some distance. When they reached him, he was dead."[21]

The National Safety Council reported that farm accidents killed almost as many as war in the twenty-eight months after the Pearl Harbor attack: 40,000 farm-accident fatalities to 42,081 war deaths. In 1945, accidental deaths of America's farm residents totaled 16,000—an increase of 8 percent from 1944.[22]

Fearing Outsiders

"The United States is going to be in a hell of a shape for food if manpower is pulled from the farms at the rate now demanded," Edward O'Neal, American Farm Bureau president, told a Des Moines audience in October 1942. "They say food is as important for victory as ammunition," he continued. "If they really mean that they have got to give recognition to the man who serves on the farm, the same as in the army." This central concern—deferment of their sons from military service—grew for many Iowa farm families who remained dependent upon the agricultural labor of the young men. Brigadier General Charles Grahl, Iowa's director of selective service, had tried to assist by notifying all draft boards to reclassify farm work into one of two deferred classifications, especially that on livestock, dairy, and poultry farms. According to a 1943 Gallup Poll, 77 percent of American farmers considered the shortage of labor to be their biggest problem.[23]

Farmers had turned more and more to expensive machinery when a labor shortage quickly developed in 1942, and this labor shortage remained the central concern that farmers expressed: the loss of sons and hired farmhands. These young men had provided the traditional supply of labor on most Iowa farms and now were lost to draft calls and war jobs. A farm deferment might keep some of these men from the armed services or war industries.

Agriculture had not initially been classified as an essential industry to make farm boys eligible for deferment, and farm labor had remained traditionally underpaid compared with industrial work, so many young farmhands and sons left rural regions to seek industrial work and earn more money. By 1943, the farm-labor situation grew progressively tighter as the farm population in Iowa declined from 776,250 in 1940 to 760,789 by 1943, largely at the expense of farm manpower.[24]

Even if they wanted to stay on the farm, many young men with deferment status faced a strong social stigma. A great deal of discrimination existed in wartime America against men who were not "fighting for their country," although farm laborers had legitimate deferrals for agricultural needs. Writer Archie Satterfield describes the context in that patriotism had "tunnel vision": "If you looked young and healthy, you should have been fighting." A reporter for the *Iowa Farm Economist* polled 202 young men and asked whether their present job on the farm was "the most important contribution to the war effort." Ninety-three percent said yes, yet a number still felt community pressure to be dressed in uniform. The Food for Freedom campaign tried to reassure these young men in various ways; one poster depicted an enlisted man placing his hand on a young farmer's shoulder—"Those overalls are your UNIFORM, bud." Fifty percent of the young men surveyed by the *Iowa Farm Economist* wanted to continue farming but believed "definite advantages" would go to returning veterans, as they remembered the "honor, privileges and prestige bestowed upon the veterans of World War I."[25]

Many young farmhands did leave, by choice or by draft, for the army or the navy. Hugh Sidey, son of Greenfield's newspaper editor, was then a high school student and remembered many of the local farm boys' departures. He described the often-repeated scene: "The old Trailways bus would come to the hotel, which was right beside my dad's newspaper, to take the draftees into Des Moines, and Dad insisted on a picture of every guy. Almost every day, it seemed, there would be another ten or fifteen, and they all lined up in their farmer clothes with their cardboard suitcases."[26]

Despite deferments and mechanization, farmers felt forced to turn to other sources of labor. By 1943, Iowa employed 70,000 fewer farm workers than before the war, and its farm machinery was aging, becoming more and more difficult to repair. The situation grew increasingly desperate. Farmers at first turned to townspeople, foreign labor, and teenagers, as well as their own families, but then officials told farmers across the nation to "abandon luxurious prejudices" that had kept them from hiring "Negroes, Mexicans, and women," as this war should produce a democratic effort from all the home fronts.[27]

Urban citizens who assisted on the farm front often belonged to organizations such as civic groups, chambers of commerce, and women's clubs. The communities of Montezuma, Chariton, Marengo, Le Mars, and Jefferson each won the Merit Award Certificate from the *Des Moines Register* for "Outstanding Accomplishment in the Great Homefront Battle of Food." Governor Bourke Hickenlooper issued an official proclamation in May 1943 commending the people of Iowa for "their fine spirit and splendid cooperation" and declared a Labor Registration Period for Food Production and Preservation in Iowa. Sometimes local businessmen and clergy drove tractors in the evenings for farmers, and advertisements even encouraged townspeople to volunteer on local farms. A Younkers department store slogan exemplified the push: "Help the Farmer—During Vacation or In Your Spare Time—It's Patriotic and Fun, too!"[28]

Although the labor shortage continued, many Iowa farmers and their families resisted the most available kind of labor, those workers perceived as foreign. *Wallaces' Farmer* asked its readers in 1943, "How do Iowa farm people feel about the bringing in of either Americans of Japanese ancestry or white Americans from the [South]?" In both cases, the proposed workers would be outside draft eligibility because of age and within family groups. It is interesting to note, however, that *Wallaces' Farmer* displayed considerable negative emotion (and no question mark) in its corresponding headline: "Would you hire Japs!"[29]

Overwhelmingly, farm people described themselves as "doubtful" concerning the possibility of hiring people of Japanese ancestry; only 9 percent of the women and 13 percent of the men favored this alternative source of labor, while over 70 percent strongly resisted. Comments often bitterly and even violently opposed the suggestion, such as this one from a Lee County man, "If a Jap came on my farm I'd kill him the first chance I had." A Dallas County woman responded in a less violent yet still cautious tone, "I wouldn't want Japanese-Americans living next to me. I just wouldn't feel safe." Potential farm laborers from Kentucky received a more positive response, with 40 percent of polled Iowa men in favor of the idea, but one Lee County man thought those men should be in the army. "Kentuckians are good fighters," the man explained. "Let them go in the Army. Keep our own boys at home." Other farmers believed that since the proposed workers were American citizens, they deserved a fair chance, but most farmers did not want to import labor, preferring to rely on their own family members. A Dubuque County man's comment was typical: "I don't want any labor but my own boy."[30]

Wallaces' Farmer asked the same labor questions a year later to determine whether Iowa farmers had changed their views in light of an even more desperate labor situation. Attitudes had changed little by 1944, when 10 percent of farmers said they would hire Japanese Americans and 48 percent would hire Kentuckians. Many Iowans felt they could relieve their labor struggles simply by purchasing more machinery; others believed the war was just about drawing to an end. Many Iowans continued to express anti-Japanese views, such as a Chickasaw County man's comment that he "couldn't trust a Jap now, even if he were American born." Other views began to sound more open-minded, such as one from Jones County: "Why not bring in Japanese workers. After all, there are a lot of German families around here, and they work just as hard and are just as true to this country as many American-born people." A woman from Audubon County expressed sympathetic thoughts based on her own exclusionary experiences as a German immigrant: "Don't bring any Japs in here. I can remember the way we were suspected, abused in 1917, because my parents were natives of Germany. This was in spite of the fact that my brother was in the American army. The remembrance rankles even now. If these Japs were brought here, they would be subject to the same treatment. I wouldn't wish that on any one."[31]

Iowa Quakers at the Scattergood Hostel near West Branch (Herbert Hoover's birthplace) considered resettling Japanese Americans in that area, but this proposal met with so much local resistance that the Quakers felt forced to abandon their plan. However, local residents displayed no resistance to the idea of relocating refugees from Nazi Germany. With the proposed Japanese American relocation, though, some of the Quakers feared local anger might be directed at themselves as pacifists, and even most Friends hesitated to personally face this "pent-up war hysteria."[32]

Other Iowans proved more persistent. One farm woman wrote to the *Des Moines Register* to persuade other rural residents to hire second-generation Japanese Americans (*Nissei*) on Iowa family farms short on labor. Alison Escher from Cumming had hired a Japanese American worker, Robert Ohki, when her husband finally agreed, perhaps from exhaustion after working from six in the morning to midnight every day that spring. Her neighbors' reactions to the new farmhand indicated some "terror" with the often-heard comment "I wouldn't have one on the place!" Despite some of Escher's initially stereotypical reactions to Ohki's wearing pants and collared shirts instead of a kimono and his being able to eat a meal without rice, she gained tremendous respect for him and compassion for his family's plight in an internment camp in the western United States. She concluded her essay by describing a recent scene between Ohki and a local youth with the statement "If I had shut my eyes I would have thought the conversation was between my own nephews."[33]

In 1942, after federal officials had established ten Japanese American internment camps, the War Relocation Authority determined that forty-two cities, including Des Moines, could act as alternative relocation centers for Japanese Americans confined in these western internment camps. Young adult Japanese Americans could leave internment camps by one of three ways: volunteer for the military, enroll in a midwestern college, or become a farm laborer in the Midwest. By war's end, of the 110,000 Japanese Americans who had been uprooted from their West Coast homes to internment camps, almost 30,000 confiscated citizens resettled in the Midwest—about 500 of them in Iowa. Most of the Japanese Americans who came to Iowa arrived in Des Moines in mid-1942; most left immediately after January 1945. By 1988, of the original five hundred, only six remained.[34]

Not only was there discrimination against Japanese American workers, but any idea of newcomers moving into Iowa farm communities met either skepticism or outright anger, no matter how much the aid was needed. Over 1,100 Mexicans arrived in August 1944 and 1,467 in August 1945 to labor on Iowa's farms, as well as 314 Jamaican workers in July 1943, 429 in 1944, and 766 in 1945. When 223 men from Barbados came to Oelwein to detassel corn for DeKalb, many residents expressed stereotypical reactions toward the black men, although the local newspaper described the Barbados workers' behavior throughout their stay as "above approach" (*sic*). Even though this imported labor was very much needed, the community of 8,000 imposed its own difficulties for the migrant workers, and five "beer shops" posted signs that read "colored trade is not solicited." One of the Barbados men revealed his feelings concerning this constant discrimination, as he commented in his English accent: "Evidently these people do not admire us."[35]

Ironically, a foreign source of labor that was officially welcomed was German prisoners of war. (German Americans were still Iowa's largest ethnic group.) The first "PWs" were brought to America in 1943, but additional secure sites needed to be built in areas that could utilize this labor on local farms. The military eventually established POW camps in forty-four of the forty-eight states, and Algona and later Clarinda became the two prisoner camp sites in Iowa. Algona's complex cost $1,280,668, and the Clarinda complex, which switched to Japanese prisoners in 1944, cost $1,300,000 and held 3,000 prisoners captive using 500 military police. Algona's camp officially opened on the twenty-seventh anniversary of U.S. entrance into World War I. The employment of POWs did have some restrictions. Prisoners could not compete with local labor for work, and the work they were to do had to be easily taught to large, supervised groups. In other words, isolated or mechanized work did not qualify because of concerns of escape. The prisoner laborers wore dark blue uniforms bearing the letters *PW* (prisoner of war) or *PP* (protected person) in white. A typical work schedule was six days a week, 7:30 a.m. to 4:30 p.m., and the military expected farmers to obey the rules and never to fraternize with the enemy.[36]

Although Iowa farmers urgently needed the labor of these POWs, the proposal still seemed a risky solution. When the nine carloads of German prisoners stepped from the train at 5 a.m. in Algona that first day, three hundred soldiers guarded them with tommy guns against any break into the Iowa countryside.[37]

Farm Family Warriors

Over 90 percent of all farm-labor needs were met by the farm family itself in 1943 and 1944. Greater efficiency and longer hours increased agricultural production by 20 percent above the 1909–1942 period. The USDA found that the workday of farm operators in all north-central states averaged 12.8 hours, an hour longer than in June 1940, and that farmers often worked every day of the week. As R. C. Meyer, a fifty-one-year-old farmer outside of Iowa Falls, summed up the labor shortage, "It's pretty hard—one man doing two men's work."[38]

Because of their own long hours, farmers continued to ridicule labor's push for overtime pay during the war. In October 1942 at a meeting of 2,500 Iowa farmers at the Des Moines Shrine Auditorium, the men laughed "uproariously" when Edward O'Neal of the National Economic Stabilization Board jabbed at labor's forty-hour week. Later, on a more serious note, O'Neal asked his audience, "How can the farmer compete for labor when these high factory wages are paid, the country going deeper and deeper into debt to do it? The war is becoming exceedingly serious, and the rate we are paying wages is greatly increasing our difficulties."[39]

During the war, farmers worked much longer days, sometimes fourteen- to sixteen-hour days, and it is not difficult to imagine the strained nerves and muscles along with the added stress created by the situation. Public record has omitted the fact, but conflicts inevitably arose on many family farms, especially with authority, creating within the farm family "a terrain of loving contest." World War II with its aura of patriotism intensified these conditions of production, commitment, and authoritative control as the federal government increasingly called upon women and children to expand their traditional spheres of duties—usually without the formal rewards of money or land. These tensions were never publicly aired during the war, however, because the farm family had to be America's greatest victory team.[40]

Some institutions continued to believe that farm families remained essentially more cooperative than urban families. The *Prairie Farmer,* one of the oldest of agricultural journals, proclaimed the farm family's wartime mission: "Because their farms are their business, their security, their very life, farm families always work together like no others. And this 'working together' has made it possible for American farming to overcome all obstacles and accomplish 'miracles' in food production for war." The *Iowa Farm Economist*'s writers also believed farm families were more understanding of work pressures because the entire family, children included, "can see, understand and share the work of others" in this war crisis, thus creating greater family unity. To honor such work, the USDA awarded some farm families certificates for their outstanding "all-out farm war production" in the Food for Freedom campaign.[41]

Perhaps families felt a sense of guilt if they complained about their added work when soldiers were struggling in desperate war conditions, especially when the young men came from their own families. For example, one headline read "Typical Madison County Family Gives Total Effort to Total War—Father, Mother and Daughters All Work." The Jobsts were trying their best "to see that every acre and every animal on the farm makes a maximum contribution to feeding Carl Jobst and millions of other men like him who are doing the actual fighting." Or, as farmer Walter Hake reflected on his military son's absence, "We'll get along all right here, although I'm alone now. The boy went in the navy, but he plowed most of the night before he left. I've sold all the cows except two. . . . If a fellow doesn't have too many chores he can get along."[42]

Young people who remained on the farm—boys and girls—worked increasingly longer hours with greater responsibilities despite the increased time away from school and added physical risks due to mechanization. Often they were quite young, preteen or early teens. But parents and government officials deemed this idea of "little adults" working as acceptable for the all-out production demands of the war effort, and big families could pay "extra dividends," such as the Allamakee County family of James Corrigan and his wife, who had eleven sons.[43]

Many articles and advertisements romanticized the children's sacrifices as building integrity along with an enhanced work ethic. The May 25, 1942, cover of *Life* depicted a determined teenage boy driving a tractor, his hands gripping the wheel in the ten-two position, his eyes focused grimly ahead. The *Des Moines Register* also proudly published many photographs in its farm section of similar boys and sometimes girls driving tractors. A *Prairie Farmer* advertisement called this work "His Place in the Sun." The ad's copy dramatically emphasized the child's added work responsibilities: "He is old enough to sense that something of grave importance is happening in the world. He felt the urgency of it when Dad gripped his arm hard, the day his big brother marched away. When Dad turned to him and said, 'Now it's up to us, Son,' he understood, and he approached the stature of manhood that day."[44]

The 4-H farm club organized Iowa's youth throughout the war, and all 4-H groups established war programs after Pearl Harbor with an emphasis on production, conservation, and war service. By 1943, Iowa had 15,055

4-H boys and girls raising products worth $2,618,133, with the largest portion of those members—almost 7,000—raising livestock valued at $1,350,000. In 1944, Iowa's 4-H clubs declared themselves a "Victory Army," and many members, ages twelve through twenty, signed Victory Pledge cards with the slogan "Feed a fighter or more in forty-four." The largest 4-H exposition ever held boasted one thousand boys and girls in attendance; it was the 1944 program, devoted entirely to war production.[45]

The Victory Farm Volunteers developed as another war effort to utilize child labor. Its members, town teenagers ages fourteen to eighteen, participated in day-haul programs to local farms. Each state provided transportation for the youth from town to fields and back at day's end, and local schools cooperated with the federal program. The total number of Iowa teens involved in the day-haul program, along with a live-in program and labor camp, amounted to 14,385 in 1943, 16,942 in 1944, and 23,404 by 1945.[46]

Because of traditional labor shortages, farm families also called upon girls to "man" the mechanized farm-front effort. Iowa had 12,600 4-H girls, and many of these female members took over part of their farms' production work by driving tractors, raking hay, and doing other chores, with a number of girls reporting more than two thousand hours of such service. Over 8,000 members worked in victory gardens throughout the war years as well as on home economics projects, bond sales, and scrap drives.[47] In a 1942 study of young farm women's labor, college student Phyllis Gough asked one hundred Iowa State College freshmen women about the tasks they had completed on their family farms, and 51 percent said they had driven a tractor in 1942, 21 percent for the first time, and they said they liked driving tractors better than any other farm activity. International Harvester boasted that young women could join the "Field Artillery" as "tractorettes": "A tractorette is a farm girl or woman who wants to help win the battle of the land, to help provide Food for Freedom."[48]

The debate over farm girls' working in agriculture versus industrial jobs aired at the Iowa Farm Bureau convention in November 1942. Maxine Burch, a Madison County farm girl, led the panel. "The place for a farm girl is on the farm if at all possible," Burch told the audience. "She can do best in freeing the hands of her mother and father for the work of boosting farm production." The counterpoint, expressed by Carl

Malone, Extension economist, was that farm girls could perhaps help the war effort more effectively in war factories, since, as Malone explained, "in those industries a girl often is able to produce as much as a man but on the farm she can't do it." An Iowa farm wife, Mrs. Lee Fredericks, believed otherwise; she told the *Des Moines Tribune* that "all our boys are girls" and explained that her five daughters completed all the necessary work on their family farm. "Each one has definite responsibilities and they're doing a swell job," Fredericks bragged. "I wouldn't trade them for boys if I could."[49]

Much of the increased farm-front labor came from adult females. Determined, resourceful farm women performed the job needed for the war effort with enthusiasm and without complaint. The *Iowa Bureau Farmer* described farm women's efforts as "keeping farmers' powder dry." Yet even when the men enlisted for war duty and the farm women stayed home, alone and in charge, society still considered women "just helping"—always second despite their production responsibilities, never viewed or described simply as "farmers," but always as "farmerettes" or "ladies of the land."[50]

Farm men themselves often delivered such a mixed message: men did not want women working in the fields, even when additional labor was desperately needed. The stigma lingered; proper women should work only in and around the home. However, the Iowa State College student publication, the *Iowa Agriculturist,* took a slightly more progressive view, one not often expressed: "Although Iowans like to think that the days of women working in the fields are practically gone, without a doubt wives and daughters will be in the fields this summer along with husbands and sons when the pinch of the labor shortage is felt."[51]

Gender-appropriate behavior always seemed difficult to define, but most farm women did not question their added roles and responsibilities. One farm woman from Monroe County promised, "I'll be glad to work to the limit of my endurance, if it will only help to bring my boys back home." A Warren County home economist described the women who gathered for one of her meetings as "helping fight the battle of food production." This Iowa county served as an example for *Successful Farming* in acknowledging the efforts of all American farm women, who, according to the farm journalist, "faced the biggest job in history." According to the article, many facets made up the farm woman's work, and she should not see herself simply as an extra farmhand but rather as essential hands—hands that drove tractors, fed chickens, planted tomatoes. The article continued to romanticize the work ("It is these same hands which so patiently tie hair bows, sew on buttons, and fasten jar tops") while also praising farm women as the busiest women in the U.S.A.[52]

Agrarian men often recognized and valued women's overall work patterns, creating a unique respect despite the inequality. Farm women always did the housework and, if necessary, field work in addition, yet men rarely, if ever, crossed their own gender boundary by working within the home. Men, then as now, also did not wish to discuss their lack of participation within the home. One glimpse of the persistent problem did appear in a humorous yet slightly reflective section of *Wallaces' Farmer,* "Song of the Lazy Farmer," which praised the unsung work of farm women. This "poet" described his day: "For help I'll never fume nor fret as long as she can wake me yet and have my pancakes sizzling hot, and go with me to pasture lot to milk the cows and slop the swine and drive the planter on the line, and keep the garden plot all hoed and help me spread the barn yard load. And then at noon like it so, a-sittin' by the radio while Mother hustles up the grub and bathes my shirts in the laundry tub." The husband's hands seemed able to rest at times, especially during meal preparation and laundry chores, while the wife's never did. No wonder he ended his song in this way: "Let's cut out talk of labor dour as long as we have women power!"[53]

Mechanization on the farms and in the homes brought not leisure to farm women, but available time for additional farm work. This was efficiency. *Prairie Farmer* reinforced this message: "With modern farm machinery to help them, the women often can turn in as good a job as the men—and still have energy enough left to keep the household running smoothly." And war-era housework loads had become even greater than the excruciating Depression years of "making do." Mrs. Leonard Schissel proudly kept her household running despite her added farm work. "I get up at 6:30 a.m. (farm time) and I do a lot of burning of the midnight oil," she described her wartime schedule. "I always iron at night, and do mending and patching then. Sometimes I do my sewing, making the children's clothes and my house dresses and slacks. Vegetables have to be canned in the morning, when they are fresh, but I can put up fruit at night. That doesn't make so much difference." That summer Schissel planned to can five hundred quarts.[54]

All in all, the labor shortage was filled largely by all the members of the farm families. Despite the worries over the shortage of labor and the rationing of new farm machinery and parts, production climbed, breaking records each year of the war. R. K. Bliss, Iowa State College Extension director, praised in 1944 the hard work of Iowa's farming families devoted to the food-front fight. Bliss believed "the job comes first." He concluded, "And that is the reason why Iowa farmers with the handicap of labor shortages, machinery shortages and now very bad weather are still making amazing progress in producing food in support of our armies and our Allies."[55]

Growing Farm Factories

General Motors in 1943 compared farming with its own factories: "The American farmer's job is a good deal like a manufacturer's. His farm is his factory. His equipment is his machinery. His soil and seed and livestock are his materials. Right now he knows that bumper food production is needed for the war effort—just as we of General Motors know that weapons of war must flow from our plants in huge volume." During the Second World War, farms became factories. Even the breakfast cereal Wheaties made the connection, calling each farm "Your Own Munitions Plant!"[56]

Everywhere, propaganda, even before the attack on Pearl Harbor, promoted the idea that to be successful, to be productive, farms needed to become like factories, "the nation's No. 1 defense 'plants.'" The national government presented awards to various farmers for their production efforts much like the Army-Navy "E" Awards given to war industries. The *Des Moines Register* conducted its own statewide "Food for Victory" campaign, in which Mr. and Mrs. Harold Schultz of Schleswig won the first merit award for their outstanding farm-family effort in production. This farm couple had solved their labor problems, as did thousands of other farm families, by the wife's taking over the hired hand's work plus gathering over a hundred eggs a day and canning five hundred quarts over the summer. A national award, the

"Superior Achievement in Agriculture," by Skelley Gas Company, was given first to the Brady Riddle family of Castana, Iowa, in January 1943 for its outstanding production record. The Riddle family operated 680 acres of "Hawkeye land" and raised 1,040 pigs the previous year. Or, as the Skelley Gas ad exclaimed, "That's 130 tons of pork!"[57]

The industrial model by the mid-1940s emphasized scientific technology and mechanization. Since the 1890s, the ideas of increased farm size and efficiency along with better organization had progressed in the United States; farmers had both resisted and accepted these ideas. The world war was transforming agriculture, seemingly inevitably, into a more and more mechanized, consolidated, and corporate venture. This "Fordism"—capital-intensive industry based on the use of the moving assembly line—transferred to the farm right along with the increased number of Fordson and Farmall tractors. The factory model, as opposed to traditional farming practices reliant on family labor, proved difficult to resist. As historian Richard Polenberg notes in *War and Society,* "The war brought the era of large-scale, mechanized, corporate farming a good deal closer." *Life* magazine also described Iowa's farm-front agriculture in such terms: "Iowa is a food factory."[58]

A few farmers openly criticized this increasing factory orientation during the war. Ohio farmer Louis Bromfield, also a popular novelist, thought too many midwestern farmers were "mining" the land rather than developing long-term soil-enhancing techniques. To Bromfield, mechanization and the use of increased acres did not simply represent progress. In one of his wartime short stories, a female character who is a former Iowan criticizes her Dakota husband's farming methods by saying, "He had made all his land and the animals that lived upon it no more than a factory."[59]

Bromfield also expressed his views about the new metal farm buildings in *Pleasant Valley,* a biographical book of essays written during the war, calling them an ugly symbol of this turn to industrialization. He predicted, "Already they appear on any country landscape commonplace and standardized without any beauty or individuality—in fifty years they will simply be eyesores." And in a speech to Iowa farmers at the Des Moines Hotel Savery, Bromfield warned against abandoning soil-conservation techniques for factory practices on oversized, mechanized farms. Still, as a commercial farmer himself, he never questioned the importance of the farmers' role in food production for the war effort because he felt the farmer was as important as a front-line soldier. "Without the farmer, we cannot win the war," Bromfield believed, "and certainly without him, we cannot win the peace."[60]

Other agricultural commentators besides Bromfield also criticized this farm-factory orientation. Carey McWilliams claimed in *Ill Fares the Land* (1942) that great changes were taking place in American agriculture as the industrial revolution had finally hit the farmer. McWilliams called this process "the vortex of industrialization." He believed that farmers were increasingly drawn into this vortex, becoming efficient and powerful but ruthless. McWilliams summarized, "Modern technology is changing the Corn Belt into a great factory district."[61]

Paul Corey, an Iowa writer, joined the debate with his novel *Acres of Antaeus,* in which a corporate farm named "Mid-West" damages Iowa farmland for mass production, destroying many farm families in the process. His title reflects the growing distance from the land that the author had witnessed in Iowa farming: "According to Greek legend, Antaeus, a Libyan giant, renewed his strength every time he touched the earth, which was his mother, and was unconquerable. At last Hercules discovered the source of his power and overcame him by lifting him off the ground." In other words, the Midwest was losing its strength through its separation from the earth with its increased mechanization and corporate management structure. Another writer, Curtis Stadtfeld, reflected much later in the century on this World War II transformation of agriculture: "In short, the farms came to be more industrial, more oriented to a money economy and to efficient production of selective products—specialized as opposed to general farming—they became less whole, more impersonal, generally more profitable, perhaps less satisfying."[62]

When the war was nearly over, most of Iowa's farms had become quite prosperous, and the income for Iowa agriculture in 1945 was at its highest level ever. Iowa's contributions to the world's food supply peaked in the years 1942, 1943, and 1944 and nearly peaked again in 1945, despite bad weather and reduced production goals.[63] Many state officials, education experts, and farmers themselves attributed this prosperity to efficient industrial methods.

The official reports in 1945 continued to be positive regarding Iowa farmers' contributions to the war effort. Extension Director Bliss spoke with an echoing of Winston Churchill, "Never in recorded history have so few people produced so much food. Never before have an equal number of people made such an enormous increase in food production as have Iowa farmers during the past five years. And it was accomplished with fewer workers and older machinery. Patriotism was placed above profit as a compelling motive to increase food output." Harry Linn, Iowa's secretary of agriculture, agreed, "It means that the Iowa farmer contributed no small share in helping to ease the starvation plight which threatened most of the globe."[64]

Agricultural historian Gilbert Fite argues that World War II solved several farm problems at once. Production surpluses no longer were a problem with the farm-front all-out production; prosperity came from wartime demands and high prices. Fewer workers were needed after mechanization, so many Americans left agriculture forever. "Within a single generation," Fite noted, "commercial farmers had become a tiny minority in American society." He poignantly asked whether something basic and meaningful had not been lost forever.[65]

Increased Production, Faster Soil Depletion

Farmers greatly expanded their production of corn, and by 1944, national corn production had increased 25 percent from 1939. Iowa became a ten-million-acre corn state, producing 20 percent of all the corn in the United States, and the state's average annual wartime production reached 552,977,400 bushels. Production also increased because of the higher production yields of hybrid corn. This "hybrid hurricane" of corn was complete by 1945, when 100 percent of commercial fields were planted in hybrid seed. W. O. Tranbarger of Conrad was declared the "Corn King" in 1945, when he won a ten-acre yield contest with 131.8 bushels per acre. War or not, Iowa had always meant corn, and writer John Dos Passos described this fact with enthusiasm in a letter to his wife, Kathy, written while he was on a trip around the country to assess war preparations. "It's wonderful here [in Coon Rapids]," Dos Passos began. "Nobody thinks of anything but corn—not corn liquor but hybrid corn (one hundred bushels to the acre) standing pale and gaunt in immense fields rising in ranks over the rolling hills."[66]

Though Iowa meant corn, the state's farmers produced many other crops and animals as well for war needs. As Homer Croy wrote in his book *Corn Country,* "Even a real corn queen has other dresses in the closet." Another "dress," perhaps, was poultry, although most farm men traditionally considered raising chickens to be "women's work." Farm women often held complete responsibility for raising chicks and gathering eggs, and the money from the flock was then considered hers in most farm families. Raising chickens had never been a simple job, and the process became even more complex with the introduction of hybrid chickens, improved henhouses, and commercial feed mixes. As the *Iowa Agriculturist* stated, "There can be no slackers in a war-time poultry enterprise."[67]

Like planting, poultry and egg production also became more industrial during the war years and after, since they could be even more profitable with a scientific, systematic approach rather than the traditional farm methods that had been used by farm women and children. Experts suggested a "wartime laying mush" for increased egg production. An example of the new poultry system and the resulting increase in men's interest was the two-story chicken parlor introduced on the Miller farm in Winneshiek County. Mr. Miller proudly described his new chicken parlor, "I've eaten in restaurants that didn't smell half as good as this place does."[68]

Raising poultry in farm flocks required constant care and attention, but it utilized land and feed efficiently. During World War II, industrial-type farms began to confine chickens in facilities to increase egg production and lower labor requirements. In 1943, Iowa's farms produced the largest number of chickens in the country at 62,350,000 and the largest number of eggs at 3,999,000,000, for a cash income of $104,650,000. The president of the Iowa Poultry Improvement Association, Floyd Bloom, said in his 1943 annual address that poultry production had become a vital part of war food production. "With a severe shortage of labor, equipment, and poultry supplies," Bloom began, "it behooves each and every one of us to put forth our every effort, individually, and as an association, to get the job done."[69]

Another division of the Food for Freedom campaign included the development of new farm products to meet war demands. The federal government desperately needed substitutes for oil and fiber when

Japan's conquests of Pacific countries cut off supplies. Soybeans and hemp began to meet these needs. Soybeans were converted from a forage crop in the 1930s to a major crop during the war, with utilization of the bean for oil and flour, and production increased from a few thousand acres in Iowa to almost two million annually by war's end, largely in the central and northwest regions of the state, with their percentage of highly tillable and level acres. A new Extension pamphlet titled "Soybeans, Iowa's Key War Crop" enunciated the crop's rapid progress. Nationally, the soybean average yield increased eight times, and some farmers believed soybeans could help "even the score" against Japan.[70]

Farmers associated the growing of new war crops such as hemp and soybeans with untold financial risks and therefore were hesitant, wanting government protection for possible crop failures. In 1942, hemp was considered a weed, growing in ditches and fencerows, but by the very next year it was listed as a war priority, and over 4,000 Iowa farmers devoted 45,786 acres to hemp in 1943. Though farmers initially worried about the profitability of growing hemp, it proved to be a very efficient and lucrative row crop. The market for hemp would never approach the level that soybeans developed, but it was appealing because it too was an easy crop to grow, with little manual labor, since its harvest could be highly mechanized—almost industrial. The John Deere Company developed hemp-cutting machinery for the war effort. For added information and drama, the USDA made and showed at local theaters a motion picture that described raising hemp for the war effort along with the harvesting and turning process. The film's title was simple and traditional: *Hemp for Victory.*[71] Farmers also listened to the government propaganda that "HEMP is a war crop for Iowa." Government advertisements for this wartime production combined the incentives of patriotism and profit; in other words, a farmer could "save a boy's life" as well as make money. The message of destruction also presented itself within these government advertisements for wartime production: "Hemp is a war crop for Iowa. . . . Every acre is a nail in Hitler's coffin. Every acre of HEMP will blow the Jap off this earth."[72]

Hemp production slowed down and eventually stopped, however, when enough straw tonnage was produced in 1943 to meet the next two years' needs. Iowa farmer Ollie Janssen expressed disappointment at this because his field had previously brought him $4,000 in one season, proving that mechanized hemp production could be as profitable as corn or soybean production. Therefore, midwestern farmers were not pleased when the federal government drastically cut back hemp production and then quickly canceled war orders for it. Many farmers had believed hemp might be a permanent, government-subsidized postwar crop.[73]

The high wartime production of row crops, however, developed long-term soil deficiencies, and extensive planting of corn and soybeans had seriously damaged the quality and quantity of Iowa's topsoil. Officials such as Extension Director Bliss argued that Iowa farmers needed to take a more aggressive and farsighted stance regarding soil conservation, since the war was over. The director of the U.S. Extension Service, M. L. Wilson, spoke at Iowa State College's 46th Annual Farm and Home Week in February 1946 about the need for a renewed soil-conservation effort in Iowa. He maintained that "the soil must be rebuilt along with the bodies of Europe's starving millions to insure peace."[74]

Native son Vice President Henry Wallace and other agricultural experts certainly had reason to be concerned about the war years' all-out production and its effect on Iowa's valuable topsoil. Researchers for *Iowa Farm Science* studied 105 farms in Pocahontas County, a level area in north-central Iowa with a substantial acreage devoted to cash grain farming. Sixty-eight percent of the 1946 corn acreage had previously been in corn, oats, or soybeans for five years or longer. Farmers had managed only 10 percent of this land with a soil-conservation method such as a first year of corn followed by hay or pasture rotation. Within the entire state, the acres of intertilled crops (cultivated rows of corn and soybeans, which contributed to more soil erosion) had increased by 2.5 million during the war, while the acres of small grains had decreased by 1.2 million. Iowa farmers had also plowed up during the war years more than 260,000 acres of what was previously considered permanent pasture. Clyde Spry, secretary of Iowa's Soil Conservation Commission, concluded that Iowa was worse off from a conservation standpoint in 1946 than in 1940.[75] One hundred percent of Iowa's corn acreage was planted with hybrid seed corn by war's end, increasing the general yield level at least 25 percent but also increasing the soil's depletion with added mechanization and chemicals. *Wallaces' Farmer* expressed its postwar concerns to Iowa readers by asking simply, "If you had most of your farm in corn the last few years, were you a patriot or a soil-miner?"[76]

And yet farmers believed international problems could again be ignored because of their own local prosperity. As historian John Blum notes, World War II was "a lovely war after all, with the fighting remote and prosperity returned. In that context, for many Americans, it was difficult to remember that the demand for guns had fostered the production and consumption of butter."[77]

Losing Sons

Iowa during the Second World War was, at times, a lovely, prosperous, and secure place to live and work, and novelist John Dos Passos painted just such a romantic word picture as he traveled across the state during the war years. "Behind the house the great stretch of country rolled pale ocher towards blue hills along the horizon moving in slow undulations like an ocean groundswell in a calm," Dos Passos began drawing the image. "Here and there in a deeper hollow was a scrap of a bright blue pond or the green smudge of a swamp."[78] From this point on the globe, most Iowans found it difficult to imagine a war-torn European landscape.

Another traveler, Hilary St. George Saunders, from Europe, envisioned a more conflicting picture when he spoke with Mr. and Mrs. Koons from Swea City, Iowa, whose son was supposedly the first in the United States Army to kill a German soldier. Mr. Koons began speaking his mind regarding the war developments: "The world is getting too old for war and such nonsense. This time it has got to end, and it's boys like my son who will end it. We've learned what peace is like out here but I guess we'll never have it for keeps till you in Europe have learned it too. That's why we're fighting—to help you learn it." As a philosopher, Saunders wondered if farmers were perhaps more pacifist than other men, that they might "view existence as the tillers of soil in all countries have always viewed and most always view it, as a struggle against drought, frost, wind, hail, rain, green-fly, and all the other foes which Nature mobilizes against them." Saunders reflected, "Why should men take on their own kind as well passes their understanding. 'It's just goddam stupid.' And yet, whatever their attitude may have been in the last war, in this one they are ready to bear their share." This may have been isolationism or perhaps the ability "to reduce life to its essentials."[79]

Iowa's farmers, however, could no longer afford to be isolationist following this devastating global war, when the world's food shortages became increasingly more severe. As early as March 1943, former president Herbert Hoover (who had managed the European famine crisis after World War I) reminded midwestern governors at a Des Moines meeting that food production remained the greatest part of the home front's responsibilities and should continue after the war had ended. Hoover warned the audience, "We can have peace or we can have revenge, but we cannot have both."[80]

The images of American abundance contrasted sharply with those of the desperate European conditions, such as the publicized photographs of American GIs handing out candy to Europe's starving children. Iowa's land of farming abundance also contrasted sharply with the degraded German landscape, which had once been beautiful with well-cultivated fields but now bore the marks of war with demolished houses and dead, bloated cattle. Some Allied leaders thought Germany should be completely transformed to a pastoral country, without war industries, to avoid the possibility of future wars.[81]

World War II ultimately became a war for food and survival. And when the Nazi concentration-camp prisoners were finally rescued in the spring and summer of 1945, the image of survival through deliberately imposed starvation conditions would be horrifying. In Dachau, some German guards tried to escape by disguising themselves in striped prison clothes, but their "well-fed faces" gave them away. Later, British nurses spoke of former Dachau prisoners whom they had tried to nourish. The survivors were free to wander the hospital, yet the nurses noticed that "they were always back in the ward at mealtimes, no matter where they strayed, silently converging on the food trolley with their tin plates, eyes riveted on the containers full of meat and vegetables." Despite the prisoners' now-regular meals, nurses would find "while making the beds, a slice of corned beef, a potato or a piece of bread hidden under a pillow, for they could not yet be sure that another day would bring more food." Almost 30,000 people had been liberated from Dachau, but 2,466 died in the following six weeks. Medical care and food could not save them at that point.[82]

Donald Willis, a twenty-two-year-old soldier from Swan, Iowa, had been drafted into the U.S. Army and served with the 3rd Armored

Division in Europe, and he kept a diary from June 6, 1944 (D-Day), through June 6, 1945. On April 11, 1945, at the opening of the death camp at Nordhausen (which he referred to as "Hell Hole!" in his diary), Willis described his horror at the slave extermination camp in which the living and the dead were mixed together. He remembered for the rest of his life the eyes of the liberated survivors who were so thankful for the rescue. As he recorded their diet, "Black bread and thin soup were their one-a-day meal, which was at the starvation level."[83]

This world war had destroyed so many people. Although Europe's destruction directly contrasted with the United States' lack of it at home, America was not without its losses.[84] Iowa's war dead totaled more than 5,000 men by early 1945, a higher per capita record than most states, and many Iowa farmers were well aware of what war sacrifices had been made although their agricultural world had prospered. Toward the end of the war, writer Hilary Saunders watched at an Iowa farmhouse as a farmer and his Iowa State College–educated son argued over aspects of contour plowing. Finally, the seventy-year-old father said, "Well, if it's going to win the war, son . . ." Saunders commented on the scene: "All his sweat and labour, all his sons save one, had to be devoted to this end. The word 'war' on his lips was like blasphemy in the mouth of a priest."[85]

When soldier Weston Nobel left to serve overseas, he remembered what his father, an Iowa farmer near Riceville, said to him: "Life is so ironical. Everything I'm touching now is turning to money. Everything. And yet, it may cost you your life."[86] In a similar scene but years later, in the early 1980s, journalist Studs Terkel wrote that prosperity did come with the war, but "boom had a double meaning." Terkel then described an aged Iowa farmer and father:

> For the old Iowa farmer, it was something else. Oh yes, he remembered the Depression and what it did to farmers: foreclosures the norm; grain burned; corn at *minus* three cents a bushel; rural despair. Oh yes, it changed with the war. "That's when the real boost came. The war—" There is a catch in his voice. He slumps in his rocker. His wife stares at the wallpaper. It is a long silence, save for the tick-tock of the grandfather's clock. "—it does something to your country. It does something to the individual. I had a neighbor just as the war was beginning. We had a boy ready to go to service. This neighbor told me that what we needed was a

> damn good war, and we'd solve our agricultural problems. And I said, 'Yes, but I'd hate to pay with the price of my son.' Which we did." He weeps. "It's too much of a price to pay."[87]

War's all-out production of food and Iowa's resulting agricultural prosperity had come with a heavy price for many family farms: resources that could never be replaced. Iowa had paid with far too much of her wealth, with both her soil and her children.

Chapter 2

"E" Awards and WOWs ~ The Production Front

We must be the great arsenal of democracy.

—President Roosevelt, Fireside Chat (December 29, 1940)

As the Reverend Dale Welch spoke to the seventh annual meeting of the Iowa Taxpayers Association in October 1941, he told the businessmen that this was "a grand and awful time." Welch elaborated, "Yes, these are grand times, at least in the astronomical figures that are used in computing defense needs, lend-lease appropriations, government expenditures and the national debt. And they are awful times in terms of the tragic happenings that occur from day to day and they have terrible meanings for not only ourselves but our posterity. I wonder whether as business and professional men we really are big enough to deal with the grand and awful times we are in." Welch continued to speak about the defense issue and the corresponding need for efficiency and economy in Iowa. War appeared imminent, and national-defense needs were changing the industrial face of America. Iowans did not want to be left behind, whether in grand or awful times, especially if national-defense industries should become more decentralized and profitable.[1]

Iowa's war-production preparations started as early as September 1939, when seventy-two manufacturing firms became ready, as the *Des Moines Register* reported, to "swing immediately into war production."

Des Moines possessed eleven such plants; Davenport and Dubuque had seven each; and Burlington, Sioux City, Bettendorf, and Waterloo each claimed five factories ready for war production. By March 1941, defense expenditures totaled $57 million in Iowa and had increased to $68 million by July, yet the industrial East and West coasts boasted the highest number of awards. Iowa's awarded defense contracts amounted to only half of one percent of those awarded throughout the nation, and factory defense employment by August 1941 amounted to 19.4 percent in Iowa, but 22.4 percent in the United States. The Midwest possessed one advantage for future industrial establishments as it was considered safer from enemy attack than either coast.[2]

By the end of 1941, defense industries in Iowa churned out a diverse list of products, including steel buildings, water tanks, airplane hangars, submarine paint, tanks, radio transmitters, tents, helmets, range finders, knapsacks, airplane parts, holsters, caps, work clothes, and machine-gun parts, cartridges, and covers. The Iowa Transmission Company of Waterloo, a subsidiary of John Deere, held the largest defense contract of $10,686,000 for tank transmissions, while the largest variety of contracts amounting to $1,400,503 went to the Boyt Harness Company in Des Moines for haversacks, gun covers, and cartridge belts. Many Iowa manufacturers literally did not know what they were producing since their piecework involved complicated subcontracts. By December 1941, Iowa defense contracts totaled more than $132 million in over 150 factories producing everything from gears to clothes, from corrugated boxes to mud lugs for tanks.[3]

To meet the industrial needs increasing at such a rapid rate throughout 1941, the United States began to build more defense plants despite the fact that, as *Life* magazine described, it was "a peaceable nation lacking the real warrior spirit." As historian V. R. Cardozier points out in *The Mobilization of the United States in World War II,* "Although the United States was definitely unprepared for war in December 1941, it was not altogether unprepared."[4]

The Japanese attack on Pearl Harbor changed the spirit of production to an all-out effort, and the *Iowa Unionist* would be one among many newspapers to pledge their full support to the war effort. As the state's union paper described the situation, "Our nation is engaged in a great struggle against the forces of evil, rampant throughout the world; wholly inspired by greed and all-consuming lust for power—forces that seek to deprive all but a small privileged class of their sacred, God-given right to Freedom, Justice, and Equality." Supporting this struggle was the mission of the production front as it strove to produce the weapons, vehicles, ammunition, and other materials needed to wage a total, global war.[5]

Most Americans believed that simply their productive capacity would win this war. Director of War Production Donald Nelson expressed a common belief in September 1942 when he said, "This Nation is beginning to produce as no other nation in the world has ever produced. The soldiers of production, just as truly as the boys at the fronts, are helping to lick the enemies of Democracy." Or, as William Knudsen, director general of the Office of Production Management, told employees at the newly constructed Burlington defense plant, "American production is going to win this darned war—there isn't any question about it."[6]

Other citizens warned fellow Americans not to become overconfident of the production front. Journalist Max Lerner called this optimism "the Superman Dream" and "a treacherous confidence in our industries." Ernie Pyle, a noted war correspondent, also reminded readers that they should remember those first American war casualties at the African front. Pyle admonished, "We were smug—had got it into our heads that production alone would win the war."[7]

As the *Iowa Business Digest* commented, businesses needed to "remember Pearl Harbor" by "remembering the strength, organization, and unity of the Japanese industrial system compared to the haphazard U.S. system of capitalism." The attack on Pearl Harbor had changed the spirit of the production front to one of urgency by ending any arguments about American involvement in the war. Iowa's isolationists, as in the rest of the nation, seemed left with "no choice" because of the "sneaky" and "treacherous" attack, and the democratic warrior, as any warrior, needed to be armed. Modern wars needed factories. America had the materials and the means for modern war; the attack on Pearl Harbor and the declaration of war by Nazi Germany provided the necessary catalyst.[8]

Two Blasts, No Sabotage ~ Iowa Ordnance Plant

Employment, according to Secretary of Labor Frances Perkins, had reached a new national high of 35.6 million by mid-1940 because of the stimulated national-defense program. Compared to a year earlier, almost a million more people held jobs.[9] With more European war clouds looming, the United States could see that it needed to prepare for its perhaps inevitable involvement. The United States government formed the Defense Plant Corporation on August 22, 1940, to further develop its war-production infrastructure since private businesses were not prepared to take the financial risks. The proposed plants under this act would be government-owned, contractor-operated (GOCO) plants: the federal government would finance and ultimately own them, but private contractors would conduct their building and operation on a cost-plus-fixed-fee basis. Construction began on a number of defense facilities in July 1940, and in less than eighteen months, by December 1941, seventeen GOCO plants were under production. A Burlington plant would be one of the first of these production facilities, and by the end of the war, there were 214 such plants across the country.[10]

The physical characteristics necessary for each potential defense plant site were considerable: geographic invulnerability to attack, supportive transportation facilities, adequate energy sources, available raw materials, and interested potential employees. Architects designed and contractors built plants as whole units, not by converting factories, so these facilities were, as one academic researcher describes, "born practically full-grown." This allowed an orderly design for administration and production, but witnesses often described the building of such defense plants as an "eerie experience" because of the rapid development, immense sizes, and strict security measures. The building of the Pentagon was an especially remarkable example of the magnitude and speed of this prewar construction; the world's largest office building began construction in the summer of 1941 and housed personnel within a year. Even before Pearl Harbor, the need for defense projects was extremely urgent as the United States needed to "out-Hitler Hitler."[11]

Government defense plants created dramatic changes in the communities where they were built. Most midwestern towns prided themselves on stability, but rapid industrial changes dramatically affected community services and housing. Willow Run, Michigan, the site of the world's largest new war factory at that time, bore the consequences of rapid change accomplished with great technological advances but few social considerations. The Ford bomber plant there possessed some of the most modern features in industrial production, yet many new laborers had no choice of housing but trailer-home communities, with few if any facilities developed for their living conditions. Other examples of rapid industrial change were two new plants in Indiana, the Wabash River Ordnance Plant and the Kingsbury Ordnance Plant; the two communities' residents expressed disappointment when a construction company failed to hire local labor, and they displayed some bitterness about arrangements for the purchasing of farmland. Professionals in Iowa's war-production communities tried to apply lessons they learned from these cases by controlling rapid development and providing for new employees.[12]

The outskirts of Burlington transformed into the location of the first federal ordnance plant in Iowa, and as a result, the community was strongly influenced by wartime production. Located along the Mississippi River, Burlington claimed a population of 26,775 and boasted Iowa's oldest newspaper, the daily *Hawk-Eye Gazette.* In the nineteenth century, Burlington's river location had made it an ideal industrial center with the only steamboat landing on the Mississippi River between Fort Madison and Muscatine. By 1940, Burlington envisioned itself as a city ready to commit to war production. The Flint Hills above their Mississippi location had been a peaceful place for Native Americans in centuries past to collect flint for arrows and axes; now these hills would produce modern bombs.[13]

When Colonel R. D. Valliant from the United States Army Quartermaster Corps arrived in Burlington on November 5, 1940, local military officials had already begun initial preparations for construction of the defense plant. This plant would ultimately cover 4,000 acres, with a total land base of 20,000 acres located southwest of the city. The federal government purchased 183 farms for the site and placed an angle in the plant's rectangular outline on the north side to avoid Middletown, population 126, whose residents were not very excited about this new development. A local gas-station operator commented, "A lot of those farmers who will have to move were my customers and I guess they are pretty worried about it."[14]

Most local residents appeared to handle the transition of land from private ownership to the federal government rather smoothly, as the government paid $3,580,887 for 200 of 206 tracts of land, with only 6 small claims going to court. The largest claim paid was for the Des

Moines County Farm at $200,000 for 396 acres, and the smallest was $337.28. Of the farmers, 130 were owners and 90 were tenants, but 50 tenants still had not been able to make definite plans for relocation by February 1941. War Department representatives praised long-established residents for agreeing to sell their farmland without any significant legal arguments. This federal government purchase of 20,000 total acres of land in Des Moines County amounted to one tenth of the county's area. Once started, the Burlington munitions plant construction seemed to gain its own momentum in the transformation from peaceful, productive farm acres to the largest detonator plant in the country. The War Department awarded the construction contract to Day and Zimmerman, Inc., of Philadelphia, and work locating building materials as well as prospective workers for the Burlington plant proceeded. The buildings' construction required steel and concrete for permanence, and the entire area was fenced and policed. Major John Lowry, a War Department representative, assured Burlington Kiwanis Club members in December 1940 that nothing would delay construction of the munitions plant. The $34,451,384 contract from early November 1940 combined with an additional $12 to $15 million for construction costs made for an estimated total of $50 million in January 1941, although that figure would be higher before it was finished.[15]

By the end of December, over one hundred train carloads of construction material had been delivered to the construction site, with many more expected. Plant officials also started accepting worker applications, and all employees were then fingerprinted and photographed for security purposes. By January 1941, the plant construction force exceeded 1,100, of whom 75 percent were Burlington-area residents. The Burlington City Council passed a resolution urging the ordnance plant's construction company to give preference to local labor after the Chamber of Commerce's mail tripled that month with job requests from other parts of Iowa, Missouri, and Illinois.[16]

Though the plant was initially to be titled the Burlington Shell Loading Plant, unofficially other names caught on, such as *the powder factory, the munitions plant,* and *the arsenal.* Federal officials decided to name the plant the Iowa Ordnance Plant (IOP) in early February 1941. (The name was changed after the war to the Iowa Army Ammunition Plant.) The rapid construction work fascinated local residents, and roads leading to the plant were officially closed in the latter part of March because of the "jammed" highways. Traffic neared ten thousand visitors on one Sunday. Admission to the plant area was restricted to officials and employees.[17]

The number of employees kept increasing in 1941, from 2,460 on February 14 to 6,254 on April 25 to 9,533 on May 24 (when the facility was 40 percent complete) to 12,217 by July 12. Shifts worked minimum forty-eight-hour weeks, with time-and-a-half pay over forty hours; crews invested 9,075,612 man-hours to make the plant 83.5 percent complete by the end of August. The target completion date was actually moved up from November 3 to September 3, 1941.[18] Altogether, the Iowa Ordnance Plant hired 16,620 workers between January and July, including replacements. As the vice president of Day and Zimmerman, E. F. Johnstone Jr., told the Iowa Engineering Society's annual convention, new employees with farming backgrounds exemplified the "best type." Johnstone explained, "Because World War [I] experience showed farm men and women were more careful and more deft at fine hand work than workers of any other background, Iowa farm people will be sought to work in the plant when it is completed." Officials expected women to make up 30 percent of the labor force, especially for fuse work, but also for loading and weighing shells. Men over the age of forty composed another group of sought-after workers; they were thought to have better safety habits since they had reached "an age of caution."[19]

The Iowa Ordnance Plant, when completed, contained machine-shop equipment worth $7 million, and its annual operating expenses reached $30 million. The plant's construction materials also made up impressive lists. For example, in one peak day, April 29, 1941, workers poured over 3,000 tons of concrete. The original amended contract of $50 million for 496 structures (of which 211 were storage igloos) increased by $7.2 million in June to include 25 more manufacturing buildings and 69 added storage igloos, along with 18 more miles of railroad track. The plant divided itself into 20 production and storage areas linked by 75 miles of railway network, 100 miles of roads, 30 miles of water lines, 15 miles of sewer pipe, and 100 miles of electrical line. Its power plant could supply enough energy for a city of 50,000.[20]

From the day officials turned over the first spade of dirt on January 17, 1941, to the plant's dedication on July 31, 1941, the creation of the ordnance plant fulfilled a remarkable story of industrial coordination and enterprise. One journalist believed this construction scene in southeast Iowa to be one in which "men and machine are winning a major battle in America's all-out defense effort. It's a battle of the production line—the first line of defense."[21]

A year after the formal announcement of the proposed Burlington plant on November 6, 1940, construction crews had transformed 20,000 acres of farmland into a nearly $60 million ordnance plant with 600 buildings. The payroll for that year totaled over $10 million. "The whole landscape has been changed," a *Hawk-Eye Gazette* journalist summarized. "What was once a placid easy-going farming community is now a bustling industrial area where Uncle Sam is loading shells to be hurled at Hitler or anybody else." The first artillery shell rolled off the melt line in September, just nine months after construction had started, yet months before the attack on Pearl Harbor. The Iowa Ordnance Plant now stood as the largest construction project ever in Iowa, turning out bombs and shells steadily by 1942.[22]

Governor George Wilson and Lieutenant Governor Bourke Hickenlooper paid the plant its first official visit on July 9, 1941, and Major Otto Jank coordinated this inspection tour. Wilson officially commented on the plant's progress, "Although I had kept in close touch with the plant through the press, I hadn't realized the extent of the project nor the extensiveness of the construction program." The governor would write on December 30 to the *Hawk-Eye Gazette* with his congratulations to this enterprising city: "I am sure that we are all gratified by the news we received from time to time of the healthy strides toward the greater prosperity of Burlington and rejoice with you in the hum of industry and the stir of commerce."[23]

The Burlington Chamber of Commerce organized a National Defense Day celebration that July to honor the plant's construction with a visit by Vice President Henry A. Wallace, an Iowa native. Wallace arrived to a nineteen-gun salute in nearby Middletown, then proceeded toward the plant, where officials honored him with a souvenir shell. A thousand soldiers from Fort Leonard Wood escorted Wallace to the Burlington Hotel, where, from the balcony, he reviewed the troops with their full equipment and field guns to the music of the 20th Infantry Band.[24]

This National Defense Day concluded with a banquet in the Burlington Memorial Auditorium with about five hundred people in attendance. "Preparedness" was its theme. During the after-dinner program,

Major Jank presented the City of Burlington with an 81-millimeter shell ("with all the dangerous elements removed") on behalf of the ordnance department. As Mayor Max Conrad accepted the shell, he said, "On behalf of the people of Burlington I accept with great pride the first shell made in the Iowa Ordnance Plant." Conrad explained that it was both symbolic of peace—since it was unloaded—yet symbolic of something else as this plant was prepared to produce "hundreds of thousands—yea millions of loaded shells if need be." Other officials also spoke of their pride in Iowa's wartime industrial production. "Something else comes out of Iowa besides tall corn . . . ," Brigadier General Norman Ramsey of the Rock Island Arsenal declared; "the state is successful in the output of shells." Brigadier General Philip P. Fleming, a native of Burlington, said that he had had mixed emotions about the plant since he had ridden a pony during his childhood over what was now the plant area, but as an adult he realized the land had to be set aside for war production.[25]

Also that evening, local shortwave radios broadcast the text of Wallace's highly patriotic dedication, "America—the Mighty." "Today we dedicate this great plant to the defense of liberty," Wallace began, "to the worship of God, to respect for the dignity of man and to the peaceful pursuit of happiness. Through a oneness of spirit we shall live." Wallace then continued with a ringing, rhythmic pride: "As days pass and factory belts move ever faster, as muscles and minds quicken to the task, this great agricultural community will have its part in the oneness of will and work which shall win not only the war, but the peace."[26]

A Cedar Rapids newspaper editorial later praised Burlington for its organized celebration and Wallace for his polished elocution. The editorial also commented that Wallace probably intended to awaken the people of the Midwest to the current national dangers by stirring them to a more "belligerent" mood. The paper seemed to doubt that Iowa's citizens in July of 1941 had fully considered war. "In any case, shells can be produced as well in Iowa as they can in Connecticut," the editorial concluded, "and the new Burlington plant should prove it."[27]

Not everyone was so enthusiastic about this official celebration. Burlington Republicans called it "a New Deal Affair" because Democrats Vice President Wallace and Senator Clyde Herring were present while Republican Governor Wilson was absent. Lieutenant Governor Hickenlooper, however, did introduce Wallace, and local Republicans could not complain too much because the plant payroll reached $500,000 a week, double Burlington's industrial salaries during "normal times."[28]

To earn this money, the Iowa Ordnance Plant workers produced bombs for the Allies. The first load line started production a day earlier than planned—on July 30, 1941; the second line started on October 27; the third line on November 20. The first production order comprised 155-millimeter howitzer shells, then 81-millimeter trench mortar shells, then 155-millimeter GPF ("grand precise firing," translated from a French term) shells, then 75-millimeter anti-aircraft shells, then aerial bombs. Most of the ordnance production turned to larger artillery, with the largest aerial bombs weighing 2,000 pounds and measuring 5 feet by 2 feet, equivalent to a "man-sized" bathtub. The assembly lines for these shells equaled mile-long conveyor systems. One journalist pictured the entire plant as a "giant baby": "Like an elephant's calf, it was born big. It will only produce big projectiles."[29]

Burlington residents certainly remained proud of the community's bomb production. For American Heroes' Day on July 17, 1942, local businesses displayed thirty 155-millimeter shells in downtown Burlington store windows. In another patriotic gesture, the Burlington American Legion Post No. 52 purchased war bonds totaling $10,000 to pay for a carload of bombs from the Iowa Ordnance Plant. And in an ironic twist of "it's a small world," two overseas Burlingtonians ended up loading several five-hundred-pound bombs titled "Kisses for Hitler" onto Flying Fortress bombers destined for the Italian front.[30]

Plant officials also wanted to maintain pride in their plant's production record and so continually stressed security and safety measures. All employees on the production lines required two entry passes—one at the gate and a separate one to a production line—and guards confiscated all matches and lighters at the front gate. In the changing rooms, far from the lines, employees switched from civilian clothes and shoes to khaki overalls called "monkey suits" and "powder shoes," which had no nails or capped toes. A number of bombproof shelters for employees were scattered around the plant grounds in case of an explosion. As a fireman explained the whistle cord on the production lines, "If anyone sees anything go wrong, he pulls that—and we all skedaddle." The Iowa Ordnance Plant initially maintained an excellent safety record, but it was soon lost. Between December 1941 and June 1942, three explosions occurred in the nation's ordnance plants, killing eighty-three people and destroying a million dollars' worth of property, and two of the three explosions occurred at the Iowa Ordnance Plant.[31]

At 1:05 p.m. on Friday, December 12, 1941, just a few days after Pearl Harbor, a single blast shocked the countryside, strong enough to rattle windows in West Burlington, twelve miles away. Residents learned that TNT had exploded in the No. 1 Melt Unit, a three-story building of reinforced concrete, steel, and bricks, and the force of the blast hurled men out of windows and doors. The roof and walls flew several hundred feet in the air, and debris fell around the injured men. No women worked on that line, but officials estimated that fifty to seventy-five men were working in the building at the time. William Pratt of Burlington, one of the injured, described the blast, "The first thing I knew there was a terrific noise and then the roof began falling in."[32]

As an immediate result of the explosion, eight men died, but only six bodies could be quickly identified. A hand from one body had to be traced back to the employee's fingerprint records. Twenty men were rushed to local hospitals, with the newspapers pronouncing them "casualties of war." Ultimately, thirteen men lost their lives. The morale of other IOP employees, however, was reputed to still be good after the accident because of the anger from the Japanese attack on Pearl Harbor. The number applying for jobs remained high. And three experts from Washington ruled out any possible sabotage.[33]

The December blast in Burlington was ranked by Associated Press editors in 1941 as the outstanding news story for Iowa. Sadly, a second accident in March 1942 would also be the outstanding news story for its year. At 11:53 p.m. on March 4, an explosion destroyed another melt unit, the No. 3 Line. There was a white flash and a huge puff of smoke, and flames shot high in the air as the explosion shattered and ripped off the top of a concrete, steel, and brick building. The blast could be heard for twenty-five miles and rattled windows in Burlington. At midnight, just seven minutes after the explosion, the police station suddenly became "a madhouse" filled with startled people and ringing phones. Throughout the night, rescue workers labored under floodlights with no reported hysteria or wasted efforts. Fortunately, the explosion occurred in the southwest section of the facility and was thus isolated from other buildings. Rescuers initially recovered fifteen bodies and sent fifty injured men to local hospitals. One employee later described the explosion, "All hell broke loose before you could bat an eye." Another said of the blast, "It looked like pictures of a volcano." The following day the editor of the *Hawk-Eye Gazette* stated that "wholesale death, grim, stark and ghastly" had moved in upon Burlington.[34] Twenty men ultimately lost their lives in this second explosion.[35]

While Burlington residents grieved for the victims, a predictable wartime response emerged from local newspapers. Since Wallace's speech in 1941, the dominant theme regarding almost any event related to war production was to praise workers for their patriotism and to cast them as soldiers who simply served on a different front than those fighting on the battlefront. The *Hawk-Eye Gazette* responded accordingly the day after the blast. Those who died were "heroes in civilian capacities," the editor wrote, who "gave their lives as gloriously and as freely as if they had fallen at Pearl Harbor, Singapore, or Manila."[36]

Morale remained high at the ordnance plant following the second blast, although several workers quit or transferred. Most employees, displaying "typical Americanism," seemed determined to "carry on." Jake Waring, who survived both blasts, enlisted in the navy at the end of March. Waring jokingly explained: "If I'm bombproof, I suppose I'll have a chance to find it out there too."[37]

Senator Herring quickly initiated an official investigation of this blast based on a report by Marc Burbridges, a discharged safety engineer from IOP. Burbridges had warned officials as early as December of dangerous practices witnessed at the plant. He had predicted another accidental blast, expressing concern for employees' safety and suggesting specific measures such as the hiring of more safety engineers and the provision of better training for employees. The general manager of Day and Zimmerman disputed all charges, and plant managers stressed strict housekeeping, claiming the plant was "at its peak of perfection."[38]

Herring, however, commented, "This explosion should not have happened." He believed that William Knudsen, director general of the Office of Production Management, should investigate. As Herring argued, "When anything interferes with war production, he ought to know about it." The general flew in from Kansas City, Missouri, and closed all melt units until after the investigation. One coincidence to be investigated was that both blasts occurred during shift changes, resulting in higher numbers of fatalities. Still, investigators found no evidence of sabotage and concluded that the cause was "the vigorous manual operation of a valve controlling the flow of TNT."[39]

From its opening, despite the two accidents, the Iowa Ordnance Plant consistently maintained high production levels, which translated for area workers into employment opportunities with good wages and, at least until the war ended, stability. The phrase often used to describe such favorable employment situations was *a booming war economy.*[40]

The Iowa Ordnance Plant outside of Burlington completed the war with an impressive production record: 25 million mortar shells, 200,000 medium-caliber shells, 5 million major-caliber shells, and 2.5 million bombs weighing between 90 and 1,000 pounds each. The plant's average annual payroll during the war came to $20 million, which should have given "a psychological lift" to Burlington's "depression-jaded business men."[41]

The plant had cost nearly $60 million, with 99.3 percent of this amount federally funded. The plant did not qualify as a surplus government plant at war's end. Instead, Burlington ranked as one of twenty top areas whose development during the war was so dramatic as to put them in the postwar classification "new manufacturing area." Still, *Des Moines Register* reporter George Mills later described Burlington as having "a serious post-war headache" when the shell-loading production stopped and over a million dollars in unemployment checks was issued.[42]

The Iowa Ordnance Plant produced nitrate fertilizer after the war ended but soon returned to the production of war weapons, making even larger and more destructive bombs than it had during the war. The Atomic Energy Commission, established in 1946 to oversee the use of atomic energy, selected the Iowa Ordnance Plant in 1947 as the first of two plants in the nation to produce new types of atomic weapons. The explosive components manufactured at IOP were designed after the original implosion bomb nicknamed "Fat Man" dropped on Nagasaki.[43]

Acknowledgment of this new bomb production, however, would not be made publicly until 1951. By then, the Atomic Energy Commission had enlarged the plant and increased the number of employees, and it continued strict security measures in the remodeled facility, which was renamed the Iowa Army Ammunition Plant. The retooled IAAP later manufactured 175-millimeter shells for the Vietnam War. Local residents continued gossiping about the mysterious "Division B," the atomic-weapons area of the plant, commenting that it was "harder to find out anything about the plant now than it was during the [Second World] war."[44]

Almost Four Billion Bullets ~ Des Moines Ordnance Plant

Nearly six thousand people over the course of three hot July days in 1941 signed up for possible jobs in the proposed $30 million munitions plant to be built near Ankeny, north of Des Moines. Although Pearl Harbor was still six months away, ordnance jobs had begun to shift the American economy to one of war and future prosperity. But for now, many men wearing faded overalls and work shirts with the sleeves rolled up, hats upon their heads and determination in their eyes, waited restlessly—pacing and speculating—in a lengthy, moblike line that pointed toward the small employment window labeled "Registration."[45]

After Burlington was selected for construction of the Iowa Ordnance Plant, state officials thought other areas could also benefit from a war plant. In February 1941 both houses of the legislature passed "with absolute consensus" a $50,000 appropriation bill to attract defense industries to the state. The bill "cycloned" through in just one day. Since a dozen midwestern sites ranked as possibilities in March 1941 for a new powder plant, Iowa wanted to ensure its success as one of the chosen sites. However, farmers in both Lee and Van Buren counties protested this supposed progress; they did not want their area to be a site as they hated to sell their family farmland.[46]

During the last week of May 1941, Governor Wilson traveled to Washington, DC, to create federal interest in defense contracts for Iowa. The War Department planned under the fifth Lend-Lease bill to spend $1 billion on new and enlarged munitions plants with a potential work force of four million people. Federal officials stated that it was the largest bill for munitions plants ever approved in a single day. As part of this legislation, President Roosevelt signed an ordnance-expansion program order with appropriations for three small-arms cartridge-plant sites: Des Moines, Iowa; St. Paul, Minnesota; and Salt Lake City, Utah. Similar plants were already being constructed in Denver, Colorado, and in

St. Louis and Lake City in Missouri since the demand for .50-caliber machine-gun shells in the European war had already exceeded any previous expectations.[47]

Six to eight sites surrounding Des Moines were originally considered for the small-arms cartridge plant, but a signed United States court order on Monday, July 7, gave the War Department immediate possession of 2,445 acres southwest of Ankeny for the proposed $30 million small-arms ammunition plant. An additional 2,000 acres for a rifle range would be added to the site later. The entire land base was approximately three miles long and two miles wide, and included thirty-nine parcels of land owned by seventy-five persons and firms. Although the War Department could have taken immediate action due to an emergency wartime statute, the land was appraised and purchased with allowance for possible legal appeals.[48]

This site was just ten miles north of Des Moines, on the outskirts of the small town of Ankeny. John F. Ankeny had established the original town in April 1875 on eighty acres, and the community had grown over the sixty-five years since to 700 people. Several small villages outside of Ankeny, such as Carney and Oralabor, had started mining coal twenty years earlier, but most mines had closed down over the first decades of the twentieth century. Local residents hoped that this industrial boom would endure.[49]

Government officials chose the Des Moines area for its available labor and transportation facilities, along with the need for decentralization of war industries. Since the decade of the Great Depression, the area's labor potential was significant, with ten thousand remaining jobless in the twenty-five surrounding communities, and Des Moines' mayor, Mark Conkling, wanted local, not migrating, labor to work at the proposed plant. "I'd hate to think the plant would create any boom," Conkling commented. "We have material and resources here without creating an unbalanced situation."[50]

The residents of Ankeny displayed "an air of bewilderment," and many locals said they would not believe it until construction work actually started. Others simply did not want to sell their land. One farmer, Elliot Purmort, was very direct: "No, I don't want it. I live over here. I don't want to move. Why should I?" He added, laughing, "I'll just drive my cows right down town. Where'll they put us?" Residents were fearful of losing their old and comfortable ways, and they did not desire a transient boom from the ordnance plant. The city council quickly passed a beer ordinance (it did not have one) to maintain local control of new liquor establishments by closing bars at midnight and not allowing dancing. Also, Ankeny businessmen realized from other boom towns' experiences that underestimating or overestimating needs could ruin small businesses, and that war workers seemed terribly hard to predict. The boom for Ankeny, however, never proved to be as big as anticipated, with the nearby capital city of Des Moines absorbing most of the housing and business needs of the plant's new employees.[51]

Construction at Iowa's second ordnance plant began in late July 1941. Senator Herring turned the first shovelful of soil under a "blistering" sun in the clover field of the old Parmenter farm as gentle breezes blew the American flag flying above the scene with a cornfield in the background. Both Senator Herring and Governor Wilson spoke at the noontime, hour-long ceremony to a crowd of three hundred. "You'll have no sabotage here—not in Iowa," Senator Herring proudly declared. "There will be no labor trouble. The men who will build this plant are just as patriotic as anybody here in America. We're all ready [*sic*] 100-per-cent Americans in this part of the country." Captain Bell spoke for the army, "The welcome we have received at Des Moines really has been magnificent. I'd like to repeat one idea—this plant is not being built by one person, or two or three persons—it is the combined effort of the whole community."[52]

The War Department estimated a cost of $52.5 million for the plant's first year of operation for maximum production of .30- and .50-caliber ball-tracer and armor-piercing ammunition for machine guns. Officials warned landowners in early July to prepare to leave the new plant site within ten days. Farmers harvested their small grain crops as quickly as they could, but their young corn would be destroyed; it was paid for by the federal government. The largest landowner, F. W. Fitch Company, owned a 750-acre model dairy farm, and its $8,800 barn would be the only remaining building, used initially as construction headquarters. As in Burlington, the Ankeny ordnance-plant construction lists comprised overwhelming statistics. Workers constructed 219 buildings to complete the ordnance complex: 70 main manufacturing buildings, 3 administrative buildings, 30 magazines for powder storage, and

116 miscellaneous buildings. Costs ranged from $300,000 apiece for some of the assorted units to $2,500,000 for some of the manufacturing buildings. And the site required more than just buildings: 5 miles of sewer pipes, 300 telephone stations, 300,000 square yards of roads, and 6 miles of steam pipeline.[53]

Security during the construction phase remained strict. A fourteen-mile chain-link fence marked the perimeter, and no one, not even FBI agents, was allowed to enter without a pass. Guards remained on duty twenty-four hours a day, both on foot and on horseback, and they worked eight-and-a-half-hour overlapping shifts throughout the war years. Construction workers signed affidavits before their employment stating that they were American citizens and would not advocate overthrow of the government, and all applicants were subjected to character investigations for un-American and subversive activities.[54]

Nearly six thousand people registered for employment at the munitions plant during the first four days since many men and women in central Iowa were still desperately searching for work after the long Depression years. (This high unemployment quickly changed to labor shortages during the war, especially on farms.) One example of a man anxious for steady employment was LeRoy Schoff, who was both father and mother to his five children. Schoff had been worrying about money, describing himself as "without a dime." He "practically slept" at the employment office after word of the munitions plant job openings was released. His efforts paid off when he received a position at $.75 an hour. He told a *Des Moines Register* reporter that he did not mind "dusty labor," adding, "I don't know how I'd ever got my children back in school if I hadn't got this job. I hope I can work here as long as I live. I never was so tickled to get a job in my life."[55]

Ordnance officials wanted employee-employer relations to be professional and equitable during the construction phase. Workers received the prevailing union wages for the surrounding area, ranging from $.75 an hour for building laborers to $1.60 an hour for bricklayers. Unions established hourly wage scales for ninety-five different employee classifications. In the first week, first one shift of one hundred employees began work, then two shifts of one hundred workers each were running. Three eight-hour shifts soon followed. By the first week of September, the ordnance plant employed 3,500 people for a total weekly payroll of

$186,000. Employees lined up outside the time shacks to received their paychecks every Friday.[56]

Work at the Ankeny plant continued at a rapid rate after the dedication ceremony in late July, when workers immediately began construction on fourteen buildings. The noise of hammers, trucks, grading equipment, concrete-mixing machines, and railroad cars all transformed these once peaceful clover and corn fields of central Iowa into bomb factories. Local residents described the buildings as unlike anything ever built in Iowa during peacetime. Each manufacturing unit measured 400 feet by 1,000 feet—a block wide and three blocks long. By mid-October, night construction began under floodlights that could be seen for miles around as men labored in ten-hour shifts. By November 28, construction had passed the halfway mark because of fair weather but still remained slightly behind schedule. "All in all, everything is progressing very satisfactorily," Lieutenant Leonard W. Winget commented. "Now if only this weather holds."[57]

Architects designed each building in the small-arms ammunition facility as a segregated unit because of safety concerns. As Captain Bell described the intent, "If one should happen to blow up, it would not set off another. However, with all the precautions that will be taken, I do not think any building will explode." Only one accident occurred during the construction phase, when a temporary warehouse burned down in September. Thousands of spectators watched the blaze, causing a traffic jam. Five men were slightly injured in the accident and were treated at the plant's infirmary.[58]

Building construction proceeded even faster the week after the Pearl Harbor attack, and workers almost reached completion on the first manufacturing unit, Building Number 1. Management still worried about safety concerns, especially after the recent Iowa Ordnance Plant explosion in Burlington, and they had heavy embankments constructed around storage houses. By early March 1942, the Des Moines Ordnance Plant (DMOP) was in operation twenty-four hours a day, seven days a week, with 3,000 employees, and management made plans to hire 9,000 more workers to produce .30- and .50-caliber cartridges. The facility had the capacity to produce 2.3 million rounds of ammunition daily. Just seven months earlier, Senator Herring had turned the first spade of dirt; now he could praise the war-production results. "From a long range point of view," Herring proclaimed, "there is no reason for the pessimism about the war situation that is reported to exist in some parts of the Middle West. We've got to take it on the chin for a while; but we are preparing to land a knockout blow."[59]

One blow to DMOP's record was its early resistance to hiring local black workers. The most frequently produced rationale for this prejudice was that white opposition to black workers would cause factory slowdowns. However, the full-employment economy of World War II had already challenged the traditional management "preference" for white male labor, and African American leaders recognized this significant wartime change. Arthur Trotter, president of the Des Moines Negro Chamber of Commerce, urged Iowa's black men and women to register for war jobs because he wanted "the Negroes of this vicinity to procure their just share of employment in this present emergency." Other ordnance plants had set positive examples, such as the St. Louis Cartridge Plant, which hired 3,000 black workers in all roles from supervisory to unskilled categories; the Hercules Powder Company in New Jersey, which hired 1,000 black workers; and the Wolfe Creek Ordnance Plant in Tennessee, which had 20 to 25 percent black employees.[60]

An early challenge to DMOP's discrimination in hiring was delivered by an eighteen-year-old black woman. Following a war training program, Elizabeth Shackelford had recently been named by the National Youth Administration "youth worker most valuable for war production" for a ten-county central Iowa area. However, in April 1942 she brought suit in federal court against the U.S. Rubber Company (manager of the Des Moines Ordnance Plant) because the company "refused to employ [people] in the capacity for which they are best qualified," a violation of President Roosevelt's June 1941 Executive Order 8802, which required the "utiliz[ation of] all available labor in defense plants regardless of race, creed, color, or national origin." This alleged discrimination became harmful "in spirit and practice by delaying the defense program." It was the first lawsuit of its kind nationally.[61]

The intent of the case was to draw attention to discriminatory hiring practices and hopefully to change these practices for the good of the war effort. John Coleman had made a number of visits to training centers and war industries in Des Moines for the *Iowa Bystander*, the newspaper serving the black community in Iowa. At first he found widespread discrimination, but later he commented that "present opportunities are improving." The Des Moines Ordnance Plant did improve its hiring practices, and black Iowans would eventually hold 4 percent of the plant positions, which matched the 1940 Des Moines black/white population ratio. Two factors, according to historian Daniel Nelson, "accelerated the movement of African Americans into industry": Executive Order 8802 and then the increasing activity and agitation of union groups that favored "an inclusive approach."[62]

During early 1942, when Americans felt the war effort was not going well for the country, the issue of defense employment discrimination became a national concern. Many Americans felt that every effort should be made to improve war production while avoiding practices of discrimination, and black leaders spoke out on the issue. Lucile Bluford, editor of the *Kansas City Call,* campaigned for black Americans in war production at the Maple Street Baptist Church in Des Moines that April. While she believed that blacks had begun making progress against war discrimination and that even non-war industries had started opening doors to black workers, she believed major discrimination still lingered against hiring black Americans. At the same time, however, she thought the attitude that the war was not going well for all Americans could bring further changes. "We are losing in the war," Bluford commented. "America has to change in a hurry her attitude toward color."[63]

Increasingly more black Iowans began to be hired at DMOP, and the ordnance plant advertised in the *Iowa Bystander* during subsequent labor shortages. By war's end, the plant was placing advertisements prominently in the black community's newspaper. Ironically, as DMOP gained an awareness of equal opportunity for black workers, it still openly displayed in advertisements the unequal wages it offered the sexes. Men received \$.68 to \$1.03 an hour, while women were paid only \$.54 to \$.78 an hour.[64]

Surprisingly, after the war, employment needs further increased. As Cuba Tredwell, an African American factory worker from Waterloo, commented, "After the war they needed men real bad." Good positions for African Americans at the Des Moines war plants, for example, had meant wage improvements but also, according to labor historian Shelton Stromquist, "greater competition with whites and a growing pattern of exclusion" of blacks from union leadership roles. Union activist Robert Jackson found work after the war years as a construction laborer for a good salary but also discovered a new sense of activism. "During the war people had been out in the ordnance plant," he commented, "and they'd been making good money. They managed to save some. They worked into some good jobs. So the first thing they wanted to do when they were working downtown was sit down and eat." Jackson believed employment opportunities in Iowa's war factories later led to the first civil rights sit-down strike in 1948 at a segregated Des Moines business, the Katz Drugstore.[65]

During the course of the war, the number of employees at the Ankeny facility fluctuated dramatically based on the ammunition requirements of the armed services. Ammunition output initially tripled within a year. By 1943, about ten carloads of ammunition were made at the plant per day despite the complex manufacturing process, which required sixty-seven operations for every cartridge. The plant employed mostly Iowans, and women consistently made up 60 percent of the plant's employees. Employment peaked at almost 20,000 in 1943, then dropped to under 15,000 in February 1944, becoming relatively stable around 10,000 by June 1944. By November, the number had dropped to 7,500. Major E. E. Gialdini proudly commended the employees' overall record, "This plant never has failed to meet its production schedule."[66]

Chairman Julius Krug of the War Production Board ordered a work speed-up in November 1944, when General Dwight Eisenhower reported that his forces had fired four times the predicted bullets. This speed-up meant hiring 8,500 more employees in Des Moines, bringing the total to 16,000, and increasing production in all three manufacturing buildings. By mid-February 1945, the ordnance plant still needed over 4,100 new employees because of the ammunition shortages in Europe, and the plant desperately advertised for employees, with "no experience needed."[67]

The military's need for ammunition dramatically increased near the war's end, after the machine guns on Normandy Beach in late 1944 fired tremendous numbers of .50-caliber machine-gun bullets. Bombers such as the P-47 added to the production requirements as each plane carried two missiles, 2,500 pounds of bombs, and 6,400 rounds of .50-caliber ammunition. American industry continued to meet most of these production demands, and by January 1945, American soldiers possessed twice the artillery ammunition of the Germans. This became the triumph of American industry: German shells had to travel only a hundred kilometers, but more American shells made it to the fighting front though they had been produced thousands of kilometers away in the Midwest. Ammunition needs did not diminish with the surrender of Germany, however, but continued on the Pacific front, as a DMOP advertisement proclaimed in May 1945: "Our gallant boys need these bullets and need them urgently."[68]

Iowa's industries certainly participated in the production-front triumph. The Des Moines Ordnance Plant produced more than one bullet for every person on the face of the globe. From its first day as a clover field in July 1941 to the end of World War II, this war plant had cost $53,113,000 to build, with a total operating cost of $379,000,000 and a payroll of $86,726,000. During the war years, DMOP's five production lines—two for .30-caliber and three for .50-caliber bullets—had produced a total of 1,710,000,000 .30-caliber bullets and 2,025,000,000 .50-caliber bullets.[69]

The Des Moines Ordnance Plant also produced the first incendiary bullets, saving $13 million in costs through operation changes, and, with no major explosions, having a good safety record compared to similar plants. Over 50,000 people had worked at the plant through the war years, with peak employment shortly after D-Day in July 1944 at 19,060. E. J. Joss, factory manager for United Rubber, praised his workers: "They have done the job. The company has played but a small part." The editors of the *Des Moines Tribune* acknowledged that the quality of production and corresponding safety record kept this plant producing "full blast" after many other plants had closed. They paid a grateful compliment of "well done."[70]

With the war nearing its end, DMOP announced that the plant would close on July 31, 1945, with orders for "stand-by" basis until the official end of the Japanese war. By August 21, management reduced the work force from 10,000 to 2,400 employees and the forty-eight-hour week to forty. On the first of August, employees had started the factory housecleaning, which required thorough scrubbings of dismantled equipment along with cleaning, scraping, and polishing all facility surfaces to remove any traces of ammunition powder. Not a fleck could be left. By December 1, workers finished the job. The *Des Moines Register* honored the Des Moines Ordnance Plant's completion: "The silent buildings which once trembled with the roar of wartime production will be turned over to the Army ordnance department." DMOP was one of 262 plants released by the army on August 22, 1945. It was the third-largest plant nationally to be released; the only two larger factories were at the Ford Motor Company River Rouge complex.[71] In January 1946, the Reconstruction Finance Corporation (RFC) purchased the facility formerly called the Des Moines Ordnance Plant. At a farewell dinner, Brigadier General James Kirk, chief of the small-arms division of the Ordnance Department, praised the plant's record as "one of the country's most outstanding from the standpoint of efficiency, economy, and safety."[72]

The John Deere Company purchased a large portion of the facility (the buildings and 528 acres) in late 1946 from the RFC for $415 million and had started manufacturing corn pickers and cultivators there by February 1948. In a sense, the land had turned away from war's destructive production and returned, not entirely to the clover and corn fields of 1940, but to the growth of farm implements.[73]

Examples of Employee Excellence

A Los Angeles man by the unlikely name of Laymon L. Looney accepted the very first Army-Navy "E" Award in the nation as an ordnance-plant worker for the Norris Stamping and Manufacturing Company of California, when his plant and all its employees became the first national example of war-production excellence. Lieutenant Colonel A. R. Baird presented this factory's award on August 10, 1942, for the public acknowledgment of "sustained production of shell casings." And so began the proud World War II industrial tradition of the "E" Award.[74]

While two federal ordnance plants were constructed in Iowa during 1940 and 1941, the state also contained many smaller industries that soon converted to wartime production. Shortly after the European conflict started, the federal government recognized that it needed some way to reward companies that achieved high production levels while maintaining excellent morale, low absenteeism, and good safety records. The result was the Army-Navy "E" Awards, which marked certain factories as the elite of the United States' war industries because only 5 percent of the nation's 85,000 defense suppliers earned this award. The award included a public ceremony, a large pennant to be proudly flown at the factory, and pins to be worn by each employee.[75]

The "E" Award had begun as a navy custom designed to create greater enthusiasm and pride on ships, and officials thought the same "E" Award flag and pin would be effective and necessary in industrial plants, where mass-production work was often terribly monotonous. The joint Army-Navy "E" Awards started on August 10, 1942, and by the first anniversary, the award had been presented to 1,910 plants in the nation. Of these, 7 percent employed under 100 people and 38 percent under 500; most "E" Awards, however, did go to larger companies and factories. When a business exceeded its previous production record after receiving the award, it received a service star to be added to the original pennant.[76]

Iowa's record of production for a diverse array of war products exemplified a strong wartime work ethic, as demonstrated by the number of firms who won the Army-Navy "E" Award: forty-five Iowa manufacturing firms in twenty-three cities flew the "E" Award pennant during the last three years of World War II. Cedar Rapids won the most awards with seven; Davenport ranked second with six; and Des Moines earned five. Clarinda, the smallest city on the list, bragged about its two awards. The two large-arms plants, in Ankeny and Burlington, won several awards. Also during the war years, two Iowa individuals received honors: Dr. Clovis Meyers for conducting superior research on unraveled nylon processing and Raymond Gilbrech at the Des Moines Ordnance Plant for asking permission to work one hour earlier without pay after receiving word that one of his three military sons was missing in action. Rodney Selby, secretary of the Iowa Industrial and Defense Commission, praised Iowa's consistent war-production record: "The awards have been presented to Iowa firms for the manufacture of almost any implement of war from minute aviation instruments to tanks and locomotives."[77]

The Boyt Harness Company in Des Moines celebrated the first "E" Award to be given in Iowa. Boyt, one of the largest contract holders in the state, manufactured the marine corps pack and the Phillip pack saddle for mules, along with haversacks, cartridge belts, and machine-gun covers. This "E" Award ceremony commenced in the Des Moines Coliseum on August 26, 1942, with Boyt's 1,400 employees present (800 women and 600 men). Reporters described the ceremony as emotionally moving, with the award flag fluttering (by the breeze of electric fans) as the audience concluded the ceremony by singing "America." Colonel F. F. Taylor wanted employees to consider their pins military decorations. "You are members of a second front," Taylor told them, "the production front without which the courageous battle front could not survive." Colonel A. W. Jacobsen also praised Boyt's marine corps pack and received a loud cheer when he boasted that "few Japs ever will see it, because it's carried on a marine's back."[78]

Boyt won a second award in March 1943, adding a white star to its pennant. As Undersecretary of War Robert Patterson presented this award, he praised the company for its high standard of production. Boyt employed black workers—it was one of the first Des Moines companies to do so—and one hundred black women worked for the company, two of whom attained the position of supervisor. The Boyt Harness Company earned four "E" Awards by September 1944; it was the only firm in that industry nationwide to win that many. Since its first war contract in September 1940, Boyt had produced forty different war orders simultaneously for the army, navy, marines, and air force.[79]

On November 11, 1942, the Des Moines Ordnance Plant won the coveted "E" Award, one of thirty-six companies in the nation to win that particular week. The ceremony was held December 15, and guests and employees stood shivering in the cold amid the red, white, and blue bunting and American flags. The Women's Auxiliary Corps Band played "The Star-Spangled Banner" to start the ceremony, and the songs "America" and "Praise the Lord and Pass the Ammunition" to close it. The theme of this program was the final six words of the Army-Navy "E" Award statement: "Achieving Today What Yesterday Seemed Impossible."[80]

Fred Knight, president of the plant's CIO union, promised the DMOP audience that they would be able to look returning vets in the eye. He supported his union members. "Maybe we didn't praise the Lord as much as we might have," Knight acknowledged, "but when it came to rushing the ammunition, we were in there one hundred per cent." Commander Lewis Strauss of the U.S. Navy's Bureau of Ordnance described the plant's production record in military style to the factory workers. "Every time you read about the Japanese planes blasted out of the sky by Navy or Marine fliers," the commander stressed, "there is at least a good chance that your hands helped make the cartridges that delivered the winning punch."[81]

Initially, the managing company (U.S. Rubber) of DMOP had had its concerns about Iowa's labor supply, but any doubts had disappeared by the first "E" Award ceremony. Thomas Needham, a native Iowan who began his career as an office boy in Des Moines but by the 1940s worked in New York as vice president of U.S. Rubber, told the audience of his personal pride. "I knew your capacity," Needham praised his fellow Iowans. "You pitched into the new work as real Americans, as genuine Iowans, and you did such an outstanding job that you are gathered here to receive this great honor from the Army and Navy." And the awards continued. The first award ceremony had been celebrated on December 15, 1942; the second was on August 28, 1943; the third was on the third anniversary of ground breaking, July 20, 1944; and the fourth award was presented on January 22, 1945. The first three were celebrated with ceremonies; the fourth, because of the increased need for machine-gun bullets for the European Battle of the Bulge, was not.[82]

On December 28, 1942, the federal government announced that Keokuk Electro-Motors Company had earned an "E" Award for its outstanding production record. The ceremony took place in the evening at Keokuk's Grand Theater on January 21, 1943, with Governor Hickenlooper present. It was the sixth such award in Iowa. Keokuk Electro-Motors started just before World War I with thirty-two employees and had since grown to over two thousand; its principal product was pig iron. At the ceremony, the company president, G. L. Weissenburger, announced to his employees, "The recognition given us by the Army and Navy assures us that our government APPRECIATES OUR WORKING DAY AND NIGHT to keep war materials coming."[83]

The "E" Award presentation for the Wincharger Plant in Sioux City took place on a Sunday afternoon, March 14, 1943, at the Warrior Hotel (appropriately). Wincharger produced motor generators and won the award seventeen months after its new "dynamotor" was said to be on every fighting front. Lieutenant Colonel Bowman reminded the employees of the need for their product, "When you feel you're not doing your part, go out and look at the E pennant flying over your plant in recognition of a good job. You're all soldiers in the production line of freedom."[84]

The Uchtorff Company in Davenport had started production eighteen years before the war as a part-time operation and later grew to thirty-six employees, but the *Davenport Democrat and Leader* claimed this company should not be considered "a war mushroom." Uchtorff manufactured many items, from restaurant equipment to tractor parts, but during the war years subcontracted for sixteen other companies. During the company's "E" Award ceremony in March 1943, its female employees proudly placed themselves in the front row in honor of their exemplary production record. Women comprised one-third of the company's work force, and the factory owner described them as "soldiers in the production line of freedom," praising their quick training and harmonious work records. He had first hired women just the previous September, and most of his female employees now worked a sixty-hour week in positions ranging from punch-press operator to welder to riveter.[85]

The Uchtorff "E" Award ceremony colorfully combined traditional red, white, and blue decorations and flags, and "The Star-Spangled Banner" was played during the introduction. The commanding general of the Rock Island Arsenal, Brigadier General Norman Ramsey, commended the employees with the refrain "You are soldiers on the production line in the battle of freedom." Governor Hickenlooper also drew war analogies: "There is no difference in the long run between the vital importance of the home front and the vital importance of the war front."[86]

Two Clarinda companies received "E" Awards, the Lisle Corporation and Parris-Dunn Associates. These two companies gained government contracts because of the persistence of "two small town boys who couldn't take no for an answer." Parris-Dunn had almost closed when Cecil Parris negotiated with the War Department to develop training rifles (wood with reclaimed iron and leather from World War I equipment). Colonel Harry Adamson, the commanding officer at Fort Creek, Nebraska, noted at its ceremony that it was not his job to overly praise the company's success, but added, "You know it well in the sweat and toil of your combined efforts day by day."[87]

Other "E" Award ceremonies continued to develop two consistent themes: unity and victory. When Brigadier General Ramsey spoke at the ceremony for Climax Engineering in Clinton, which was managed by Day and Zimmerman, he stated that these employees were the heart and soul of all America and were in the war as all Americans had been since December 7, 1941. The president of this company, E. F. Deacon, declared simply, "Climax and all America's legions of production shall march with your boy or mine to ultimate victory." John Wood, president of the CIO Local 143, pledged cooperative war work by all Day and Zimmerman employees in hope for their children's future.[88]

Another pattern to emerge during the ceremonies involved comparing the "E" Awards to military medals for all conscientious soldiers. During the ceremony at Fisher Governor Company of Marshalltown, executives and hourly employees alike praised their company as "the picked troops of the production line" and the "top-flight soldiers of production." At the only aircraft company in the state, Solar Plant in Des Moines, Colonel Robert Finkenstaedt compared its industrial award to the Soldier's Distinguished Service Cross. "It is given to you not because you have done your duty—that is expected of you," Finkenstaedt explained, "but because you have accomplished things over and above the call of duty." The Most Reverend Gerald T. Bergan, bishop of Des Moines, praised the Solar war workers, who "without benefit of publicity, praise, and glamour of battle have done a good job and remained devoted servants of God."[89]

Maytag, a prominent Iowa business, successfully converted its manufacturing processes from washing machines to defense production during the war. Its plant was located in Newton, a town that had grown rapidly along with the company itself; Newton's population was 3,000 about forty years earlier, but had grown to 18,000 by the late 1930s. Although it was a "one-industry town," it was also described as a typical Iowa community complete with a central business square, wide streets, and medium-sized homes.[90]

The company's founder, Frederick L. Maytag, personified the creative, inventive, and resourceful businessman. He started by purchasing, with a partner, the Persons Band Cutter and Self-Feeder Company in 1893, an innovative threshing-machine company with a design that reduced accidents involving farmers. In 1909, Maytag bought the sole interest to the company and shifted from the seasonal threshing equipment to a product needed year-round, the washing machine. His capital investment of $2,400 in 1893 had increased to a net worth of $5,452,356 by 1938, when Maytag was producing 2,000 washers a day.[91]

Despite the Depression, the record month of production for Maytag was August 1933, with 2,200 washers produced per day. This plant emerged as the largest washing-machine factory in the world, with

50,000 local people directly dependent on the Maytag industry. Maytag's business leadership could sometimes be described as an "industrial autocracy"—benevolent, perhaps fatherly, but controlling. When Frederick Maytag died in March 1937, he was eulogized as Iowa's "first citizen," leaving behind a $7 million estate and a tremendous business legacy.[92]

Labor strife had affected Maytag employees before the war. The factory workers had struggled in 1938 with a prolonged and bitter labor dispute resulting in "partisanship" and "emotional hysteria" throughout Newton about their ninety-day strike over a possible 10 percent wage cut. The National Labor Relations Act of 1935, or the Wagner Act, which established workers' right to collective bargaining, had recently been declared constitutional, and employees met this action with enthusiasm and a new union motto: "Let's make Newton a model C.I.O. town." Other residents believed negotiations were selfish and divisive, especially within a small, one-industry town. In May 1941, Maytag employees negotiated through their union for a 10 percent wage increase to an average rate of 90 cents an hour for 1,000 employees. But that summer, war seemed imminent and everyone desired cooperation for the approaching war effort.[93]

Maytag had always prided itself on its innovative design of washing machines. It was the first to develop a cast-aluminum tub; by 1940, it was advertising the "Gyrafoam Water Action" in the Maytag Commander, and the 1941 series grew more militaristic, with model names such as the *Brigadier,* the *Champion,* and the *Major.* Each day its factory used 30,000 pounds of aluminum and 160,000 pounds of iron, and in May 1941, the four millionth Maytag washer rolled off the assembly line.[94]

In August 1941, the Office of Price Administration and Civilian Supply initiated a program to drastically reduce the number of domestic washers made in the country because of the need to conserve resources for war. This cutback resulted in a temporary suspension of 225 Maytag employees, but the company developed other continuous factory work through defense contracts. The last Maytag washer was made in April 1942, slightly ahead of the War Production Board schedule. This marked a temporary, wartime end to forty-nine years of continuous manufacturing.[95]

Because the company could no longer produce washers, it converted to defense production as early as March 1941, with an initial $150,000 contract for tank-track pins. Maytag workers were soon producing shell adapters, machine shafts, and pinions, as well. By September 1941, the company was manufacturing an assortment of intricate aircraft parts for Martin bombers and fifteen other combat aircraft, a contract worth $1.5 million. The entire Maytag company underwent a drastic transformation with this defense production, starting with the installation of a high wire fence around the plant. The number of employees ballooned from 1,200 to 3,000, and women began working at Maytag for the first time, eventually accounting for one-third of its work force. During this time, 97 percent of the company's production was devoted to war needs; only 3 percent could be devoted to washing-machine repair parts.[96]

Maytag's war production escalated from a value of $100,000 in the beginning of 1941 to $15 million in 1944, but the company prided itself on rejecting all offers of cost-plus contracts, which its corporate leaders felt contributed to waste and unnecessarily high war profits. Instead, the company initiated "savings through redesign," resulting in about $1 million in reduced costs by 1944. Maytag remained particularly proud of its aircraft hydraulics—hydraulic actuating and lock cylinders designed by Tom Smith, a Maytag engineer, which reduced the number of required parts in one unit from 136 to 69 and in another unit from 145 to 28. Maytag's postwar pamphlet boasted that its "continuous improvement ethic" had never stopped during the war years.[97]

Governor Hickenlooper praised all of Iowa's production-front efforts during the Mason City Tent Company "E" Award ceremony, as Iowa had exceeded other states of comparable population and wealth in its output of man-hours, war bonds, and supplies for the war effort. These were the production-front success stories—the manufacturing plants that exceeded both production and efficiency goals. The ceremonies, like those for military awards, provided a proud moment of formal recognition of the focused energy and talent of Iowa's production-front soldiers.[98]

Iowa's companies had certainly performed successfully in their wartime efforts on the production front, producing such varied items as mule packs, airplane parts, machine-gun bullets, and bombs. Its industrial output had been heavily concentrated in subcontracts, so in the postwar era, Iowa would not enjoy the continued government contracts that benefited other regions. And no longer would there be an equal of the "E" Awards to recognize employee excellence.

Real Rosies

"Do you approve or disapprove of the way Mrs. Roosevelt has conducted herself as First Lady?" the Gallup Poll asked in March of 1940. A resounding 68 percent of Americans approved of Eleanor Roosevelt's work, giving her a popularity rating greater than President Roosevelt's at the time. Iowa leaned Republican in 1940, giving its electoral votes to Wendell Willkie, but interest and support remained with the First Lady.[99] "Everywhere Eleanor," as her wartime nickname emerged, certainly represented over these crucial years a hard-working, extraordinary woman concerned with a world at war.

Labor issues had been an increasingly significant part of factory life during the Depression years, but as Shelton Stromquist notes in his oral history of Iowa labor, two labor conditions had changed with World War II production: unemployment was replaced by labor scarcity, and the federal government desperately needed uninterrupted production. Factories needed to produce without fear of strikes or employment shortages slowing the war effort.[100]

As historian William O'Neill describes in *A Democracy at War,* popular opinion during the war strongly disfavored such previous labor issues as strikes and demanding higher wages because of the desperate need for war production. However, as he points out, no one at the time seemed to question farm or business profits related to war production. David Hinshaw in his analysis in *The Home Front,* published during the war, maintained that although labor was very patriotic, it also remained concerned about union membership maintenance. Unions argued, though sometimes faintly, that the wartime era should not jeopardize recent labor gains because veterans would need to return to a fair labor environment.[101]

Labor scarcity suddenly replaced unemployment, and this factor challenged the composition of the industrial labor force during the war years. Unemployment totals for Iowa dropped considerably, from 95,088 in March 1940 to 17,000 in November 1944. With increased employment opportunities, the labor force itself also changed. By the spring of 1945, the national labor force exceeded the average number by 7.3 million, of which the largest new groups were 2.8 million teenagers; 1.9 million women over thirty-five years of age; 1 million men over sixty-five years of age; and 600,000 young women with servicemen as husbands.[102]

Teenagers working in factories for the war effort met with mixed community reactions—emotions of both pride and concern. Between 1940 and 1944, nationwide school enrollment of fifteen- to eighteen-year-olds fell by 1.2 million, or 24 percent, while the number of employed fourteen- to seventeen-year-olds increased by 2 million, or over 200 percent. In November 1942, the federal government lowered the required age from eighteen to sixteen for girls to be employed in war industries, except in hazardous factories such as ordnance plants. During the war years, the employment rate of fourteen- to fifteen-year-old girls would jump four times, and work loads would be increased and hours lengthened as many adolescents dropped out of school altogether during this period.[103]

In addition to younger people working, accidents were another concern. According to a 1943 article in *Collier's* titled "Children for Hire Cheap," many children, some as young as ten, appeared caught up in this youthful craze for earning, which caused worries for their safety. Charles Harness, state labor commissioner for Iowa, commented that "the number of minor children working now for pay in Iowa is about five times that of a year ago, and many of them are girls."[104]

World War II not only renewed patriotism and the work ethic but also placed an emphasis on materialism and youth culture. Two values seemed in conflict—the traditional work ethic vs. the modern value of education. As Alma Jones, a child development specialist, believed, some "reconverting" after the war might be needed to get teenagers back to school; otherwise young people with little formal education would not be able to compete professionally after the war, especially against veterans with GI Bill advantages.[105]

Although teenagers became the largest group of new workers, married women gained the most attention in that category. Society never perceived wives as full-fledged workers, and researchers of World War II have described most women's employment status as remaining that of second-class employees. The commonly recognized elevation of Rosie the Riveter as a real worker is really a romantic myth. D'Ann Campbell in *Women at War with America* notes that unions considered women to be "until" workers: "working until they get married, until they have a baby, until the house is paid off, or until they retire." Deborah Fink comments in her Iowa study, "World War II and Rural Women," that the established pattern always utilized the word *help* with women's work, while Karen Anderson points out in *Wartime Women* that wartime propaganda stressed that women were only aiding soldiers overseas. Ruth Milkman in *Gender at Work* considers the constant mixed message of war jobs: women could *do* these jobs, but only temporarily, since women ranked as family members first and workers second. In his book *A Democracy at War,* O'Neill notes the fact that society considered women's employment efforts always as secondary or temporary and goes so far as to say that "the failure of democracy to recognize women as equals jeopardized the war effort."[106]

Not only did women suffer from the societal view of them as less valuable and less capable than male workers, but their male coworkers often resented any competition, especially when the numbers of employed women for the war effort rose quickly. Nationally, the total number of employed women rose from 13.8 million in December 1941 to 15.6 million by December 1942. Allan Winkler finds in *Home Front U.S.A.* that these new women employees felt frustrated by the "cold welcome" they were given, and Winkler contends that the Rosie the Riveter propaganda was mostly intended to persuade the resistant men that women could be capable workers.[107] One mistake in propaganda that added to men's resentment was the same mistake the military made with references to the women in the Women's Army Auxiliary Corps—emphasizing the concept that each woman working was "freeing a man to fight." Later officials softened and changed the phrase to "The Woman Behind the Man."[108]

The character of factory work itself transformed during the war effort. When workers became the soldiers of production, taking a factory job became a patriotic action, not a socially demeaning one. For example, the largest organized group of women in Iowa, the Iowa State Federation of Women's Clubs, decided in 1943 that all members should register with the U.S. Employment Service for industrial and agricultural work. As Mrs. F. W. Weitz, Federation publicity chairman, told the press, "We've got to do everything possible on the home front to win this war. We can't be highbrow in wartime." That same year, Jessie Walker, who was actively involved in Des Moines war work, spoke about black women's wartime roles in a speech at the Fortieth Annual Meeting of the Iowa Association of Colored Women.[109]

Iowa's war factories, like those nationwide, needed "womanpower." Of the 90,000 people employed in Iowa's war-production plants in March 1943, approximately 22,500 were women (25 percent). In Des Moines' war plants, starting salaries for women ranged from $20 to $25 per week, and many women left other jobs for the better paycheck in war plants. By October 1943, two-thirds of the Des Moines Ordnance Plant's employment ads were listed as women's positions. Lillie Cordes Landolt was one woman who filled a position there. Landolt had worked previously as a telephone operator in Gilmore City, until she married. When the family moved to Des Moines after her husband found training as a riveter, Landolt also decided to work at the new ordnance plant and found the experience to be interesting, though the machines seemed huge and the work dangerous. She described her decision, "Even though we had five small children, I went to work at the ordnance plant, and I really loved it." The Landolt family really needed this second paycheck, and so Landolt spent the war years making 55,000 bullets a day.[110]

The "feminine motive for work" may have officially been patriotism, but strong economic incentives encouraged most female enlistments in paid production work. Two studies of Iowa women's employment during World War II found war workers to be patriotic and committed, yet most women were working primarily because they needed the paycheck. Donna Sciancalepore found that five of the seven women from Waterloo that she interviewed remembered the appeal to patriotism that initially attracted them to the workplace and kept them motivated. Yet many American women also appreciated the fact that the work offered them an alternative role. Alice Nield, one of the Waterloo war workers, said she took her job to escape housework and "dullsville."[111]

For her article "Women on the Home Front: The Iowa WIPEs," Jacqueline Smetak studied women who had worked for the North Western Railroad, cleaning and servicing locomotives in Boone, Council Bluffs, and Clinton. "Women worked tough jobs," Smetak comments, "in spite of discrimination, unequal pay, notions about what they could and could not do, the difficulties of taking care of children and a house in the days before modern household appliances were common, a lack of help and child care, and the frustrations of chronic shortages and long lines at the grocery store." Despite every hardship and hurdle encountered from employers, other employees, and community businesses, these women workers believed their efforts were valued and needed. And as Smetak concludes, "In a very real sense these women—of all ages, races, creeds, and colors—helped spell the difference between victory and defeat." The *Waterloo Democrat* described one of these working women, Sadie Kling, a mother of eighteen who donated her seventh day of work each week at the Rock Island Arsenal to the war cause, as "a REAL War Worker."[112]

Factory work remained an ongoing struggle for many female employees. Iowa's women factory workers, as did women industrial workers across the country, worked for equal opportunity, adequate training, equal pay for equal work, safer working conditions, equal union participation, child-care centers, and adequate housing despite the fact that the official message, repeated endlessly, remained that this work would last only for the duration. Women factory workers also experienced much loneliness, boredom, fatigue, and depression as underpaid production soldiers at monotonous jobs, day after day, with seemingly no end to the war. Women ordnance workers, for very good and various reasons, earned their acronym: WOWs. Women Ordnance Workers, Inc., was organized in Chicago, and its membership eventually numbered 33,000.[113]

One problem many employed mothers faced was finding adequate child care. The absence of day-care programs also confirmed the temporary and secondary status of married working women. The *Iowa Farm Economist* interviewed 297 employed mothers with a total of 537 children under age eighteen. Of these women, 171 worked six days a week, and 145 were away from their homes from 6 a.m. to 6 p.m. Two-fifths of the school-age children were left alone, another two-fifths were cared for by relatives, and one-fifth were watched by hired girls. Almost half of these mothers stated that they would be quite interested in approved child-care programs, if available.[114]

One alternative to developing child care within the industrial sector was to adjust and shorten shift hours to encourage mothers with school-age children to work. These "victory shifts" started in September 1943 at the Des Moines Ordnance Plant as special daytime hours for housewives as well as evening hours for businessmen. The housewife victory shift was from 9 a.m. to 3 p.m., while the businessman shift was from 7 p.m. to midnight. The victory shifts, officials believed, enabled housewives to get children to school along with making breakfasts and dinners as well as contributing to the industrial war effort. By the second week, the plant had enlisted 150 new workers. One such woman was Alice Albers, mother of four, who wanted to join the nation's army of women workers in war plants. Before, she had considered herself "just another housewife," but now she made $28.80 a week (working seven days a week) as an inspector at the Des Moines Ordnance

Plant. She took the job to "pay back bills." After a month, victory shifts at DMOP enlisted over 300 married women, and Employment Manager Dean Price commented, "They are doing their bit and doing a good job, too. The largest share of the money they earn is going into war bonds to help further the cause."[115]

Some parenting experts, such as Geneva McKinley, a family caseworker for the Iowa Humane Society, which was incorporated in 1893 for the prevention of cruelty to children and animals, felt that mothers should not work no matter what the cause. "There is too much glorification of the working wife in war industry," McKinley explained, "and too little credit to the mother of five to eight children who stays at home." Mothers working in factories also met with skepticism from such groups as the Iowa Parent-Teacher Association, whose board drafted a resolution in 1942 concerning industrial employment of mothers with young children. The resolution stated that the first responsibility of mothers should be to give "suitable care" to young children, and therefore mothers should be deferred from war work. However, the resolution also stated that employers should not create barriers against hiring mothers. The PTA believed that if women should work, it should be in those day shifts that were least disruptive of family life, and if child care could not be in the home, then it should be provided by the community. Still, PTA president Nelle Kenison added a final note of guilt, "As mothers are engaged in war work, what of the children?"[116]

At the end of July 1945, when the Des Moines Ordnance Plant prepared to close on what was declared T-Day (Termination Day), many women (who represented 50 percent of the payroll at that time) wondered what to do next: housework, self-employment, unemployment, or another job. Many women returned to housework because of their overwhelming responsibilities, but for some women, returning home symbolized a sign of success and security. "I may get another war job," Janita Smedden said, "but I want to get my canning done first. We've got a nice garden." Lillie Cordes Landolt opened a dressmaking shop from her house so she would also have time for her children. "I wanted to be home with those kids," she commented. "They were too precious." Virginia Larson planned to use her savings of $600 to train for her own business in "beauty culture."[117]

Unemployment checks gave some Iowa women time to look for other positions. Seventeen-year-old Evelyn Immes had had experience in factory work, but she wanted to sleep for a very long time after the work at DMOP ended. Immes described her plans, "Sleep for days. Then I'll look for a job, something essential. And I'll be getting my unemployment insurance till then, anyhow, won't I?" Others, like Mary Grund, had found factory work far more rewarding financially and socially than domestic work. "A girl'd be foolish to go back to that," Grund critiqued. She immediately applied at Firestone Rubber and Tire Company in Des Moines after hearing about the ordnance plant closing. She declared, "I'm going to get good money while I can." Nellie Griffin was another who applied for further factory work, at Newton's Maytag as a machine operator, now listed as "a woman's job."[118]

However, few industrial positions remained for women by mid-July 1945, and officials advised women to consider maid service again. By August 1, a thousand women faced unemployment in Des Moines while 1,131 job openings remained for men but with no excess men available. Some employers had decided arbitrarily, before the war had officially ended, to replace their women with men even when men were not a present, viable option.[119]

Still, women had been valuable workers throughout the war, and according to an Iowa Poll conducted immediately after the war, 84 percent of Iowans held the strong belief that women should receive the same pay as men. Labor union members answered the same way, with 84 percent saying "yes." The Poll concluded, "Iowans are generally agreed that 'Rosie the Riveter' should have equality with men at the pay window."[120]

Sadly, however, "Rosie" never found such equality, although wages for women had increased somewhat. Gone were the victory shifts and the ads for hundreds of available positions at the local ordnance plants. Employment options for women were once again limited and segregated—perhaps summarized by a 1946 Northwestern Bell Telephone advertisement headed "Girls! Looking for a Good Job?"[121] The real Rosies once had eagerly earned and now sadly lost their good jobs.

Spedding's Eggs and the Largest Bomb Ever

All of this production of bombs and bullets throughout the United States led in many ways, almost inevitably, to the largest and most destructive of bombs—the atomic bombs dropped on Hiroshima, Japan,

August 6, 1945, and on Nagasaki August 9. At 8:15 a.m. in Hiroshima, a solitary B-29 released the first bomb with a "noiseless flash"; then came the explosion, then the fire. The bomb was aimed at the center of a city of 350,000 residents. This atomic bomb weighed 4 tons, but equaled 20,000 tons of TNT, making it almost 2,000 times more powerful than any other single bomb.[122]

Shortly before what Americans would call V-J Day, August 14 in North America, employees in Japan's war plants stopped working to listen to their emperor declare the end of war, although he never did announce surrender. Afterwards, as historian Lester Brooks describes the reaction in his work *Behind Japan's Surrender,* "sobs and tears sprang irrepressibly from the listeners." Brooks continues, "They were tears as much of relief as of grief. It was the end of fourteen years of war. Whatever was to come could scarcely be harsher. As soon as the broadcast ended, factories all over the nation shut down." Millions of conscientious industrial workers in Japan suddenly found themselves without jobs for the immediate postwar period, a time in which their government leaders said they must learn to "endure the unendurable."[123]

On August 15, American citizens received official word that Japan was surrendering. Dramatic times caused dramatic emotions, such as the ones in this recollection from journalist William Shirer in *An August to Remember:* "Now for me, as for no doubt everyone on the globe—friend, enemy or neutral—that mid-August day when the Japanese surrendered, there was an overpowering sense of relief. Peace would settle again on what was left of a stricken world. But our planet would never be the same again."[124]

Historian Robert Westbrook contends that Americans decades later have remained sharply divided in their opinions about the bombings of Hiroshima and Nagasaki, but in 1945 they appeared unified. Other historians agree. Richard Rhodes, in his lengthy work *The Making of the Atomic Bomb,* explains this simply, "We were at war." He adds that our nation by 1945, like others, had been brought to a "psychic numbing" regarding the bombing of cities and civilians. Fears during the war years had dramatically accumulated from the threat of Germany's potential nuclear research to the predicted invasion scenario of Japan, and as Studs Terkel found in his oral histories of the war, no one at that time could really grasp the destructive horror of this new, atomic bomb.[125]

Memoirs from Iowans also contained few mixed reactions to the atomic bomb. Jim Skahill, in his collection of memoirs *Way Back When! 1924–1944. Hundreds of Characters Stumbling through the Great Depression,* maintains that attitudes then were contagious. He continues with a description of the Iowa home front, "If you asked a multitude of old women about the Japanese people ninety percent would answer, 'Bomb the Bastards.' If you asked the younger people what they thought of the war, they would answer, 'Let's go get them.'" Skahill explained the harsh reactions, "World War II was like a Jap or a German holding a Luger to your head. We were all anxious to get it over before they swallowed us. There weren't that many political issues present in 'our' war."[126]

Robert Edson Lee was a soldier in the Pacific and distinctly remembered the day the first atomic bomb was dropped. He noted in his memoir, *To the War,* that he was as physically remote from the bombing as his Iowa parents, but he was affected psychologically by it. "We had all been in the war too long and seen too much that we could not comprehend," lamented Lee. "The bomb meant simply to a generation that we could go home, and that ended our moral concern." Still, Lee remembered living with a lingering feeling in the following days that something was terribly wrong in the world.[127]

Iowa had contributed to the atomic bombs in two ways. One Iowa connection was pilot Paul Tibbets, from Glidden, who unexpectedly painted his mother's name, *Enola Gay,* on his airplane, the single bomber that would drop that first atomic explosive. The second connection was that Iowa State College sent over two million pounds of high-purity uranium metal in the form of 2¼-inch cylinders to the Manhattan Project. Frank Spedding, professor of chemistry and later physics and metallurgy, led this secret process by converting a college laboratory to mass production of the cylinders, nicknamed "Spedding's eggs." Spedding had been contacted on December 6, 1941, about participating in a highly secret government project, and his developing techniques led to the production of the pure uranium, thorium, and plutonium necessary for the Manhattan Project. He went on to found the Institute of Atomic Research in 1947. Iowa State College received an "E" Award in October 1945 for this contribution to the atomic bomb of a quick and inexpensive method for the quality production of uranium metal, saving the federal government more than $100 million over the course of the war years, according to Ned Disque. It was for this time the major producer of uranium metal, and its process dropped the cost of producing uranium from $22 per pound to $1 per pound.[128]

The excellence awards, however, could not conceal the results of these atomic bombs, and the comparison between the cities of Japan and the towns of Iowa was unforgettable. One soldier from Iowa described the aftermath of the atomic-bombed Hiroshima for the *Iowa Bystander* after he witnessed two-thirds of this Japanese city absolutely destroyed by this single bomb. He wrote that Hiroshima differed from other bombed cities with its continuous charred, ashen heaps instead of crater holes: "The atomic explosion had the effect of seemingly flattening everything within the radius affected by it. . . . For blocks on end throughout the city not a wall is standing."[129]

Shortly after the Hiroshima bombing, the *Des Moines Tribune* tried to imagine the result if such a bomb should be dropped on Des Moines. The newspaper printed a diagram imposed on a map of Des Moines that included four square miles of possible devastation, an area equivalent to "East 14th Street to West 18th Street and then University Avenue to the Des Moines River." Although the bombed area in Iowa was only an imagined square on a map, the concept of an isolated and protected America, even in the Midwest, was now completely destroyed. The following summer, an Iowa Poll found that 62 percent of Iowans supported world atomic control, wanting civilian or scientific rather than military control.[130]

The small lab at Iowa State College that had produced highly purified uranium was converted after the end of the war to a center for the Atomic Energy Commission, but it conducted atomic research rather than production. In other words, the former "backyard laboratory" became a facility of four buildings worth $6 million with a payroll listing 550 people, including many scientists and highly trained technicians. Much of the old wartime secrecy disappeared, but the facility was still a heavily guarded operation.[131]

Iowans had been extremely productive soldiers of war, producing items from mule packs to airplane parts, from bullets to bombs. And Spedding's eggs from Iowa State College and a solitary plane named after an Iowa mother became part of bringing the world into an atomic age.

Chapter 3

Bonds, Scrap, and Boys ~ The Community Front

In 1941 the world wasn't at peace, and it wasn't running smoothly.

—MacKinlay Kantor, *Happy Land* (1942)

When Thomas Lutman, a pastor from Sheldon, addressed the Iowa Retail Hardware Association's annual convention in February 1942, he professed that the efforts of men and women on Main Street would win the war and write the peace—phrasing that became quite commonly used. "The nation will become one vast machine shop for the duration of the war," he began, "but Main Street will endure long after the war." Lutman envisioned farmers and small-town folk as "the backbone of America" and contended that Sinclair Lewis had captured only the "shabby" side of Main Street in his popular 1920 novel and not its strength or "basic simplicity." Lutman added, "Main Street has grown the wheat and the corn and the men that have nourished America. Just as the city draws its water supply from the hills beyond, it also draws its leadership."[1]

But Main Street had always represented a rather complex community setting, despite its seeming simplicity. Iowa in 1940 remained a state of small communities; no large urban center dominated either business or social life. The capital, Des Moines, was Iowa's largest city, but its population measured only about 150,000. Federal and state governments developed, cultivated, and needed this sense of the small community to organize and even pressure citizens to contribute money for war bonds and gather scrap for collection drives. The men sent to war, whether draftees or volunteers, especially drew communities together through their common concern, sacrifice, and grief.

Main Street became the memory and the motivation for fighting World War II. The federal government perpetuated this mythology of the small town during the war with pamphlets such as *Small Town U.S.A*, which emphasized the strength of American communities as contained within their small businesses and small talk. The strong beliefs many townspeople held about concepts such as classlessness and cooperation along with a sense of pioneer heritage all contributed to a community's cohesiveness. This small-town image even became an effective wartime advertising strategy, with such slogans as "Main Street goes to war!"[2]

Iowa developed and strengthened its own mythology of the perfect small town throughout the war with stories like the pictorial reports on "the old hometown" published in the *Des Moines Sunday Register.* Boone featured its main drag, old drugstore, and pretty girls; Oskaloosa its soldier honor roll, friendly town police, and more pretty girls; Stratford its bakery, barbershop, and "a country boy in town on Saturday night"; Earlham its town band concerts playing "America the Beautiful"; and West Liberty its return of the horse-drawn milk-wagon and an attentive local barber listening to customers discuss the war. Within this idealization of grassy town squares and tree-lined streets, war seemed hard to imagine, but Iowa's citizens would be forced to look beyond their state borders to the developing global war.[3]

Modern war meant total war and involved the entire population. World War II, "the civilians' war," meant sacrifice. The community front did not consist of an undirected group of overworked, striving, and sacrificing citizens committed to victory through an unconscious sense of unity. Rather, the resources needed from the community front by a government ill-prepared for war were quite specific: money, salvage, and young men. The first resource—money—people believed to be valuable, of course, but realized it was not such a sacrifice to make the needed war loans. People generally perceived the second resource—salvage—as waste and needed to be persuaded only of its actual worth. The third—their young men—represented a resource the community knew to be valuable but only later would find out how much they had sacrificed in them to the machine of total war.

To be successful from the community front, citizens needed to agree with the war effort by understanding expectations, feeling sacrifices equally, and completing definite war jobs. The idea of war sacrifices continued to strengthen people's sense of their significance, as Frank Miles, editor of the *Iowa Legionnaire,* reminded his listeners in a radio address, when he declared that the war was "a job for everyone." Miles continued, "This war to save our independence is the war of every man, woman and child in America. Only by the turns of fate are some of us here and others in the armed forces. Every one should, therefore, strive to serve as if whether the nation is to live or die is upon his or her shoulders."[4]

Another leader, Nellie Kenison, president of the Iowa Parent-Teacher Association, which had 63,514 members in 1942, offered her perspective on the community front's wartime role: "We are in war whether we like war or not, and who is there of us who does not hate war. It is our job to win the war and write the peace. Our men are fighting all over the world and WE must fight on the home front."[5] Iowans on the community front were ready to begin the struggle.

"Vim, Vigor, and Vitality" within Victory Drives

The car had been "riddled by Jap bullets" in the Pearl Harbor attack and now went on display as a patriotic symbol in a number of community squares, including those in Red Oak, Clarinda, and Winterset. In Winterset, this publicity car perched on the southeast corner of the square for five hours on a Saturday morning. The State Automobile Insurance Association of Des Moines had purchased the car from a former Iowan to further motivate fellow citizens to buy bonds, and local newspapers promoted the display. One newspaper noted that "the Japs played a dirty trick on Miss Salem Thompson, Des Moines girl, who left her car parked on Hickam Field in Honolulu the night before the surprise attack of December 7."[6]

Iowans, like other Americans, translated fear into concrete images to raise more money for the war effort through the sale of war bonds because the first resource the community front needed to devote to the machine of war was money. The federal government conducted eight war-bond drives during the course of World War II to help pay war expenses but keep the national debt down and control inflation at home. Although the government offered a variety of bonds for investors, the E bond was issued in small denominations and designated "the people's bond."[7] The smallest bonds sold were in $25 denominations; people paid $18.75 for them, and they matured in ten years. The government also sold ten-cent stamps, which could be collected and turned in for bonds.

Citizens remained suspicious of propaganda because of the manipulation and "rhetorical excesses" of 1917 and 1918; many Iowans remembered the Committee on Public Information during World War I and its legacy of hate and hysteria. As Nancy Derr concludes in her research concerning Iowa's fund-raising efforts during those years, the state lost prestige in the first two Liberty Loan drives by finishing in last place. But, with "a new surge of organization, exhortation, and extortion," Iowa placed first in the third and fourth Liberty Loan drives, although this triumphant first place met mixed reactions as Iowans criticized the "public shaming" of citizens, often German immigrants, into purchasing Liberty Loans. Derr describes the methods used in these drives: "The extraordinary haste with which a rural state could meet its multi-million dollar quotas indicates the overwhelming coercive power which the threat of ostracism held for Iowans, still heavily dependent on the small town bonds of face-to-face cordiality."[8]

During World War II, officials utilized every means possible to sell war bonds, but they organized focused drives rather than continuously calling for citizens to purchase bonds. The four major themes they pursued were the need for Americans to sacrifice; the need for all Americans to participate in the war effort; the need to support military family members; and the need for a safe American future. Attempts to garner familial support were particularly effective when emphasizing devotion, courage, and death. Kate Smith, a popular singer who served as a national bond-drive speaker, utilized this tactic effectively about those "boys we want back": "Those boys are our own boys and they have the greatest right in the world to our support."[9]

The challenge was to convince the average citizen to purchase "a piece of the war" in this patriotic campaign. Though some people felt manipulated by sentimental and emotional appeals, others were offended by the idea of private gain from the war. Many Americans preferred to view contributions like church collections, as a simple offering. In the early 1940s, war-bond drives had the advantage of selling a popular and dramatic war, and the disadvantage of pulling money from citizens who had suffered economically during the Great Depression and had only started to recover financially and emotionally.[10]

Officials often attempted to instill guilt into citizens to promote bond sales, as in an image of Uncle Sam pointing his finger and stating, "Your War Job Is—Buy War Bonds!" The *Red Oak Express* asked its readers, "Is One Dollar Gift Enough to Pay Them?" and framed the ad with photos of the thirty Montgomery County "boys" in German prisons. Injured servicemen served as models for the Norman Rockwell *Saturday Evening Post* cover of a serviceman, supported by a crutch, looking sentimentally at his $100 war bond.[11]

Along with guilt, war-bond advertising emphasized both power and paranoia. War bonds bought the power needed to defeat an enemy's way of life along with the promise of future prosperity in America. Paranoia presented itself as well in bond advertising, with extreme dualism such as hatred of "Hitlerism" or the evil nature of the Japanese, which was always contrasted with the pure and untainted image of the Allied cause. The words *Nazis* and *Japs* punched out this hatred. Japanese soldiers were constantly portrayed as subhuman or little men, as primitives, and referred to as "the Yellow Peril." They were pictured as vermin, rats, or monkeys, and conflicts such as the Battle of Attus added fuel to this depiction of them as animals or madmen. The racist perception of the Japanese grew stronger and lasted throughout the war years—that is, until the discovery of the Nazi death camps.[12]

Secretary of the Treasury Henry Morgenthau Jr. believed people could be convinced of the need for war bonds if "properly urged," and the Treasury started selling bonds on May 1, 1941, and raised over $6,023,707,000 nationally without "overmuch effort." Funding tactics needed to change after Pearl Harbor, however, to quickly raise even more money for the declared war effort. In Iowa, the total sales of defense savings bonds and stamps from May 1941 through March 1942 amounted to $49 million, but by July 1, 1942, the federal government had increased its drive for funds and was demanding specific war-bond quotas from each state reaching as high as "a billion a month."[13]

A number of Davenport citizens strenuously and successfully sold war bonds that spring of 1942 in what *Life* magazine called "an inspired campaign." Sixteen hundred "minute men" committed to training for this campaign and then scoured the city for donors. The two most inventive ideas were having firemen scale ladders to astonish office workers at their windows, or Marilyn Boeck's sitting in a wheelbarrow to sell bonds and having each new buyer take turns pushing her around the downtown area. *Life* insisted that other American cities "might well plagiarize from inventive and patriotic Davenport, Iowa."[14]

Des Moines sponsored a large, creative two-mile parade on a Wednesday afternoon in July 1942 with over 50,000 spectators and 10,000 marchers. Parade attractions included the "Iowa Pattens" (Father Floyd and his eight sons, all in military uniforms); the Drake University band with two hundred girls in red, white, and blue; and two hundred sailors from the electricians' mate school at Iowa State College. Other marchers included troop units, store employees, state and federal employees, veterans of World War I, and Gold Star mothers (women whose sons had been killed in the war). Iowa civilian-air-patrol planes circled overhead and dropped war-bond leaflets to remind spectators of the celebration's purpose. Throughout the entire parade, flags waved, bonds sold, elders socialized, and youth jitterbugged. Local officials declared the day and the drive a success.[15]

But sometimes the war enthusiasm during these events seemed "over the top." After the Des Moines parade, spectators tore "to shreds" an Adolf Hitler effigy in front of the *Register* and *Tribune* building. Instead of having the scheduled Fireman's Jump, a group surprised the crowd by flinging an effigy of Hitler from the top of the building. A *Tribune* reporter commented on the mob in front of its building: "Did they catch him? They did not. They dropped the life net, let the Nazi dummy crack his head on Locust Street and then leaped on him with heels—to grind him into the asphalt." This crowd watched with "smiles, cheers, and rapt seriousness."[16]

"Pearl Harbor Week," beginning December 7, 1942, focused the bond campaign with such slogans as "Make your own declaration of war." Iowa ranked third in war-bond purchases with $180 million in bonds purchased in 1942, with eleven counties each raising enough money to purchase a bomber. Still, one ad continued to warn, "Don't kid yourself! We could lose this war!"[17]

Fund drives from 1943 to 1945 were focused into shorter, finite periods of time, with two a year in 1943 and 1945 but three in 1944. The Second War Drive by the U.S. Treasury Department enlisted this theme: "They Give Their Lives—You Lend Your Money." This campaign opened on April 12 with a national goal of $13 billion and closed by the 30th. Iowa finished second with 154.1 percent of its quota, or $13,870,000.[18]

Children also joined in the fund-raising efforts. The U.S. Treasury, Office of Education, and Wartime Commission jointly sponsored a "Schools for War" program to coordinate war activities, exhibit information concerning efforts, and give recognition to participating schools. The motto was "Save, Serve, Conserve," with each *V* in bold type. By February 1943, Iowa students led the nation in war-bond purchases; five thousand schools participated, buying a million dollars of war bonds and stamps each month. In Mason City, grade school students raised $4,568.40 in twenty-one days to purchase five jeeps. Several WACs (Women's Army Corps members) personally drove the purchased equipment to the school, and at the ceremony one little girl walked up to the jeep and touched it carefully. She exclaimed, "Why, it has tires like a real car."[19]

Throughout the war, teachers and parents encouraged children to behave as "good American citizens." As the editor of *Children's Activities—for Home and School* wrote, "We can all do much to help win this war and bring it to a speedy end." By the end of the war, the nation's schoolchildren had contributed over a billion dollars in war-bond purchases. In 1945, the *Iowa Parent-Teacher* justified the federal Schools for War program by stating that youngsters had paid for bombers while also saving for their future college expenses. An *Iowa Farm Bureau Spokesman* caption best summed up the bond propaganda toward children, "I'm too little to fight . . . but I do buy bonds."[20]

Iowa women also contributed many hours and dollars to the war-bond effort, both selling and buying. In fact, Iowa's women provided a national example of a successful fund-raising organization. Harriet Elliott, director of the National War Savings Staff's Women's Division, agreed that Iowa's record of war-bond sales gave her "the best rainy-day reading of all" to brighten her gloomy hours. Why? Because Iowa consistently achieved totals well beyond its quotas, more than any other state in the union. Elliott advised other states, based on Iowa's success, to follow three simple words: "form women's divisions."[21]

Mrs. Harold Newcomb headed the Iowa State Women's Division of the War Finance Committee and Iowa's "Women at War Week" during November 1942. She believed that "as soon as women understand the reasons for buying victory bonds they will see that their men folk purchase them." Newcomb knew women were "instrumental" in 85 percent of household purchases and planned to educate many of Iowa's women and sell them bonds using the slogan "This Is My Fight Too."[22]

On September 9, 1943, the Third War Loan Drive began with the slogan "Back the Attack" and a national goal of $15 billion. Each community's and citizen's particular job remained simply to scrape together every dollar to buy that extra war bond. Des Moines held a three-mile bond parade including 1,200 WACs in twenty-three platoons, marching in open ranks. An army of 30,000 bond workers planned to call upon every person in the state to "donate," as they referred to it. By the end of this campaign, the drive had topped $13 billion nationally, and Iowa had reached $248 million.[23]

The "financial offensive," the Fourth War Loan campaign, began with a $14 billion goal, visualized as a stack of $1,000 bills as high as New York's Empire State skyscraper. This campaign lasted from January 18 to February 15, 1944, with "Let's All" added to the Third Drive's motto of "Back the Attack." Iowa's quota was $177 million, and Governor Bourke Hickenlooper warned Iowans about "a danger that optimism may prompt a slowing up in our effort." On the last day, total Iowa sales amounted to $139,900,000, which was 79 percent of the quota.[24]

Along with the eight specific war-loan campaigns, various groups successfully conducted special drives to directly purchase war weapons. From 1943 through 1944, Iowa bonds bought one liberty ship, fifty-four planes, and thousands of jeeps. The Iowa Federation of Business and Professional Women raised enough money in 1943 to have its name placed on an ambulance plane. The Iowa girls 4-H campaign in 1944, "Bonds Buy Mercy," financed a C-54, an evacuation plane that carried wounded soldiers. The enthusiasm of Edith McBeth, chair of the Iowa Clubwomen, helped that group raise over $687,000 in their women's campaign "Buy a Bomber." And by war's end, the Iowa Federation of Women's Clubs had raised over $1.5 million in bonds.[25]

When the Fifth War Loan Drive, or the "Big Push," was gearing up, its organizers did not change the slogan significantly from the Third Drive, going with "Back the Attack—Buy More than Before." The Fifth campaign ran from June 12 to July 8, 1944, and addressed "Mr. and Mrs. America, Everywhere U.S.A." National goals climbed higher as war costs accelerated, and Iowa's goal was $202 million. An Iowa Poll taken during the fifth drive revealed that 82 percent of Iowans were buying bonds, and of those, 91 percent were saving money through bonds. Just slightly more men than women were buying, and higher-income groups were the most consistent. By place of residence, of the people in cities, 83 percent purchased bonds; towns, 77 percent; and farms, 82 percent. In President Roosevelt's fireside chat on June 12, he made a specific request: "I urge all Americans to buy war bonds without stint."[26]

In Iowa, women again energized the campaign with bonds for babies, a grandmothers' league, and bond queen contests along with club and church projects. In almost every county, women planned that unspectacular but important job of house-to-house canvassing to promote the idea that "just one more bond won't hurt anything." Mrs. Frederic Leopold, an immigrant who had become a block leader in Burlington, boasted that she was willing to "walk her feet off" for the bond drive because her old country had not given her much: "Hard labor and cucumbers—and no opportunity for an education."[27]

By campaign's end, Iowa had fallen down on the job in E bond sales, with only $57 million of the $74 million quota raised. Random research conducted by the state bond organization blamed the "in between donors," who supposedly were "ducking." Professionals or owners of factories or large businesses were possibly buying just $25 in bonds to "save their faces," when they should be purchasing bonds of $75 or more. Bond organizers also found another group to be slacking—farmers and small-town business owners. Still, the Iowa Finance Committee could find no true "rhyme or reason" for the shortfall, except perhaps false optimism about the battlefronts.[28]

The Sixth War Loan Drive started on November 20 and was to run through December 16, 1944, but was extended to December 31. Determined officials decided that this campaign should not lag, although it was the third drive that year. For that purpose, one of its slogans was "Get Behind the VI War Loan with VIm, VIgor, and VItality." The official emblem was a bomb with "6th War Loan" printed on it, aiming for the center of the rising sun on the Japanese flag. With the third anniversary of Pearl Harbor, most bond ads angrily focused on fighting the Japanese, as in one ad's caption "Yes, only bombs and shells make any impression on Japanese minds." A Gallup Poll found that nine out of ten Americans thought that war bonds represented a good investment. However, most people wanted to purchase them voluntarily, not on a compulsory basis.[29]

At the end of the Sixth War Loan Drive, Iowa's total sales reached $281,700,000, which was 180 percent of its quota of $178 million. Iowans exceeded their quota of E bond sales as well, with $72,111,000 in bonds sold, for 116 percent of the quota for that category, though this was $4 million less than what they raised in the Fifth. Still, Iowa's 1944 year-long record was second nationally, with 10.91 percent of income spent on bonds, coming in only after North Dakota's 11.12 percent.[30]

The Seventh War Loan Drive ran from May 14 through June 5, 1945, with the theme "Pour Out Your Might in the Mighty Seventh!" Capitalizing on the popular Iwo Jima photograph, this drive utilized the symbol of three soldiers raising the flag in front of a "Mighty 7." The national goal was $14 billion, with Iowa's quota set at $189 million. One special event for the Seventh involved thirty army planes landing in one-minute intervals at the Des Moines Airport before a crowd of 10,000 spectators. The Iowa Mother's Day Ceremony featured music played by the Za-Ga-Zig Band as two hundred forty veterans—including nineteen Iowans, to "give an extra punch to the war loan drive"—from the Tax Navigation School stepped from planes.[31]

Sales still remained behind schedule, however, and Iowa was down by $5 million in E bond purchases by June 7. To encourage more sales, Vernon Clark suggested the slogan "On to Tokyo with War Bonds." By the drive's end, seventy-nine counties zoomed over the top to put Iowa second in the nation, two-tenths of a percent behind Montana. State officials agreed that last-minute buying greatly aided the campaign but lamented the fact that just a quarter of a million dollars more would have landed Iowa in first place. The war-bond ads tried expressing the military fighting concerns in the Pacific that early summer, with lines such as "Their 'Quota' may be DEATH, *Your* Quota is Bigger Bonds."[32]

The Eighth War Loan Drive leaders "rechristened" it as "America's Great Victory Loan" when Japan surrendered during their planning phase. The revised campaign began on October 29 under the new title "Peace and Prosperity" and was originally scheduled to end December 8 but would be extended to December 31. The national goal was $11 billion, with a continued emphasis on individual rather than corporate purchases, and the slogan of the Victory Loan again piled on guilt: "They've finished their job . . . let's finish ours."[33]

This drive strove to remind citizens that the price of victory was both blood and money. World War II had cost $336 billion, or eleven times the cost of World War I. As a *Des Moines Register* editorial titled "Victory Loan" stated, "The people on the home front cannot relax their bond buying yet." This last campaign was carried on over four important dates—Armistice Day, Thanksgiving, Pearl Harbor Day, and Christmas. First Lady Eleanor Roosevelt, through her syndicated column "My Day," captured the essence of this period: "It should be up to us, not to veterans, to sell bonds."[34]

Bond organizers introduced several special choices that season such as Thanksgiving Bonds, Roosevelt Bonds (sent from the Hyde Park post office with a photograph of FDR), and Christmas Bonds with the slogan "The Finest Christmas Gift in the World Is a Victory Bond." In the final count for the Victory Bond Drive, Iowa tied with Alabama for fourth with 148 percent of quota. In this last drive for victory, Iowans had purchased $68,252,000 in E bonds—more than $22 million over the $46 million goal—as every county in Iowa landed over quota for the first time.[35]

The end figures for the eight war-bond drives in Iowa totaled $2,408,456,163, which was certainly over the quota of $1,777,000,000. The eight specific war-bond campaigns had raised $1,924,445,847, while the months between drives had raised $484,010,316. Iowa's final record, though certainly respectable, did not earn the best ranking; rather, North Dakota set the overall record for contributions, measured per capita, in the combined eight bond drives during World War II. War-bond sales for the Second World War had created impressive records as total sales were four times greater than those in the Great War. In Iowa, World War I bond sales had totaled $500,532,500, and the quota had been $462,715,510.[36]

On October 2, 1946, sixty regional and county chairmen attended the Iowa Alumni Association of War Bond Workers meeting in Des Moines. Vernon Clark, now national director of the United States Savings Bond Division, congratulated the state's members on the fact that more E bonds were being sold in Iowa after the war than were being cashed. As reporter George Mills quipped in 1946, Iowans did have the advantage of possessing more "folding money" in both their pockets and their savings accounts than ever before.[37]

Scrappers

Some scrap collectors certainly were eccentric. One such person was Walter Smith of Council Bluffs, who accumulated 36,288 typewriter-ribbon spools prior to the war. Another was "Farmer Bush" from Corning, who turned in a very large collection of license plates dating back to 1914. And Anson Ritigers from Polk County donated a twenty-eight-year-old accumulation of scrap iron amounting to 4,100 pounds.[38] For most Iowans and Americans, however, becoming "scrappers" took some doing and some organizing.

The second resource, after money, that the United States Armed Services needed was recycled metal, paper, rubber, cloth, and even milkweed pods to become the raw materials needed for new weaponry, ammunition, medicine, and other military supplies. Scrap collections involved everyone in the community—every man, woman, and child—in this effort to "re-educate" citizens to save, conserve, and contribute. Collection campaigns became very serious affairs throughout the war years, and every neighborhood started some sort of a salvage committee. Many Iowans, at first, thought a great deal of money could be made by selling to "the junk man" because of this desperate government need, but ceiling prices from before the start of the war remained in place. Most people, however, remained committed to the continuing salvage campaigns solely for patriotic reasons.[39]

Women and children proved to be especially strong soldiers in this campaign. The War Production Board created a Women's Salvage Army in each of the forty-eight states to spread information and ensure community cooperation. Every county in Iowa established a chairman with assistants for the Women's Salvage Army, creating a total work force of 99 chairmen and 835 women workers. Mrs. Fred Weitz, the state's salvage board chair of the women's division, issued a summons she headed "A Call to the Women of Iowa for Salvage Army." Weitz proved to be an able leader, with reporting and writing experience, and she described herself as an "ardent feminist." She said of her salvage duties, "It's so easy to do the simple thing, and so hard to sell a simple truth, to arouse interest."[40]

Unlike too many adults, children stayed focused throughout the war years on the country's need for scrap, truly becoming the heroes of the scrap drives. "Children's Crusades" became "the shock troops of salvage." As historian Jordan Braverman comments on these young Americans' efforts, "They supplied the earnestness that might have been lacking in their elders; they, at least, were not guilty of complacency."[41]

Children knew their neighborhoods; they liked to scrounge and get dirty—those needed ingredients of a scrap drive. Imagination was also a necessary element that they could provide. Often children or their teachers organized quasi-military units in which the children could earn rank and insignia, and the U.S. Office of War Information created a cartoon character, Kid Salvage, to encourage children to participate in scrap hunting. The *Saturday Evening Post* called this salvage army of children "30,000,000 soldiers for our New Third Front"; this army included schools, informal neighborhood groups, and clubs such as the Boy and Girl Scouts. The U.S. government seriously described these young people as "the seasoned veterans in the Battle for Scrap."[42]

Almost every community in the country organized a school scrap army that started a "locust-like invasion" of American homes on October 7, 1942. Children felt the urgency, as *The Saturday Evening Post* noted, because "grownups lack the imagination their children have to translate an old overshoe the dog has chewed, a broken discarded lawn mower, a rusty golf club, skid chain or flatiron into hand grenades, machine guns, shells, bombs, fighting ships and planes." The schoolchildren of Winterset, for example, gathered twenty-one tons in their first two days of the organized search as they scoured the town. The local paper praised their efforts: "They hauled it in play wagons, baby buggies, and every sort of conveyance. Ponies and a team of goats were pressed into service." Though the children's work efforts became quite impressive, historian Marc Miller in *The Irony of Victory* raises an important point about children's all-too-consistent and almost insistent participation: "The question arises why in the midst of an extremely popular war, this nation went to such lengths to indoctrinate its own children."[43]

The drive for iron became the most dramatic scrap campaign, in sheer volume and direct military use. Usually men directed the iron drives because of their access to used equipment, especially on farms, and the piles of scrap iron they collected often became quite large, which added to the drama along with the aggressive competitions between towns and regions. Also, citizens—young or old—did not have much difficulty connecting the transformation of scrap iron into guns; people could easily believe in this process and therefore in their needed contributions to the war effort. Slogans for the campaign included guilt-inducing queries: "Whose Boy will Die because *You* failed?" and "Can Men call *You* 'scrap-slacker'?" Herbert Plagman, Iowa's salvage executive secretary, echoed this guilt: "Lack of cooperation on the home front in the scrap drive might be the cause of the death of an American soldier for lack of arms and equipment."[44]

Iowa responded with a newspaper-directed scrap-iron drive lasting from September 28 through October 17, 1942. Each Iowan's quota reached one hundred pounds of almost anything that could be translated into military use. Madison County saw its scrap mission concretely tied to the war effort as stated in the Winterset paper: "To supply our fighting men with the bombs, bayonets, guns, gas masks, hand grenades and other fighting weapons they need, the American people must gather millions of tons of additional scrap material."[45]

The local Future Farmers of America provided one success story for Winterset by the end of the year through their salvage collection. The FFA instructor, Simon August Ossian, described the boys' salvage work in military terms: "They worked like troopers, never giving up until they had combed ditches, junk piles, and other remote places to find scrap metal and rubber." The boys collected 20.8 tons of metal along with 400 pounds of rubber, which netted $155.12 to buy war bonds. Their high school yearbook called it "one big achievement."[46]

Several communities in southwestern Iowa met the scrap-iron challenge through healthy competition. Clarinda decided to treat its initial iron drive exactly like a military operation, with "a scrap force" of one hundred business and professional men in "a motorized division of twenty bannered trucks." Their orders drilled as follows: "The scrap force was to mobilize at 6:30 p.m. on the south side of the square, men being asked to come in work clothes, overalls if available, and ready for work. Upon arrival they will be assigned to trucks and districts and will receive orders to 'move out.'" Whistles blew regularly to remind every person in town to get the scrap metal piled up, and Clarinda's citizens ultimately gathered twenty-eight tons in this one-hour drive on a Tuesday evening.[47]

Red Oak participated in "a civil war" between a northern tier of Mills, Montgomery, and Adams counties and the three counties south of them, Fremont, Page, and Taylor. The *Red Oak Sun* rallied support, "Another civil war is on. Not a war of rebellion, nor to free any slaves (although it may help to keep men from becoming slaves), but a war for Scrap!" By the end of the drive, the volunteer fire station donated its 2,550-pound bell to join the courthouse contribution of its historic cannon. In another small town, Villisca, the mayor delivered a proclamation: "We cannot leave it for somebody else to do—we must all get in and work: everybody, right here in Villisca, must help." Stanton, one of the smallest towns in Montgomery County, proudly stacked up the largest scrap pile in this civil war, with the entire town and local farmers working toward the effort, led by E. E. Wigstone, the "hustling" scrap chairman.[48]

But at the beginning of 1943, almost half of Iowa's ninety-nine counties reported "no scrap iron or steel collections whatever." Plagman warned fellow Iowans, "We're slipping. We agreed to back our fighting men with plenty of heavy scrap so they could have all the ships, tanks, guns, and planes they need, but we're letting them down. That's not like Iowa." By spring, the scrap metal drives still lagged, and Plagman described this situation as "nothing short of shameful." The state fell from twelfth place in the 1942 national ranking to 1943's bottom of the list.[49]

The National Jalopy Campaign initiated a creative approach to the scrap iron drive that the War Production Board assigned to the American Legion. The campaign slogan used alliteration—"Jolt the Japs with Jalopies"—and the "Jalopy Recruiting Pledge" read: "I have a jalopy that wants to enlist. It is O.K. with me." American Legion posts awarded the largest numbers of contributions with Certificates of Recognition, and Fred Chandler led this Iowa campaign with that legendary "legion spirit." "As we read the headlines from North Africa each day, I think we can visualize why more and more steel is needed," Chandler noted. "We of the last World War are in this battle too! Let's go over the top now." He later quoted his own pun, "Keep scrapping for scrap until the scrap is over over there."[50]

Iowans tried to go all out for the scrap metal drive, sometimes even donating historical items such as courthouse cannons. Ironically, this scrap was supposed to create artillery described as "too big for a courthouse square." Vernon Sietman from Marshall County noted his sadness that several Civil War cannons donated from the Marshalltown courthouse square were melted down for the war effort. Sietman strongly believed this to be quite a sacrifice, but that was how strong the community feeling of cooperation for the war effort was. By the end of the war, some historically minded individuals had compiled a partial list of the many relics of historical significance that had been lost in Iowa's rather frenzied scrap drives.[51]

Wastepaper became the target of another salvage drive that helped support the tremendous amount of packaging required to ship 700,000 different items from home front to battlefront. This national drive in which every scrap of paper was needed opened on January 3, 1943, and the Iowa salvage division reported that a third of Iowa's counties had collected between July and November 1943 a total of 5,452,580 pounds of wastepaper. "Just a minute Mr. and Mrs. Iowa," one ad directed, "don't throw away that old newspaper or that old sack, or that cardboard carton!"[52]

By 1944, each person in the nation needed to salvage seven pounds of paper for a total quota of eight million tons set by the War Production Board. Both Girl and Boy Scouts proved to be especially active at the local level. The Boy Scouts of Winterset, for example, collected 68,283 pounds of wastepaper in a one-day drive, enough to fill a railroad freight car. The boys rallied in their resourcefulness, using a goat-drawn cart, coaster wagons, bicycles, pony carts, dog carts, and wheelbarrows. In 1945, each Scout unit nationwide that collected one thousand pounds of scrap paper received a General Eisenhower medal and a genuine shell case used on a European battlefield.[53]

The country experienced a rubber shortage at the war's beginning as the United States still remained completely dependent on foreign imports for rubber and tin. The government needed to quickly develop and produce a synthetic rubber for the many essential war needs, but in the meantime, scrap seemed to be the answer. In 1942, Roosevelt called for an all-out, nationwide rubber-salvage campaign from June 15 through the 30th. As one slogan cracked: "Make that rubber s-t-r-e-t-c-h."[54]

Iowans responded generously, especially after Roosevelt extended the drive until July 10. Iowans collected 9.54 pounds per capita, for a total of 12,105 tons. The Des Moines County chair of the rubber drive, C. L. Scott, reminded local citizens of needed contributions, "All scrap is worthwhile—a bathing cap, old hot water bottle, unusable tire or tube, the country needs scrap rubber." By the end of the year, the nation collected 454,155 tons of rubber. Iowa ranked sixth in the effort.[55]

Other miscellaneous drives for wartime scrap included a copper and brass drive that, for each pound, gave one free admission to a Des Moines movie theater. In yet another drive Iowa Clubwomen contributed worn stockings to be manufactured into gunpowder bags. Their newsletter encouraged this unique salvage: "Our county courthouses are our common symbols of democratic government. Let us contribute enough discarded silk and nylons stockings to go many times around the squares upon which they stand."[56]

Even books became a salvage item in a collection sponsored by the American Library Association, the U.S.O., and the Red Cross. The Victory Book Campaign started in December 1941; by the end of 1943, volunteers had gathered over eighteen million books throughout the nation, and ten million were distributed to men in the armed forces. Iowa's libraries had collected a total of 286,177 volumes to earn a twelfth-place finish.[57]

One last salvage search occupied the fall of 1944: milkweed pods. These pod hunts are still memorable for Iowa's residents who participated in them as schoolchildren. The milkweed-pod campaign aimed at collecting 2.5 million bushel bags to produce 1.5 million pounds of floss for a million life jackets. In Kossuth County, for example, schoolchildren collected enough pods to fill half a train car and received $450 as a donation to their school for the effort. Ellen Witham earned the title "bag champ," as she collected 44 of her rural school's 58 bags. Iowa's children collectively gathered between 100,000 to 150,000 bushel bags, but Michigan led the drive with 700,000 bags of milkweed pods. Whether any of this floss was every used as flotation for life jackets is still being debated.[58]

At war's end, many communities proudly remembered their salvage record, but the patriotic groups disbanded when the defense work appeared done. Scrap drives were successful if the need was colorfully expressed in military terms and adequately explained to citizens, but the United States government sometimes had to openly confess its need for resources in order to persuade people to donate to the national war effort. The scrap-drive organizers structured national, state, and local committees, and their drives had preset, democratic quotas. Local newspapers and business organizations directed most campaigns with men as generals and with women and children as support troops.

Company M

The third resource that communities sent to war, the most valuable by far, was their young men. The boys certainly represented the most significant "contribution" from the community front, as the war continually touched towns' residents and families directly through their soldiers, and the *Des Moines Tribune* recognized this almost universal fact: "Along the streets and roadways of Iowa, every home has been affected in some way by World War II." Locally, Priscilla Wayne answered an East Coast accusation that "the middle west scarcely knows that a war is being waged" by countering, "It is true we might see more bombers and be closer to some of the war activities if we lived in the east, but we know there is a war going on, make no mistake about that. Ride through the streets of Des Moines and note the service flags in the windows."[59]

National Guard units, often regionally organized units of soldiers, were among the first troops sent overseas. A joint resolution by Congress in August 1940 had called the entire National Guard of the United States to federal service for extensive military training. Southwest Iowa's Company M was one such troop called for active duty. This company boasted a long history, having been organized in 1893 and fought in the Great War. The World War II farewell for 123 men of Company M at the Red Oak train station certainly became emotional, with two thousand relatives, friends, and well-wishers present. The local newspaper described the scene as one of "great morale building" that "put that certain something into the hearts of every member of Company M." The paper's reporter painted the emotional picture: "The crowd remained on the tracks after the red light on the train's caboose had faded around the bend." One soldier, Robert Conrad, later wrote from Camp Claiborne in Louisiana that training seemed to go fairly smoothly after "a swell trip" to this "enormous and new camp." Congress voted the following August (1941) to continue Guardsmen's terms to eighteen months.[60]

After training, Company M shipped out to Ireland, then to the North African front. A letter from Lauren McBride, commander of Company

K, commented on both companies' experiences that "this travel is very nice but that the best place in the world is back home." He especially sent his thoughts "to the loved ones at home whom we know are enduring hardships and doing just as much to win this war as we are in North Africa." Corporal Dennis Smith's letter got straight to the point and described the relatively comfortable beginnings of the North African occupation. "We are issued free of charge a pack of cigaretes [*sic*] each day," Smith detailed. "I'm getting plenty to eat. Wine is dirt cheap and I'm having quite a bit of fun learning French."[61]

These experiences, however, quickly changed, and Company M became tragically involved in the battle with the Nazis at Kasserine Pass on the North African front. Iowa's southwest region's communities sustained the heaviest blow from this early battle when 311 Iowa soldiers were reported missing from a national list of 814 from 41 states. One-half of Iowa's casualties hailed from this southwestern region, many from Red Oak, and *Life* magazine featured the tragic event, running the headline "War Hits Red Oak." The article stated, "A small prairie town gets word that 23 of its boys are missing in action after a battle in North Africa." *Life*'s editors tried to depict the impact of such news on a small community by publishing an aerial photograph with the names of missing men printed above their homes to give a dramatic visual of the town's losses. A decade later, a reflection in a local history noted, "For the people in Red Oak, it wasn't just a casualty list."[62]

The community residents were devastated partly by the sheer number of losses, and war consciousness increased by the hour as everyone seemed more and more stunned by the flood of telegrams: "Missing in action." Those "crisp words" on the printed telegrams were carried to each of seventeen Montgomery County homes on March 8, 1943. More telegrams would follow. As Kate Smith began her popular radio show the next day, she paused to comment that Red Oak, Iowa, had cause to go in mourning for all her sons missing on the African battlefield. The first southwestern soldier able to write back to his family from this critical African front was a Stanton resident, Phil Swanson: "I have been in action here in Tunisia. I've seen enough to last me a life time, I assure you. Greet everyone for me. Will never have time to write all."[63]

Iowa's communities would honor the military men and the loss of life in symbolic displays. Clarinda paid tribute to all its World War

II soldiers with an archway engraved with 2,000 names located on the square. The *Red Oak Express* suggested a similar monument for its courthouse square, "Let's give to the service men the tribute they deserve." The first reported death in Red Oak was Corporal Dale ("Swede") McCormick, 25, who had recently been in a military hospital but returned to Company M just before its tragic battle at Kasserine Pass. The total number of Iowa's war dead by July 1943 amounted to 412, placing it eighth in the nation though twentieth in population. Governor Hickenlooper felt this fact should answer eastern states' charges that midwestern states lacked "equality of sacrifice." The governor proudly responded, "There is no question that this state is making its share of sacrifices."[64]

Months later, *Life* magazine described the autumnal mood in Red Oak with the eerie quiet of mostly older men and women along with the children, all waiting for the return of their young adults. The writer tried to capture the strange silence of this small town:

> "Return to normalcy" is not a suspect phrase there. It means simply when the young men and women are home again, and the stores that the draft and the shortages have closed reopen, and the children go to bed in their parents' new small houses and early evening is a bustle of shopping and young laughter.
>
> Evenings are quiet now. The grandparents tend to drift to the green near the courthouse. It is a pleasant place for talk or a game of checkers in the summer. And big in the center, much bigger than the plaque which lists the dead of 1917–18, stands the boards that give the names of the Red Oak men in the service. The dead are marked plainly, but every father and mother in Red Oak can tell you too just who has been wounded or taken prisoner.[65]

Many families in Red Oak suffered from that deep and lingering pain of grief. In September 1944, Gordon Gammack, a *Des Moines Register* war correspondent, confidently told a near-capacity audience at Red Oak's high school auditorium that this small town had certainly felt this war. "You have made a tremendous sacrifice," Gammack acknowledged, "and no one could say that you do not know there is a war on."[66]

Little Lana Kay McKee, an infant in Red Oak then, could not say anything of her sacrifice, not yet realizing she had once had a father, Private

First Class Joseph McKee, whom she had never seen. This infant numbered only one of hundreds of "Iowa's War Babies" who either never met their fathers during the first years of life or would never know their fathers at all.[67]

The 34th "Red Bull" Division was on the Italian front by the beginning of 1944 and had weathered considerably since its early days on the North African front in 1942. Having started with large numbers of Iowa, Minnesota, and North Dakota men (who had originally enlisted in 1941—the original in-for-a-year, $25-a-month gang), the unit now had few remaining Iowa soldiers, and they found themselves surrounded by men from all over the United States. Ernie Pyle, noted war narrator, described these remaining Iowa soldiers as "wise and worn, like a much-read book, or a house that wears its aging stone stoutly, ignoring the patchwork of new concrete that holds it together." Another veteran found the Iowa men not quite so "stout" and deeply weary from the years' "constant turnover." "They were old timers," soldier Tom Kindred commented, "and among the infantry units there were real problems because those who were still there were thinking they couldn't last much longer. Something had to hit them. . . . Their morale was very bad."[68]

In 1946 the nation noted its military losses as the *Saturday Evening Post* remembered Red Oak's: "If New York City had lost as many sons as this Iowa town, the dead would have numbered 70,000." Red Oak now suffered as "a community despoiled of its finest youth by war, but rich in cherished memories." The article continued, "Red Oak, Iowa, looks like the home town we dreamed of overseas; rich and contented, with chicken and blueberry pie on Sundays, for whose sake some said we were fighting the war. It is the kind of town we wanted to be the same when we came home, at the same time hoping that somehow it would know what the war was about." The article concluded:

> But now, one year after, Red Oak hasn't forgotten the war, for too many of her sons are gone. On the green grass of the town square, between a Civil War monument and a bronze plaque honoring the dead of World War I, are new honor rolls, as big as billboards. On them, blazoned with gold stars, are the names of fifty Red Oak men who lost their lives in World War II, marking one of the highest mortalities any American town has suffered.[69]

While many young men did not come home to their hundreds of small towns, thousands did return. The iconic soldier's return seemed exemplified in a Pulitzer Prize–winning photograph taken in Villisca, another town in southwestern Iowa. In the photograph, a soldier is bent over to hug his young daughter in front of a boxcar at the depot while his wife weeps and touches his arm. Their young nephew looks on, dressed in a striped shirt. The hidden faces in this homecoming photograph could have been anyone's—yet the roles remained clear and powerfully expressive. *Life* magazine told the story behind the image:

> Three years ago Bob Moore was running a corner drugstore in Villisca, Iowa. Then he joined the Army, leaving behind his wife and child. In February he led his company to safety through German lines in Fald Pass, winning promotion to lieutenant colonel and the Silver Star. Last week Bob Moore came home, a soldier, officer, and hero. But to the ones who waited for him in Villisca he was still more importantly father and husband. After 16 months at war a hero comes home to Iowa, welcomed by his small daughter's big hug and the joyous sobs of his lonely wife.

The photograph soon captured the public's imagination. *Look* magazine called it "a hero's reunion," and *Time* characterized the photo of Moore being "greeted by his sobbing wife, ecstatic daughter, and interested nephew" as "timeless." A *Newsweek* writer described the image: "A picture that ranks with the war classics, this photo tells its own story more movingly than any words could." Today the most popular photographs at the National Archives are those from World War II—images that capture "a defining mood": "an element of surprise, an unexpected juxtaposition, an ironic contrast." This photo of Moore's homecoming, with his bowed head, his clutched daughter, and his nearly hysterical wife certainly captured the intense emotion of the community front. Along with Moore's family but not included in the photograph were "a crowd of townsfolk"; most were parents and relatives of the men who had served with Moore on the North African front.[70]

Red Oak's postwar recovery, like that of other American communities, could not easily or quickly be brushed aside, as a hometown journalist commented decades later when analyzing the town's response: "The 1940s had told Red Oak something. Shouted it into its face, actually. War is never kind, but sometimes it can be down right cruel. And World War II was cruel to Red Oak. So when the Korean War flared up in the early 1950s, the town wasn't all that easy to convince Korea was the place to be."[71]

Even in 1993, Lois Bryson of southwestern Iowa still possessed her World War II telegram that listed her husband, Fred, as missing in action. She remembered not just her pain, but the community's. "We all hung together," Bryson began. "Everybody had somebody who left. Like rural areas today, a lot of people befriended you and helped you out."[72]

The sad cost of the Second World War for many communities has been an excruciatingly extended silence about war's true sacrifices. Alan Spitzer, a World War II veteran from Iowa, wrote in 1995 that people should honor "all of those truncated lives, those lives that were never lived." Spitzer also remembered that returning veterans were never expected to speak about any of the consequences of war. "Wounds were expected to heal," Spitzer commented, "and veterans were 'supposed to get on with life.'" In 1998, Jim Johnson, who was eleven years old in 1945, still recalled the veterans, many wounded or prisoners of war, returning to Red Oak. "They came back and went on with their lives," Johnson commented poignantly. "They never talked about what happened to them. It was something they did as young men and they paid a terrible price."[73]

Sent Sons and the Sullivans

Although Red Oak's unusually large number of war casualties gave it a "dubious honor," as veteran Lloyd Dunn from Clarinda later described it, many other Iowa communities and families had also sacrificed their young men to the machine of total war. So many families had sent so many sons to fight. As the wartime editor of the *Annals of Iowa* wrote, "Into every community, town, city, and farm of Iowa the war has already reached its harsh hand."[74]

The community of Odebolt boasted the most Iowa men from a single family serving in the armed services when in September 1941 Clarence Patten at age fifty-two joined his seven enlisted sons in the U.S. Navy, serving on the same ship as his sons, the *U.S.S. Nevada*. "We are proud," Chief of Naval Operations Harold Stark declared in a special broadcast, "to salute this typical American father and outstanding citizen, who stands shoulder to shoulder with his sons, ready to defend the fundamental traditions of liberty. This is the kind of men that make this the finest navy in the world."[75]

Later, another brother joined his siblings to make nine family men in all, making the Pattens the navy's largest family. Seven of the brothers were later stationed on the *Lexington* and in near-tragic circumstances survived the sinking of this aircraft carrier. Several of the siblings served as part of the engine crew—the "black gang." All seven escaped injury after the explosion, but in the aftermath the brothers became scattered and separated, not knowing one another's fate for almost a month. Shortly after the near-fateful accident, the navy asked all nine sailors to tour the country as a publicity stunt. Reporters described them as the "breezy Patten brothers" who "never stop kidding each other with a routine of back-slapping and handshaking." The *Des Moines Register* published a photo of the Pattens' young nephew, mouth open in amazement, surrounded by "His Heroes—8 Uncles and a Grandfather."[76]

The Pattens would not be the only large Iowa family to serve in the military. The second-largest family had seven sons in the navy, the Davis brothers from Davenport: Oscar, Marshall, Ivan, George, Melvin, and Marvel Davis would follow their brother Sheldon's example when he enlisted in 1940. Another family, the Sniders of Williams, set a record for Hamilton County with six stars on their service flag for sons Donald, Gilbert, Glen, Marion, Wendell, and Wayne. In yet another Iowa family, six sons of Edith Aldrich of Harvarden joined the army—Joseph, Anthony, Glenn, Eugene, Robert, and Edward. Aldrich said her "hobby" was waiting for the mailman and pacing her apartment floor.[77]

Other mothers anxiously paced as well. A Mexican immigrant mother, Virginia Reyes of Des Moines, also witnessed her six sons going off to war: David, Ralph, Dan, Robert, Henry, and Richard. The *Tribune* featured the Reyes story with a focus on their mother's endless waiting: "Within the last two years the modest frame Reyes home with its shady, flower-brightened yard which once echoed with the shouts of eleven Reyes children at play, has grown quieter and quieter. Tuesday Mrs. Reyes sat alone in a silence that was almost complete." She missed her sons, terribly. "The apple-pie order of the house, and the spicy aroma from the kitchen," concluded the article, "are signs that Mrs. Reyes is a busy woman. Besides the familiar home tasks she writes to each twice a week and waits for letters from her sons, who 'write often and well.'"[78]

Other Iowa families had several sons serving in different branches of the military. Mr. and Mrs. Emergy Dull of Cherokee had five sons—Paul, Max, Glenn, Ivan, and Burton—in the armed services, with two in the navy, two in the army, and one in the marines. "The sun doesn't set on this Iowa family," the *Iowa Bureau Farmer* quipped. Another family, the sons of Mr. and Mrs. Herman Hahn, joined the Five Star Service Circle with five brothers serving in the army. The Hahns were described as "a fighting family" because seven uncles had served in World War I.[79]

While many Iowa families sent a number of their sons to war, the family nationally believed to have made the greatest sacrifice was the Sullivan family of Waterloo, Iowa. The five Sullivan brothers—George, Francis, Madison, Eugene, and Albert—had always been known to the townspeople simply as "the Sullivan boys," growing up in a working-class family during the Depression years. The Sullivans suffered childhood economic hardships but always remained a tightly woven group of six siblings, five brothers and one sister. The Sullivan "boys" became a unique and recognized group because they sought special permission to be shipmates despite warnings from navy officials of what this might do to their parents if tragedy struck. No family should lose all its sons to war. They eventually served aboard the new *U.S.S. Juneau.* When the five sailor brothers gathered around an open hatch cover on the *Juneau*'s fantail for a photograph, it became one of the most widely distributed images during the war years. The movie *The (Fighting) Sullivans* (1944), directed by Lloyd Bacon, develops the exaggerated and romanticized theme that this American family produced fighting but loving sons. The producers later added *(Fighting)* to the title, perhaps to boost civilian wartime morale.[80]

An explosion during an attack sank this unsinkable ship, and nearly all the crew members of the *Juneau* died during a complicated sea battle. At first, authorities reported the brothers only as missing, but months later the Sullivan brothers received national recognition because of their tragic deaths together after this battle. *Life* reported the catastrophe as the heaviest blow ever suffered by an American family.[81]

But it was later learned that George Sullivan had survived the ship's sinking, desperately coping in the ocean water for several days before dying. A letter from one of the few survivors, a Nebraska sailor named Lester Zook, described the aftermath of the battle to Alleta and Thomas Sullivan: "It was a sad and pathetic sight to see George looking for his brothers, but all to no avail. George and I made several liberties together and we were always kidding about going back on the railroad after the war was over. I don't know whether this sort of letter helps or hurts you, but it's the truth."[82]

Though the Sullivans became popularly known throughout the war years as heroes sacrificing themselves in battle, the recently told story is quite different: sailors abandoned for days by the navy due to communication errors, left to battle sharks, dehydration, and exposure. This was the true story—that the explosion and aftermath took 683 lives, not the battle—but most Americans preferred the heroic version of the brothers' sacrifice, such as the Younkers department store advertisement that read, "The *Juneau* went down fighting in the battle of Guadalcanal. It was one of the most brilliant victories in the annals of our Navy: twenty-three Jap ships were sunk and nine of our own were lost. The *Juneau* was one of them and aboard her as she sank, were the five gallant Sullivan boys from Iowa."[83]

The Sullivan parents held a mass in their five sons' honor at St. Mary's Church in Waterloo on February 9, 1943. Archbishop Francis J. L. Beckman proclaimed that the spirit of the *Juneau* would live forever, for these five boys came from "fighting stock." He tried in his sermon to comfort those assembled. "It was the American spirit," Beckman began, "that indeniable [*sic*], that oh so noble impulse gushing forth from the land of the free, which moved the five boys whom we particularly commemorate this morning, to offer the supreme sacrifice for God and country."[84]

One of the first letters from a public official to reach the Sullivan parents came from Vice President Henry A. Wallace, originally from Iowa. "Guy Gillete and I were talking last night," Wallace wrote, "about the marvelous spirit which you and your wife have displayed in facing one of the most extraordinary tragedies which has ever been met by any family in the United States. It is the spirit of the Sullivans which will enable the United Nations to gain a complete victory." Eleanor Roosevelt sent her condolences as another anxious mother with military sons: "You and your husband have given a lesson of great courage to the whole country, and in thinking of this war and what it means to all mothers of this country I shall keep the memory of your fortitude always in mind, as I hope other mothers with sons in service will do."[85]

When the Sullivan parents visited Washington in mid-February, even experienced newsmen described the event as "a difficult and throat-catching one." *Newsweek*'s report was uniquely emotional: "They might have been any middle-aged American couple. The woman was stout and motherly looking. She wore a plain dress—one of the two she had brought with her on the long trip east. Her husband was equally inconspicuous in a dark suit of depression vintage."[86]

The Sullivan parents then volunteered for a home-front mission to visit a number of shipyards and war plants. "The boys always wrote to 'keep my chin up,'" Alleta Sullivan said simply. "After their ship went down I remembered what they said and made up my mind to see what I can do to help win the war—to kind of carry on for their sake." The message delivered to industrial workers from the bereaved forty-nine-year-old midwestern housewife and her husband remained simple: "Whatever your jobs are do them a little faster than you ever did. Every day you cut the war short means that many more sons will come home to their families."[87]

President Roosevelt even wrote personally to praise the couple's war efforts. "Your unselfishness and courage serves as a real inspiration to me as I am sure it will for all Americans," FDR praised. "Such faith and fortitude in the face of tragedy convinces me of the indomitable spirit and will of our people." Unfortunately, not everyone viewed the Sullivans' war work in the same light. Writer John Satterfield concludes his research on the Sullivan brothers by observing that a number of Waterloo residents resented the Sullivans' fame and believed their mother had deliberately sought the national publicity. Satterfield poignantly considers the town's response: "Local hostility dampened the acceptance and support they sought and needed in later years. For the rest of their lives, Tom and Alleta were less than completely welcome in Waterloo." Obviously not all of Waterloo's residents felt this way, as the town dedicated an eight-acre park in 1967 as the Sullivan Memorial Park.[88]

Eight months after the loss of the *Juneau,* U.S. Navy Secretary Frank Knox finally sent the official letter to the Sullivan parents: "This lapse of time, in view of the circumstances surrounding the disaster as officially reported by close witnesses, forces us reluctantly to the conclusion that the personnel missing, as a result of the loss of the JUNEAU, were in fact killed by enemy action." Knox also wrote that he regretted the parents' "extraordinary loss." When the Sullivans finally found out that all five sons were not possibly still missing but actually dead, their grief became profound. Alleta Sullivan later tried to explain her initial feelings: "Your first temptation when the news comes is to lock your door and retire into your own private grief. You want to sit alone in your room and cry your heart out."[89]

Thomas and Alleta Sullivan would ultimately attend 235 rallies across the nation and speak to more than a million war workers. Still, some Americans later remarked that they felt the navy used this tragedy in a way that they felt was both exploitative of the family and offensive to others—that it implied that loss could be measured by the number of children who died. For the family, however, the public appearances helped to ease and postpone what writer Satterfield describes as their "deep, lingering grief."[90]

Their true story merged into legend. The later Hollywood movie, *The (Fighting) Sullivans* (1944), portrayed the Sullivans as an ideal American family from small-town Iowa, joyfully living through the Depression years through the sheer strength of family. The movie seemed not so much a war film, but, as film historian Bernard Dick explains, "a film about a family, an exemplary family capable of practicing the art of nobly wrought grief."[91]

On August 14, 1945, after President Truman announced Japan's surrender, a reporter called on Alleta Sullivan in Waterloo for her reaction to the final ending of the Second World War. Her daughter answered the door, replying that her mother could not speak right then. "I think you know what Mom's reaction is," the Sullivan daughter told the reporter. "She feels quite bad. She told me she's glad for other boys coming home but hers won't be back."[92]

Many people who were children during the war long remembered a sadness and a helplessness surrounding their nameless wartime grief. Such was Mary Maloney's experience when she was a grade-school student in Davenport. One day she saw a woman sitting on the front porch of a house with a gold star hanging in the window, which indicated that a son had died in the war. Mary remembered how she felt that day: "I stopped and looked at her. I wanted to say I was sorry. . . . I stood there for what seemed a long time and finally gave a little wave."[93]

For other Iowa families, the end of the war brought long-awaited reunions, such as when four of the five Cooper brothers from Des Moines returned home for Christmas. The following month, all five Cooper brothers posed in uniform for a *Tribune* photographer. Though they joked about which brother outranked the others, all agreed that "Ma" remained "the boss." ("What she says goes, brother.") Their mother, however, was "too busy" to pose with her sons: "doing dishes, gathering uniforms and civilian clothes to be sent to the cleaners, and doing a hundred other household tasks." "Pop" would not pose unless Ma did, but still the newspaper depicted a happy and busy Iowa family whose soldier sons were finally together again.[94]

Harold L. Smith

The immediate postwar period seemed one of peace, but also one of pain. The money spent on war bonds had been an investment, the scrap given in drives was never missed, but the boys who went to fight and their ultimate sacrifices shaped the immediate and lingering years of the postwar period. Both the soldier and his "Main Street" became symbols of the war. John Blum, in *V Was for Victory,* summarizes all that the soldier represented in this fighting effort of the "good war": "The hero of World War II stood for blueberry pie and blond sweethearts, for the family farm and for Main Street, for perseverance and decency—for Americanism as a people's way of being."[95]

A war novel by Iowa author MacKinlay Kantor titled *Happy Land* became a Hollywood movie that portrayed the fighting effort in such terms when it described a small-town Iowa father's grief after his son's war death. The *Time* movie review described the story as "a tender, folksy elegy for a typical American boy who is killed in the war, and for his typical American father, who is thereby killed in spirit." Still, the story's strong moral message remained strangely optimistic, stressing that "the boy's brief easygoing, generous, small-town life was worth dying for because it was worth living."[96] Though the emotion in the sentimental phrases may not seem authentic, the community front had truly sacrificed far too many young soldiers.

General Dwight D. "Ike" Eisenhower remained a general who always understood the value of his young men and their importance to the people back home. Eisenhower's first question whenever he met any group of soldiers was to ask, "Where are you from?" War historian Stephen Ambrose describes Eisenhower's beliefs and expressions as decidedly "Main Street"—the general undoubtedly had the common touch. In a letter to his wife, Mamie, Ike reflected on the sacrifices people back home were making for this war: "Mothers, fathers, brothers, sisters, wives and friends must have a difficult time preserving any comforting philosophy and retaining any belief in the eternal rightness of things. War demands real toughness of fiber—not only in the soldiers that must endure but in the homes that must sacrifice."[97]

This war, like all wars, left behind so many deaths along with the shattered lives of grieving loved ones. The death of one son, Harold L. Smith of Winterset, symbolized the many other young lives lost, and his family and his town portrayed all the families and communities that tried to cope with the aftermath of those deaths. Smith entered the service on March 25, 1944, a year after his graduation from Winterset High School as valedictorian, band letter-winner, and basketball co-captain. His nickname was "Smitty," the class prophecy called him "Professor," and the yearbook described him as being "as merry as the day is long."[98]

Smith received military orders to be sent overseas in October to England, then to Luxembourg, where he fought in General Patton's Third Army. During that excruciating winter in Europe, many teenagers, barely trained, were fighting on both the Allied and German sides during the Battle of the Bulge. Ambrose, in his combat history *Citizen Soldiers,* comments that in the winter of 1945, "America was throwing her finest young men at the Germans."[99]

On February 12, 1945, Smith died of wounds received in battle while leading a machine-gun action against the enemy. The official letter to his mother, Harriet L. Smith, stated, "The War Department has informed me that your son, Technician Fifth Grade Harold L. Smith, has given his life in the performance of his duty." He was nineteen years old.

The Smiths held a memorial service on Sunday, March 25, 1945. Another letter to his parents, from his commanding officer, Captain Lamont Pinkston, told them, "The loss to our purpose of a man with such character, courage, and ability is great and will be felt for some time." The *Iowa Legionnaire* also expressed its condolences: "Comrade Smith and your brave wife, all Legionnaires mourn with you in the supreme sacrifice paid by your heroic son. There is little we can say or do at this hour to relieve your anguish, but God and Country are thankful for the service of your soldier." Years later, Harold Smith's parents requested that his body be sent home. He was buried on August 31, 1948, in the Winterset Cemetery.

Madison County residents installed their permanent Memorial Plaque in their courthouse hall on July 11, 1951, to replace the temporary wooden honor roll on the courthouse square. This memorial bears Harold Smith's name along with the 1,500 other young men from this one Iowa county of ninety-nine who served in the military during the Second World War, and the names of the men who made the supreme sacrifice are starred on the bronze plaque.

A later memorial, dedicated in 1984, would also be composed in bronze—but across the world, in Luxembourg. It too remembered those who served and sacrificed. In a letter dated October 1984 to Harold Smith's relatives, a soldier who had served with Smith on that fatal day emotionally describes this newly dedicated memorial. This letter, written in longhand on Thunderbird Motor Inn stationery, anxiously attempts to describe the European memorial and the significant moment to his friend Harold's family. "The people of Luxembourg are very appreciative of what our people did for them—we gave our young men's lives—we returned their country to them—and their way of life," began George L., as the letter was simply signed. "You can be reassured, the Luxembourgers are thankful—they have not forgotten. Forty years later they are still saying thank you to the men of the U.S. Army and they wrote it in bronze!"[100]

Important words have been engraved in bronze memorials for those who died in the Second World War, those sacrifices that all communities should remember for a very long time. Finally, fifty years after the war ended, the Iowa World War II Memorial was erected in Des Moines on the statehouse lawn. This memorial with its title "The Freedom Flame" was dedicated to both veterans and civilians alike so present-day Iowans can continue to remember that their freedom was "purchased at a price."[101]

Chapter 4

Mrs. America's Mission ~ The Kitchen Front

The life of a Stay-at-home can be dramatic. Even minus the martial music and the uniform one can march in step with a world that is carving a new freedom from the mistakes of the past.

—*Iowa Clubwoman* (1942)

A thousand members of the General Federation of Women's Clubs gathered in Washington, DC, on January 24, 1942, for the National Defense Forum. The secretary of agriculture's economic adviser, Mordecal Ezekiel, solemnly addressed the Federation and its guest of honor, Secretary of Labor Frances Perkins, about homemakers' future duties for the defense effort, such as watching food supplies and controlling waste. "It is quite possible," Ezekiel began, "that every housewife will have to keep a can or jar in her kitchen to pour fat drippings into." Giggles rippled through the audience. He seemed surprised and stated that he was not joking. Now laughter filled the room. Mrs. John Whitehurst, president of the Federation, whispered to him, and then he finally understood. "Oh—," he said. "I'm informed you already do. I'm embarrassed. Well, maybe it will have to be a bigger jar." The audience "roared."[1]

This was the beginning of the kitchen front: the combination of government directives and homemakers' efforts. Every civilian had a responsibility, a patriotic duty, to contribute all possible efforts toward winning the war, and the homemaker would be no exception. The wartime housewife would have consistent though perhaps sometimes overwhelming demands from the government placed on her productive and resourceful work in the kitchen. Iowa's housewives, like homemakers across the country, would contribute to this war effort through cooking, salvaging, gardening, canning, and working with the rationing system. Many homemakers would even exceed these extra orders while maintaining their routine work of home and child care, and most women would meet these demands with renewed patriotism and enthusiasm. The war had moved into the kitchen.[2]

American housewives, though, had tackled war's food problems before—during the Great War. "Food will win the war" was renewed as a slogan from that war. The winter of 1917–1918 had proved to be a difficult one, as many housewives had played that grim game of meatless Tuesdays, wheatless Wednesdays, and porkless Saturdays, and they learned to "hooverize"—to ruthlessly conserve, following the directions of Herbert Hoover, the newly appointed food administrator. The recipe juggling and the canning were voluntary acts of patriotism that women wanted to engage in since they believed their kitchen efforts were needed. This war with Hitler reminded many older homemakers of the last war with the Kaiser, bringing back many of the memories and experiences of that time for those generations old enough to remember, and they became the ones to now encourage the younger wives and mothers to be cheerfully patriotic and "keep our aprons on!"[3]

Aprons aside, the historical image of Iowa continued as one of good food. In an *American Cookery* article titled "Hearty Dishes from the Hawkeye State," Doris Watabaugh described the mix of memories that good Iowa food held for her husband as she tried to replicate the old recipes in her modern Des Moines kitchen. "Each dish he liked in his boyhood," Watabaugh stated, "makes him think of those glorious days when he lived on a Midwestern farm. His father was a thrifty farmer who reaped rich returns from the fertile black soil of Iowa." Her husband was not alone. Good food and good cooks remained highly praised in Iowa as in most rural areas. A well-stocked kitchen from the garden or farm meant security, thriftiness, and pleasure.[4]

The kitchen began a transformation from a family resource to a war weapon as the kitchen front boasted of its new status as "the front line to keep this nation strong." The United States promised to be the best-fed nation in the world, determined to have the best-fed soldiers. The Armed Services now demanded an unprecedented amount of food, and the average soldier gained six to ten pounds in the first few months of training. The Army stated that the *V* of a soldier's diet meant both variety and vitamins, although realistically C, D, or K rations in combat zones offered little of each. And the home front needed to be constantly aware of the Armed Services' and the Allies' needs. This world war was "our war," to be fought without complaint as the homemaker with her new duties emerged as the kitchen soldier.[5]

The kitchen front represented a strong and abundant force on the home front. In 1941 the largest group of workers nationally was the thirty million housewives, and *Life* magazine praised the constant work of these women who labored "just for love" to make America's homes the best in the world. The writer waxed on, "They do most of the wash, make most of the beds, cook most of the meals, and nurse practically all of the babies of this continental nation." After a year of war, the numbers had changed very little: 27.2 million women remained full-time homemakers.[6]

The war effort from the kitchen stayed specifically "hers." In Ann Oakley's *Sociology of Housework*, the definition of *housewife* is one who is responsible for most of the household duties. Yet housework has often remained "invisible," with little emphasis placed upon it as actual work because its rewards, never monetary, have remained "invisible." The idea that the final responsibility for cooking, cleaning, and child care remained with women was seldom, if ever, questioned. The work, especially during war, was viewed as necessary, taxing, yet emotionally rewarding—serving one's family. Now, during war, housewives were also serving their country.[7]

"Mrs. America" became a needed image for war-effort advertisements, and this title represented a limited persona. She was always portrayed as a married, middle-class white woman, approximately thirty to fifty years old, with children who were young or grown but never babies. Though working-class and minority, younger and older women certainly contributed to the kitchen front, the only public recognition of this fact was an expressed anger at the present inability to find "a good maid." The public often viewed women who did not fit the narrow "Mrs. America" image simply as lost domestic help, not as homemakers and war workers with their own family concerns and patriotic motivations.[8]

And so during the war years, housewives became workers only sometimes deemed as important as war-plant workers. Helen Loudon of *Kitchen-Klatter,* an Iowa-based magazine for homemakers, examined the wartime housewife's role. "Have you noticed that sooner or later," Loudon analyzed, "in every crisis in National affairs, an appeal for help is made to the housewives of our nation? Why should we care if the assessor lists us as 'housewife—no occupation' when the very wisest men in our country are agreed that our work is important, indeed!" The housewife needed to do her war duty in many ways: to conserve effectively, to substitute efficiently, to ration cheerfully, to preserve proficiently. Mrs. America had orders to produce, create, and salvage, and she was to be the central point of all the home fronts.[9]

Rationing with Ingenuity

Leanna Driftmier, editor of *Kitchen-Klatter* during the war years, offered advice to many Iowa women in her editorial letters as well as in her daily radio broadcasts of the same title about homemaking. "There has never been a time," Driftmier noted in 1943, "when the homemaker has had the opportunity to serve her country as now. So much depends on the efforts of each one of us as individuals in our own homes." Later she commented, "I can't understand anyone doing anything that would hinder the progress of our fight for victory. I am sure all *Kitchen-Klatter* mothers are doing what they can on the homefront."[10]

Driftmier began airing her half-hour radio show in 1939, ten years after the magazine was started, and the *Kitchen-Klatter* show would become the longest-running homemaker program in the history of radio. Driftmier, mother of four sons serving in the service and three daughters working on the West Coast, shared "the concerns, frustrations, fears, and sorrows of parents all over the country." Besides family empathy, Driftmier also possessed the criteria for successful radio homemakers, according to radio historian Evelyn Birkby, which were "friendliness, neighborliness, and a willingness to try new things."[11]

The productive and resourceful work of housewives took on a new significance during World War II, one enhanced from the "making do" days of the Depression. Also, Americans continued to place a stronger emphasis on health and urged homemakers to learn the basics of nutrition, thus producing strong citizens needed for the war effort. Paul V. McNutt, director of the Health and Welfare Service in the Office of Defense, emphasized this point by saying that "to be truly strong, Americans must know and eat the right foods." Vice-President and former secretary of agriculture Henry A. Wallace, himself once an Iowa boy, echoed this sentiment: "Food is fundamental to the defense of the United States—on a foundation of good food we can build anything. Without it we can build nothing."[12]

This emphasis on nutrition had also played a part in the "Homemaker's Creed" during World War I, and officials in World War II repeated the philosophy in slogans such as "There's a war job in my kitchen—to keep my family fit with well-planned meals!" The National Nutrition Program's promise was to provide "What every housewife should know about preparing *WAR* FARE." Iowa's home economists and homemakers followed this national emphasis on nutrition; Wilma Phillips Stewart edited a daily food column for the *Des Moines Register,* and in her "1943 Food Picture" she admonished her readers, "Promise yourself that you will make a study of planning meals." Ruth Cessna McDonald led the Iowa Nutrition Council's promotion of wartime nutrition programs throughout the state in 1944, a campaign titled "Make Iowa Strong."[13]

Though the ideal remained perfectly balanced, wonderfully nutritious meals lovingly planned by housewives each and every day, the reality became trying to cook two or three times a day on a limited budget of everything—limited availability of sugar, meat, butter, and canned goods; limited time; limited patience; and always the unlimited backdrop of noisy children and stressful war news. Keeping all family members, much less those war workers, happy and healthy was no easy job. It required planning and, most of all, ingenuity. As Margot Murphy proclaimed in the cookbook *Wartime Meals,* "Pencils and paper are our primary weapons as we wage our kitchen battles." Journalist Studs Terkel compliments the efforts of family women in his oral history of the Second World War. He savors the memory of wartime meals: "Housewives during the war were far better cooks than they've ever been since. Can you believe it? We had so little to manage with we became inventive."[14]

Ingenuity in the kitchen certainly required a talent, but war conditions demanded that it be further developed through various educational sources. As Mary Ann Kidd pointed out in her column "Modern Home News," "destructive war does make some constructive contributions." She then described the local "Ingenuity Show," a display of new products for the home front despite war shortages. Kidd declared, "American ingenuity is finding the path to Victory."[15]

The *Burlington Hawk-Eye Gazette* initiated a number of innovative, educational, and promotional campaigns for the kitchen front when it published "Cookbooklet," the first in a series of twenty collections of inventive ideas for the wartime homemaker ranging from snacks to leftovers to eggs. In 1943, the *Hawk-Eye Gazette* published a cookbook priced at twenty-five cents titled *Wartime Cooking and Canning*, by Josephine Gibson, that had over three hundred recipes and hints that reportedly told "how the food front is as important as the battle front." Within a month, thousands of Iowa housewives had mailed their quarters to order this cookbook that promised "to help you in these unnatural rationed days."[16]

Every day seemed to bring more work for housewives as grocery shopping and food preservation took longer than ever. Historian Karen Anderson notes in *Wartime Women*, "Household responsibilities were not significantly lightened by either the family or the community during the war years." What added to the shopping and cooking time was the wartime rationing system. Although rationing seemed to go against the American ideas of limitless opportunity and resources, the federal government portrayed it as an essentially American and democratic opportunity. Those with and those without money would, in theory, be on an equal footing to compete for scarce consumer resources. Deprivation seemed an acknowledged condition of wartime, yet not being able to purchase was considered, for Americans, "a heavy blow to the psyche."[17]

Americans needed to view sacrifice as a war effort. Although they found it difficult, most U.S. citizens realized that their shortages never approached those in Great Britain or Russia. Britain's Minister of Food Lord Woolton announced a strict rationing system in 1940, and these restrictions continued well after the war's end—until 1954. Rationing in America, however, was always viewed as a short-term solution to a wartime problem. The following goods were rationed for the war effort: automobiles (February 1942), sugar (May 4, 1942), fuel oil (October 12, 1942), coffee (November 21, 1942), gasoline (December 1, 1942), processed/canned food (February 2, 1943), shoes (February 7, 1943), and meats and fats (March 29, 1943).[18]

The reasoning behind rationing involved two key concepts: since resources were rare, they should be shared equally; and to control inflation, rationing should be used rather than leaving distribution to the free-market system normally in place in America. Because most civilians accepted and agreed with these concepts, criticism was minimal and was directed at administration rather than the idea of rationing itself. Families would sacrifice comforts and conveniences in exchange for the protection of the American way of life. Winning the war required sacrificing at home as directed by the government; consumerism could no longer remain simply a private choice.

Every American home faced the rationing of needed and wanted goods, which was sometimes frustrating but always democratic. Since the shortages were largely related to the kitchen front, most of the rationing was considered "women's work." Historians Karen Anderson and Doris Weatherford each find that women managed a disproportionate share of the burden of coping with civilian deprivation, but they also deserved the credit for its success. The women who coped with rationing the best lived in small towns and on farms, the locations with resources such as "land and supplies—and foresight—to garden and preserve their own supply." Young families, especially those with small children, faced the most discrimination since they had few resources of time and land and were less able to grow their own food in gardens and prepare food from scratch. As Weatherford comments, there lingered "a sad irony in that the people who were most badly provided for by rationing were the wives and young children of soldiers asked to lay down their lives."[19]

Rationing equaled patriotism in the new "red-white-and-blue rules of eating," admonished Mrs. Gerrit Samson, wife of a farmer near Pella. "We might just as well get used to rationing first as last. All of us ought to co-operate and try to get along the best we can. After all, we're doing very little compared to what the soldier boys are doing." Patriotic citizens considered hoarding unpatriotic, undemocratic, and reactionary. Citizens should trust their government's planning, they believed.

Mrs. John Dwight, with eight in her family on a farm near Des Moines, reflected on this point: "Well, we won't enjoy it, but no one enjoys war. Food is scarce and the government is wise in enforcing rationing. It's absolutely essential. We have a farm out here, and so will have plenty of garden produce."[20]

Government advertisements presented the concept of rationing in pioneering terms: it was a way for citizens to prove they could do without, just like their ancestors had. This call for toughness proclaimed that rationing would be "good for us" and that as American citizens once again faced hardship and sacrifice, it could only develop character. And rationing could even be viewed as a way to enforce dietary self-control for middle-aged, overweight people—especially women. As statisticians for a life-insurance company claimed, "Wartime rationing of foods may prove a blessing in disguise to American women." Some people considered overweight women to be a national health problem. So not only were women to be the most responsible citizens for the smooth flow of goods to individual homes, but sadly, they were also the ones most likely to be targeted to internalize guilt about consuming resources, to feel the least deserving of any extra food.[21]

In his book *Let the Good Times Roll,* Paul Casdorph explains that rationing in 1943, when "approximately thirty-five million housewives trudged to thousands of schoolhouses in late February to get the books," was extremely difficult. The distribution of ration books, as described by historian Mary Martha Thomas, became "the biggest job ever undertaken by our government—the issuance of a food ration book for every citizen." Ration books, with their limitations, registrations, and regulations, did not seem quite American even during war, and civilians, although they consciously understood the need and never wanted to be considered soft, did resent the limitations, especially when they finally had money to spend after the long economic depression. As journalist Cabell Phillips observes in his work *The 1940s,* rationing became the most common social irritant of the home front since it equaled regimentation. Nevertheless, ration books ultimately became a part of everyday war life.[22]

Sugar rationing started with the first war ration book, but the second book became more comprehensive and more complicated as the government placed over two hundred foods on the ration list. Most canned, frozen, and dried fruits and vegetables, along with canned soups, required ration-book stamps and points. The system was so complex that a number of women volunteered to act as "explainers" in local grocery stores; they were trained in this operation and wore armbands for easy recognition. Ration books were now not only complicated but valuable. The town of Red Oak stored its ration books in a vault upon their arrival from the federal government. Housewives received warnings from Washington, "Don't lose your ration books! They're worth more than money for they can buy things money can't—food, gas, shoes, and eventually clothes."[23]

The government presented rationing in military terms: food was needed by the American and the Allied countries' fighting forces. The first ration book's stamps were numbered plainly, but the second book had four types of greenish adhesive stamps displaying drawings of artillery guns, tanks, warships, and bombers. Ration Book No. 3 also had these military symbols, but Ration Book No. 4 utilized such peace symbols as a cornucopia, ripened wheat, and the torch of liberty. The backs of the ration books admonished consumers never to buy without ration stamps and never to pay more than legal price. On Books No. 2 and 3 consumers read warnings not to lose the valuable books or even to throw them away and reminded them, "If you don't need it, DON'T BUY IT!"[24]

Sugar was valuable as both food and ammunition. The stamps in the sugar ration book told Americans they needed to consume less sugar because military needs were high, because some ships were now hauling supplies to battlefronts instead of to American consumers, because manpower was scarce at sugar refineries, and because sugar-beet production was 500,000 tons short. *Collier's* magazine explained to its readers in the article "Your Sugar Bowl Blows Up" that sugar was needed to produce a smokeless powder to shoot at enemies. In a propaganda ad, the military reminded consumers of its need for sugar and explained how much of it was being used: "If ever you catch yourself chafing over the empty sugar bowl, remember this: Every time a 16-inch gun is fired, it eats up the distilled product of a fifth of an acre of sugar cane."[25]

Dietitians offered ideas for sugar substitutes such as honey for baked goods or corn syrup for canned fruits, and since Iowa ranked second nationally in honey production and first in corn production, both sources of liquid sugar were locally available. Home economists suggested sugarless recipes (but with honey or syrup) for homemade ice cream, pies, puddings, and cakes. Even the famous Toll House Cookie recipe could be made without processed sugar. And the "furlough bride" could keep her reception patriotically simple in such ways as displaying a small wedding cake, if any, and serving a sparkling tea punch with no sugar.[26]

Despite the necessity of the many switches and tricks, America remained a land of many sweet tooths, especially prizing its pies, as is clear in the popular 1942 song "Ma, I Miss Your Apple Pie." In the 1940s, baking a good pie could still be a woman's claim to fame, as in the case of Mrs. C. H. Taylor of Earlham, who earned a front-page photograph in both county newspapers for earning the title "Queen of the Madison County Pie Baking Contest."[27]

Even after the war ended and Germany surrendered, the United States still experienced a shortage of sugar. "Why?" asked Martha Duncan, editor of *On the Home Front,* a radio show from WOI in Ames, in 1945. "Because we in this country," she explained, "don't fill our own National Sugar Bowl. Only a fourth is grown in the U.S. The sugar situation can be summed up in two words, short and sweet, we'll have less of it, right through this year."[28]

Meat, especially good cuts of beef, was also rationed throughout the war. Though farmers produced record amounts of beef and pork, the military also consumed record amounts. Consumers took most rationing in stride, but some people, especially older men, felt a certain desperation for meat. The meatless and meat-stretching dishes never truly satisfied people accustomed to "meat and potatoes" meals. With improved economic conditions, people wanted to increase their meat consumption, and being able to have good cuts of meat, especially beef, had traditionally implied wealth and status. Because of the large number of farms, many Iowans did have better access to beef and pork than most Americans, but most nonfarm citizens had to make do without much meat.[29]

"Mrs. America's" job was not only to serve nourishing food but also to conserve food during the war. She could accomplish this in one of three ways: make meat cuts go further, use "stretched" or "variety" meats, or serve meatless dishes. Nutritionists recommended that one way to make a cut of meat go further was to stretch it into three meals. A four-pound pot roast could be a patriotic dish if served first as a meal in itself, then in a meat-and-vegetable pie, and then in a creamed-meat dish. Using meat again in this way could also help make a "Wash Day Oven Meal," saving fuel, time, and effort.[30]

Stretched meats such as canned Spam, Treet, or Prem presented another meat-conservation option. Spam, the most popular nationally, is still associated with World War II through numerous jokes, yet very few ads for the product appeared in Iowa newspapers during the war. Another conserving effort utilized "variety meats" such as livers, kidneys, hearts, tongue, tripe, sweetbreads, and even brains. Purchasing variety meats saved on ration point totals, with pork variety meats having the lowest values, from three to six points, while the highest point values, ten to twelve, were assigned to quality beef cuts such as T-bones, sirloin, and round steaks. Mid-range meats such as bacon and roasts registered at seven to eight points. The *Iowa Farm Bureau Spokesman* reminded "Mrs. America" to again use her "ingenuity" in such dishes as fricassee heart or liver patties. The spokesman also suggested lamb pie, ox joints, spiced tongue, and veal waffle shortcake, all possibilities for the "Share the Meat" campaign.[31]

The most radical idea was to cook without meat altogether, or to practice vegetarianism (though seldom called exactly that), never a popular view in Iowa, with its large production of both pork and beef. One author, Barbara Rae, somewhat disguised her views under the title *Cooking without Meat* (1943). Rae believed that Americans required reeducation to shift their dietary emphasis to vegetables, beans, and eggs instead of meat as the central focus. Her progressive views revealed themselves, however, in her preface: "And when the world has finally rejected violence for the kindly state of cooperation and peace, you may wish to take some of these recipes with you into a new era of plenty which lies ahead, somewhere."[32]

Butter was never officially rationed but was often unavailable, and the precious butter supply needed to be stretched as far as possible. Even in June 1945, butter pats were still almost nonexistent at Des Moines restaurants, and substitutions such as apple butter, cottage cheese, marmalade, and jelly somehow sufficed. Nutritionists regarded this fat deficiency as not "medically serious," but many dieticians seriously considered fat a wartime necessity for the satisfying feeling of being full. *American Cookery* stated its belief in the importance of butter in the diet:

"Edible fats cushion the nerves. People who lack butter, or lard, or margarine, or oil, may be healthy but will be nasty."[33]

The decades-old oleo wars continued in Iowa when the pamphlet "Putting Dairying on a War Footing," by O. H. Brownlee, came out in 1944 as part of the *Wartime Farm and Food Policy* series published by the Iowa State College Press. Brownlee's pamphlet argued that margarine could be as palatable and nutritious as butter. Brownlee also pointed out that margarine was perhaps more sensible to produce in wartime simply because it required less manpower. He was essentially advocating current national wartime policy, but the Iowa Farm Bureau protested his views as "disloyal in a cow college." As a result, Iowa State College's president, Charles Friley, demanded that the author revise the pamphlet. *Time* magazine interpreted the event as college officials perhaps having been "cowed" by Iowa dairy farmers. In northern Iowa, the *Kossuth County Advance* called it simply an overreaction to "Iowa dairy hotheads," especially when a recent Iowa Poll found that 70 percent consistently preferred the taste of butter to margarine. No war pamphlet, however strongly it was worded, would change that opinion of taste.[34]

Some citizens resorted to "butterlegging" or "meatlegging," but most did try to make the best of rationing. Thirty years after the war, Elizabeth Clarkson Swart, a writer for the *Des Moines Tribune* during the war years, remembered the advantages Iowa's farm economy had had for her dinner table. Iowans had lived in "a land of plenty" during the war compared to people in more industrialized states, and, as Swart noted, "many visitors from Detroit or Denver went home with ham and butter in their luggage—and almost empty ration books."[35]

Coffee, however, had a limited availability all across the country, and its rationing began with the first Sugar War Ration Book, which was distributed in 1942. Although the coffee shortage did not affect quite as many people as did the sugar or meat shortages, those who were coffee drinkers dearly loved their beverage. Afternoon coffee, as described by the *Des Moines Register,* remained "an old Swedish custom in Iowa—coffee at 3:30." Everyone in the towns of Stratford, Stanhope, and Stanton stopped for coffee break, sometimes given as an excuse in 1942 to avoid "war nerves."[36]

During rationing, coffee lovers received advice to make the most of what they had—to simply drink less—and not to try blends with fillers such as cereal grains, chickpeas, or nuts. *Business Week* advised "holding the second cup," but did suggest such coffee fillers as chicory and roasted acorns for historical reasons as both had been utilized in the American Revolution and the Civil War. The second cup of coffee could be considered a forsaken luxury, although the Hotel Burlington offered an additional free cup of coffee with the purchase of a twenty-five dollar war bond. Hills Brothers' developed a new coffee slogan: "'Waste' is a fighting word today." Butternut and Folgers sold their coffee in containers that could be reused as canning jars, termed "double duty in the housewife's arsenal."[37]

After the Office of Price Administration and Civilian Supply announced a larger coffee ration at the end of June 1943, from one pound every six weeks to two pounds, homemakers still considered leftover coffee "precious." The federal government lifted coffee rationing after seven months, when shipbuilding and antisubmarine efforts proved more successful.[38]

Rationing required continual rethinking and retraining. It was very complicated: forty-eight points were allotted per month per person (including children), and individual point values were assigned to each food item. Very few packaged foods remained unrationed except olives, mincemeat, and popcorn. Ration points certainly turned housewives into mathematicians, but people also considered the effects on society as a whole. Some Americans believed that rationing might provide a "leveling" of American diets since upper-income families could no longer consume as much expensive meat. *Kitchen-Klatter* reminded Iowa readers that rationing was always better than directly facing more-drastic wartime conditions, as the magazine's editor, Leanna Driftmier, always remembered to count her blessings. "When you have time to fret over the things we can't have like coffee, sugar and tires," Driftmier pointed out, "remember the other things we don't have like bombings, invasions, starvations, etc."[39]

On January 1, 1946, the county war price and ration offices ceased to exist, and officials either burned or shipped ration records to their central state offices. Government officials congratulated volunteers and workers with "expressions of gratitude for jobs well done under trying circumstances." Still, much of the production and conservation efforts remained in the kitchen after the war despite the official end of rationing.

Civilian consumption of meat did increase in 1946 because the military's decreased, but a number of meatpacking strikes nationwide raised many concerns about the availability of choice cuts of beef. Iowa had 18,000 strikers in meatpacking companies in 1946. Local papers continued to offer recipes during the immediate postwar years as a way to economize with such dishes as leftover lamb or "savory vegetable pie."[40]

Over Seven Million Acres and Four Billion Jars Nationally

One arena of the kitchen front for which there was no lack of enthusiasm was the victory garden. Though people did complain about the physical labor, most Americans associated a great deal of pride with this type of gardening, whether it was their first gardening year or their seventy-fifth. The folk survival of this practical skill involved frugality and coping with scarcity, as well as hope for the future, especially during wartime. And Iowa's gardeners prepared themselves for the challenge: four thousand men and women belonged to the Federated Garden Clubs of Iowa, which in 1941 chose the motto "A Forward Looking Program for Victory Gardens."[41]

War gardens had been officially encouraged by the federal government during the Civil War and the Great War for the strength of both civilians and soldiers, but at the beginning of World War II, the U.S. Department of Agriculture reacted differently. Shortly after Pearl Harbor, Secretary of Agriculture Claude Wickard informed an audience of 175 delegates to a federal conference, "It's different now from 1917." The agricultural conference adopted Wickard's proposed slogan, "Vegetables for Vitality for Victory," and started the National Victory Garden Program, which also recognized the need for the conservation of lawns and flowers, the development of community and school gardens, and the need to grow "right things," but it decided that only certain gardeners should be encouraged.[42]

The USDA wanted to guard against "the misguided garden zeal of 1917–1918" by discouraging beginning gardeners because they might waste the seeds, fertilizer, chemicals, or tools needed during wartime. The department set a federal goal of 5,760,000 farm gardens nationally, an increase of 30 percent, to meet nutritional needs and ease transportation costs but not because food shortages were possible, which the USDA did not care to admit. City, suburban, and small-town gardeners, however, were not to be overly encouraged unless they were experienced.[43]

Gardeners can be difficult people to restrain, however, as American citizens control their individual plots of land. *Life* magazine still predicted that there would be 1.3 million new gardeners, for a total of 6 million nonprofessional gardeners who would work their soil for victory in 1942. A recommended model vegetable garden, twenty feet by forty feet in size, with rows of corn, tomatoes, squash, beans, peas, beets, carrots, Swiss chard, lettuce, and radishes, could provide enough food for a small family without too much work for a backyard gardener during these troubled times. Iowa State College specialists distributed a regular column to small-town newspapers titled "Better Iowa Victory Gardens" that offered technical and specific garden advice, with each of the informative paragraphs separated by a "—V—."[44]

Despite warnings from the USDA about "imprudent gardeners," Americans grew ten million victory gardens in urban areas, producing over eight million tons of food. In Des Moines alone residents planted about 2,000 gardens, with a majority of those put in by men and women who had not gardened before the start of this war. In Council Bluffs during the summer of 1942, over 2,100 children as part of the Junior Victory Gardeners harvested 11,500 bushels of food. After the nation's autumn harvest, Secretary Wickard reluctantly confessed that the amateurs had "surprised a lot of people." In truth, many Americans gardened out of necessity, and many who had done so during World War I now gardened for patriotic reasons. As historian Bruce C. Smith notes in his study of the Midwest during World War II, "What had been an economic necessity in the depression became military assistance in the war."[45]

Iowans were not unusual in their gardening passion. Many Americans recognized not only the physical health benefits but also the mental: gardening eased war anxiety. As historian David Tucker points out of the World War II era, "Victory gardening came from private rather than government desire." Still, the negativism continued from the USDA until early 1943, when officials admitted their need for effective amateur growers. By 1944, the USDA had effectively joined the campaign by distributing a five-cent victory garden pamphlet titled "Growing Vegetables in Town and City."[46]

In January 1943, a State Victory Garden Conference organized participants to discuss Iowa's garden potential. By the end of 1943, Iowans had planted more than 455,000 victory gardens, amounting to over 70,000 acres. In Polk County alone, people harvested over 40,000 gardens. The 1943 *Iowa Year Book of Agriculture* announced at year's end that Iowa had produced "more garden food than ever before in its history."[47]

A factor in the dramatic 1943 increase in gardening was people's desire to meet their own needs on items that were in short supply and items that were being rationed. As *Prairie Farmer* announced, "This year, it's 'grow your own, brother, if you want to eat.' Every bit of garden stuff you raise and can this year will be a direct blow for Victory." The three most popular vegetables to grow were tomatoes, lettuce, and carrots. Nationally, gardeners produced eight million tons of food valued at $500 million in 1943, and the reasons they gave for such extensive victory gardening were to contribute to the war effort, to conserve ration points, to save money, and to help the overall food situation. Gardeners received particular government encouragement to grow tomatoes since each regular can of tomatoes took thirteen points from an individual's forty-eight-point-per-month ration total. In the victory garden, therefore, harvesters considered tomatoes to be the most important "soldier."[48]

For those who did not own gardening space, group victory-garden plots also proved successful as well as motivational. At the Iowa Ordnance Plant, between 500 and 600 employees planted neatly arranged vegetable gardens around Gate 2, and they usually worked on weeding their lots during the evenings after their regular shifts. Iowa State College's faculty also joined the national efforts with their collective garden plot, divided into forty-foot by one-hundred-foot sections, with more then two hundred academics tending these "Friley Lots." One of the college magazines commented, "Only Hitler and his cohorts fail to see the benefits accruing from the Iowa State College faculty garden program."[49]

Gardening may have been isolated from government support initially, but it was not an activity separated by gender, age, or class. As the *Iowa Homemaker* advised its readers, women should not be alone in this project as it could involve the whole family. Men especially helped with plowing, spading, planting, and harvesting, while parents often assigned the weeding to their children. One young person who did it all was fifteen-year-old Margaret Yeggy, who planted a fifty-foot by one-hundred-foot garden and canned three hundred quarts of food from it to win the 1944 Iowa 4-H Victory Gardener award. She, along with seventeen other winners, claimed a $25 war bond.[50]

The federal government designated the first week of April 1944 as "Grow More in '44," and two million gardeners joined the effort, bringing the national total to twenty million victory gardeners. The Iowa Garden Clubs' goal for 1944 was to increase Iowa gardens by 45,000, and their president, Mrs. Gordon Elliot, advised, "Plan and plant your garden wisely, waste nothing, preserve the surplus."[51]

In 1944, approximately 476,680 of the 701,000 families in Iowa planted victory gardens. According to an Iowa Poll, Iowans planted one garden for every five people in the state. Ninety percent of 1944 gardeners were already planning the following year's plots at an average size of 8,400 square feet, or .2 acres, creating a total state garden area of 90,987 acres in 1945. Victory gardens in the nation had collectively amounted to seven million acres, an area the size of Rhode Island, in 1944. Although Illinois ranked first in overall victory gardening efforts, Iowa went "all out" for its gardening activities during the war years. Governor Robert Blue considered himself a gardener and commended the state's "splendid work": "Gardening in Iowa offers great opportunity."[52]

Although growing victory gardens was often a family effort, the canning of the produce remained specifically a woman's job. Occasionally, a man might be interested in the process, but only from a scientific, chemist's point-of-view or if absolutely "pressed into helping." The president of the Iowa Parent-Teacher Association suggested one summer that Iowa mothers could, again, use their "ingenuity" to create productive recreational activities for their children such as victory gardening and canning. She promised it would not be "drudgery."[53]

Hermetic sealing, the process of preserving food in glass jars, had been invented by a Frenchman in 1809 for the Napoleonic Wars. After 1900, machines made glass jars more affordable and available for home canning use, and the high cost of sugar in the 1800s that had prohibited much fruit preserving had also dropped by the 1900s, so home canning increased. During World War I, citizens had regarded canning as a patriotic activity, and the Committee on Public Information had encouraged this feeling with slogans such as "Can the Kaiser in the Kitchen." The patriotism only increased during World War II, as housewives heard their order "to fill the shelves with jars of victory." They were told that a patriot should be in every kitchen. The choice was quite simple: "fruit cellars vs. bomb cellars."[54]

The work of preserving extended the garden's harvest to year-round consumption. Canning was often hot, tiring, messy, and detailed work, and carefully planned instructions had to be followed to avoid spoilage or even food poisoning. The canning calendar intensified from July 4th through Labor Day, with muggy August canning's busiest month, but the winter months were considered the "pay-off," when people could eat all that canned garden produce.

Housewives became very productive in the summer, when they made a sincere effort to fill their shelves. Some instructional booklets "streamlined" wartime canning, but there was really no way to get around the hot, sticky work. The canning process required strict cleanliness to prevent any food spoilage, a waste of both time and materials. Demetria Taylor in *The Complete Book of Home Canning* instructed that the best rule was "not to undertake too much in any one day." She added, "Many jars hastily prepared by a tired, nerve-wracked homemaker are not apt to prove a good investment. Carelessness, haste, and overwrought nerves were enemies of the home canner." The "stars" of canning—those women who had canned perhaps over five hundred to a thousand quarts in a summer's time—sometimes stopped long enough to pose for newspaper and magazine articles. In the photos these women stand peacefully and proudly next to their neatly lined shelves.[55]

The resources needed for canning—glass jars, rubber lids, pressure cookers, canning baths, spices, and sugar—were limited during the war years. Rationing held sugar down to fifteen pounds per person by 1943 but increased the limit to twenty-five pounds in 1944, with application forms required for special stamps, which would allow extra sugar for applicants. Wartime rubber rings were produced from reclaimed rubber but were not to be reused.[56] *Good Housekeeping*, among other publications, recommended the sharing of canning equipment, especially pressure cookers, which were in short supply, or the formation of community canning centers. Iowa City established the first community canning center in the state, and on its first day, five homemakers there canned more than forty-eight jars of peas, beans, and beets. Mrs. George Glocker, chairman of the Iowa City food-preservation committee, developed the center, which later directed consultants, or "master canners."[57]

Iowa State Cooperative Extension initiated canning schools through its home extension agents, and they sometimes added films and skits for entertainment at these educational canning meetings. A canning clinic in Spring Creek Township showed the film *Canning Your Victory Crop* (in Technicolor). At the canning demonstration in Charles City, along with that film, leaders performed a skit titled "Mrs. America Preserves Her Future." One Iowa County food preservation meeting presented the film *You Can, Too.*[58]

Home canning definitely provided a significant part of the home front's food supply, which freed up industrially processed food to be sent overseas to U.S. servicepeople and the Allies' troops. Nationally, the USDA estimated that American housewives had prepared 4.4 billion quart jars of home-canned food in 1943. Though canning remained a rather unglamorous task, nearly 25 million housewives had processed an average of 165 jars of food each in their own or community kitchens.[59]

In 1944, the national numbers dropped to about 3.5 billion quarts of home-canned fruits and vegetables, although the government was counting on civilians for even more home-canned food for home consumption because army requirements had increased. In Iowa, 62 percent of the families had excess garden produce to can, and the average number of quarts preserved per family was 120. Collectively, Iowa women canned more than 80 million quarts of fruits and vegetables, with a market value of $23 million. Nationally, home canners had processed half of all vegetables and two-thirds of all preserved fruit consumed by civilians. In 1945, American homemakers again canned 3.5 billion quart jars of fruit and vegetables, preserving 8 million tons of food. As Jewell Graham, an Iowa State College Extension nutritionist, believed, home canning was "the nation's most important of wartime programs on the home front in 1945."[60]

Canning had indeed been an important home-front process across the nation. Robert Heide, in an essay about his childhood titled "Hometown U.S.A.," recalls that his mother regarded her "Victory canning" as serious work. *House and Garden's Wartime Manual for the Home* maintained that "home canning not only helps feed your own family but it helps relieve the shortage for other people. It's a very real form of war work." Another publication, *Home Canning for Victory*, encouraged homemakers to march on: "Imagination as to what you are doing and its importance will give you endurance. Multiply your little pack by millions and remember you are helping to feed our fighting men and the devastated regions of the whole wide world—children who will die or grow up only half alive without 'you all.' Let's go!"[61]

Patriotism only added to the already huge sense of pride that gardeners felt at the end of each season. Driftmier described the harvest season's finish in *Kitchen-Klatter:* "The 'Last of the Garden' relish has been made and jars are labeled and tucked away on the cellar shelves. I can't see how anyone can dislike the job of canning. Every time I screw a band on a fruit jar I have that satisfied feeling—money saved, points saved—food for my family when they need it." That feeling often continued years after the war, across the nation. Some American homemakers remembered their accomplishments with pride many years later. As one wartime homemaker, Emily Harper from Florida, reflected, "To see the beautiful canned good that's on the shelf, and say, 'Well, I grew it, and I preserved it, and now we're eating it.' It's great."[62]

The USDA, despite its beginning-of-the-war jitters over victory gardens, tried to keep this amateur gardening spirit alive after the war because of overseas food shortages. In its 1946 National Garden Conference, the USDA set a national goal of 20 million gardens (1.6 million over 1945's total) to meet the world food crisis.[63]

Many Iowa gardeners planned to continue growing food, according to General Chairman William Kidder of the Des Moines Gardening Program, but much of the garden space in vacant lots started quickly disappearing for new home construction. Members of the Federated Garden Clubs of Iowa believed victory gardeners could be enlisted to continue with peacetime efforts. Howard Mill, vice president of the Iowa Farm Bureau, and Herb Plambeck, farm editor of WHO Radio, tried to persuade Iowans to continue gardening because of the starvation conditions they had each witnessed in Europe and Asia. Still, the wartime urgency faded quickly, along with the catchy wartime slogans, and the new garden motto seemed as dull as an old garden hoe: "There's a Need for Food—Have a Garden."[64]

Although the need for home-canned produce continued after the war, the urgency about it began to diminish, even as *Wallaces' Farmer* declared canning "the patriotic thing to do." Martha Duncan carried on with her radio show *On the Home Front* (using the same title) into the next decade. She reminded her listeners in September 1945 that "winning the war didn't end the task we have before us." She continued with her urgent food-saving plea: "A hungry people, whole nations of hungry people won't be friendly people—especially when they know we throw away the food here that might save their lives and the lives of their children." Duncan advised her radio fans to can everything available from their gardens despite the fact that tinned vegetables could again be easily purchased without having to use ration points. Grocery stores also tried to encourage a continued canning effort, but without the wartime urgency of rationing's limited supplies and point system, the slogans only sounded stale: "Can more . . . Store more."[65]

W-I-V-E-S and WAHs

The kitchen front, like the other home fronts, utilized military imagery to create and strengthen the connection between the home front and the battlefronts. Alice Winn-Smith, in her preface to *Thrifty Cooking for Wartime,* likened the American housewife to "the general on the field of battle," and argued that "American housewives of today are united in one great army, for one noble purpose—VICTORY. Just as necessary as shouldering a rifle, is the shouldering of our responsibilities in the home." Sometimes homemakers became "kitchen commandos" simply by standing at their sinks—or, rather, their "battle stations." Some advertisements for products such as Sunkist juice or Easy Washers suggested giving medals for all this conscientious kitchen-front work, since American women fed eighteen times as many people on the production front as were fed by the Army on the fighting front.[66]

The women who actually served in the military became known by official acronyms such as WAACs, WAVES, or SPARS. "WAAC" (later WAC) stood for Women's Auxiliary Army Corps; "WAVES" were Women Accepted for Volunteer Emergency Service of the navy; and "SPARs" were Coast Guard members, their acronym coming from the Coast Guard motto, "*Semper Paratus*—Always Ready." Iowans were exposed to these servicewomen more than most states' residents because the WAAC National Training Center was Fort Des Moines and a WAVES training center was located at the Iowa State Teachers' College in Cedar Falls. For the "Victory Homemakers," a number of catchy titles eventually surfaced, but no amount of seriousness attached itself to the role. Still, war work called for acronyms.[67]

The acronyms abounded in advertisements. Alka Seltzer, in a magazine campaign seemingly designed to give a person indigestion, portrayed a mother marching with her son, complete with a broom for a rifle and a cooking pot for a helmet, singing, "Not a WAAC, Not a WAVE,—just a WAH*—Yes, I'M JUST A WAH (* *W*oman *A*t *H*ome)." In an ad for its percale sheets, Cannon pictured a woman in a ruffled apron holding an iron and saying, "Me—I'm one of the W-I-V-E-S!" Its copy then explained, "You know . . . the gals who stay at home and keep things going. Doesn't sound as exciting as the WAACs or the WAVES—but it's every bit as important."[68]

World War II propaganda did love a trite line, and women's magazines carried on in this vein. Youngstown Kitchens started advertising the WONS—Women's Own Nutrition Service—as those who "supplied the health-giving food that keeps the nation strong." Its copy continued, "Housewives are the WONS who will still be wearing their uniform, the kitchen-apron, in peace as well as wartime." *Ladies' Home Journal* called its readers WINS—Women in National Service—and stated that housewives were "the largest army in the nation fighting on the home front."[69]

If this kitchen army carried acronyms, it also needed uniforms. The *Journal* designed for its WINS dirndl-style dresses and functional overalls, keeping housework's demands in mind while dismissing the fact that few women dared to wear pants in public in the 1940s. For publicity's sake, Verna Hickenlooper, Iowa's first lady and honorary state WINS chairman, modeled the housedress version of the uniform, a dress in Air Force–blue cotton gabardine. The WINS claimed twenty million housewives involved nationally, with only one requirement for membership: "Any housewife who is doing a good job in spite of emergency handicaps."[70]

The role of homemaking was never really seen as glamorous, and any efforts at uniforms were meant to add respect to the position. The Iowa State Extension Service developed a pattern for homemade kitchen-front uniforms, which it described as "attractive yet serviceable house dresses," and the new design took into account "all the extra walking, bending, and stretching that her duties on the home front require." Iowa homemakers could also select designs from an Extension leaflet titled

"House Dresses for the Job," and Elizabeth Peterson, Extension clothing specialist at Iowa State College, said on the Iowa radio show *News for Homemakers* that the standard of efficiency should apply to house dresses as it did to military uniforms.[71]

Despite the cute acronyms and not-so-cute uniforms, a sense of women's toughness and aggressiveness surfaced. Everyone believed an angry or threatened mother could be a strong opponent, and during war the fighting trait was admirable in these new warriors. As historians Margaret Higonnet, Jane Jensen, Sonya Michel, and Margaret Collins Weitz suggest in *Behind the Lines*, there were paradoxes to war because violence was to somehow contain violence, and the role of women could also be as battling soldiers.[72]

By far the most popular example in culture of the woman as defender of the traditional domain became the "housewife-mother heroine" Mrs. Miniver, the British character in the popular 1940 novel and then 1942 Hollywood movie by that name. Women during the early 1940s could be compassionate and still not be considered passive or helpless, as M. Joyce Baker finds in her analysis in her work *Images of Women in Film*. In fact, the character Mrs. Miniver encounters a German soldier in her garden and captures the tired and frightened young man by offering him a cup of tea in her kitchen. Also on this spectrum of the strong housewife loomed a completely different image, one of the stereotypical heavyset, middle-aged woman with rolling pin in hand who could take on almost anyone.[73]

Historical images of women, both from the American Revolution and from the westward pioneering era, blended these seemingly contradictory images of nurturance and militarism. World War II, as historian David Fromkin notes in his book *In the Time of the Americans*, seemed unusual because during it Americans, who had usually walked away from their past, enthusiastically looked back to an idealized history. During the American Revolution, politics had entered the private sector with home production and rationing in the forms of homespun cloth and tea boycotts; women in both time periods played an active role with added home labor and coping with shortages in the combined public and private spheres of war.[74]

Propagandists frequently used the pioneer analogy during the war, as historian Maureen Honey explains in *Creating Rosie the Riveter:* "The pioneer represented a capable, supportive, and stoic partner who could keep the home going single-handed until things returned to normal."

Eleanor Roosevelt also praised pioneer women as a modern-day example. "I doubt very much," she wrote, "whether any of the men could have accomplished what they did without the backing of their staunch and courageous women." The cosmetic company Avon developed an extensive magazine advertising campaign during the war years based on this historical analogy of wartime women to Revolutionary-period and pioneer women. Its Avon Medallion of Honor paid tribute to the fighting spirit of women throughout America's history.[75]

Although homemakers received praise for their domestic work as a necessary wartime contribution, it remained traditionally devalued due to its exclusively feminine and unpaid status. Housework, cooking, and child-raising still garnered far less value in society than other forms of work, especially paid employment. Every kitchen-front day seemed to bring more work for housewives, with more time being required for grocery shopping and food preservation. Emily Nervell Blair, an editor of *Good Housekeeping* and self-described feminist, also worked for the Women's Interests Division of the War Department and believed that women with full-time jobs should be relieved of household tasks—her "feminist code." She asked as she waved her hand toward officers at the Pentagon, "You don't expect any of these men to go home and do their laundry, do you?"[76] Yet, Blair had the money, education, and social status for an occupation in which she could claim her time as valuable—and hire two part-time maids. Most women could not.

Several historians, however, have recognized the value of domestic work for the wartime home-front effort. As historian D'Ann Campbell emphatically states, no one has written the history of housewives in World War II (a third of the American people) despite the fact that "the entire logic of full war-time mobilization depended heavily on the behavior of housewives." Mary Thomas argues in *Riveting and Rationing in Dixie* that housework was and is "essential to family life and the economy, but it has often been unnoticed, unrecorded, and unappreciated." Thomas explains, "The conditions of war made the usual tasks of homemaking—buying, cooking, nursing, washing, cleaning, and childrearing—more difficult."[77]

Though the kitchen felt the war more than any other room of the American household, traditional family roles and the division of duties did not sufficiently change to meet the old needs of the kitchen, let alone the new war demands. Men resisted most work within the home, seeing it solely as a woman's realm. Excuses were numerous: women were better at the work or women could better survive the boring, tedious nature of it. For example, an advertising series in *Business Week* for *McCall's* magazine subscriptions included copy written to business executives illustrating a scenario titled "This woman needs help!" The ad did not imply that the woman needed help in running the house, but that she needed help in recognizing her natural role as a homemaker. In each illustration, a dismayed man returned from his career to find a neglected house and an absent wife. The ad's recommendation was not to remove this burden of imposed work from women by sharing it within the family, but rather for industry or education to improve women's household performance and efficiency.[78]

Unlike *Business Week,* the United States Army proclaimed in its home-front handbooks that it was producing "husband material," men with new domestic skills. However, these were the very men absent from the home front, so their potential contributions to it would not be realized until after the war, like so many other improvements in the situation. In another format, newspaper cartoons repeatedly acknowledged and exaggerated masculine fears of being coerced or even forced into housework (complete with frilly apron), along with the more subtle idea that housework remained too trivial even to discuss. Housework wars appeared in the comics, but never the editorials.[79]

But if married women considered taking jobs in industry, society reminded them that their first job remained in the home. The War Manpower Commission found that the strongest barrier to recruiting women for industrial war jobs was the husbands' reluctance to give up their "cook and bottle-washer." Ironically—or predictably—no national propaganda ever developed that encouraged men to take over their fair share of housework and child care to enable the overall war effort. As historian Annette Chambers Noble points out, American society has never once excused married women from home duties. Noble notes the irony, "National and local propaganda throughout the war, even when luring women into the workplace, reminded women that their household and family responsibilities could not be neglected."[80]

Mixed messages about women's wartime contributions continued throughout the war years. *Good Housekeeping* offered such an example in an article titled "Join up . . . but Don't Let Your Family Down." The article reminded women of their double duties: "Nobody expects you to be on the sidelines these days, when so many defense jobs are begging to be done. So get in there and pitch! But don't forget that a big part of the job of winning the war is keeping the nation's morale and health at grade-A levels. Reorganize your 'family front' so that it will run smoothly despite time out for defense activities." The article completed the intended message that a married woman's first responsibility remained cooking for the family with a photo of a husband and two children waiting at a set table with no food as the children cried, "Goodness, Dinner is late!" And another common guilt-inducing refrain for wartime advertisements was "I'm hungry, where's Mom?"[81]

After the war ended, the prescriptive advice for married women centered on restoring the family, especially for the returning soldiers' sake. This country desperately wanted some sense of "normalcy," or rather status quo, after a decade of depression and half a decade of war, and this responsibility rested squarely on married women's shoulders. "Rosie the Riveter" or one of the W-I-V-E-S was never to be a "new woman," but a quasi-historical model of the Revolutionary or pioneer woman. After the crisis, she should return to her family's needs, carrying even more guilt for having made the temporary departure from tradition.

As historian Susan Hartmann comments about the immediate aftermath of the war, "Civilians could never compensate veterans for their sacrifice." The result for the demobilization period and the following postwar years would be a public stress on femininity and "secure" families in which women were never to compete, especially with returning veterans, for any employment opportunities.[82] The early 1940s had attempted to celebrate and honor women's labor within the home, and the concept of the kitchen front had infused these traditional domestic roles with a strong sense of patriotism, but only the sense of duty seemed strong enough to carry them into the next decade.

Salvaging and Saving for the Future

Gardening and canning produce certainly were contributions to the war effort. Conserving resources was another, and housewives repeated the making-do refrain from the Depression ("Make it over, wear it out. Make it do, or do without.") as wartime advertisements reminded them of the constant attention necessary for conservation efforts. *Kitchen-Klatter* especially prompted its midwestern housewives, with questions like "Have you asked yourself lately if you are doing all you can to help win this war?" In other words, "Be a Waste Warden."[83]

Government officials considered homemakers to be "the backbone" of the conservation effort, and the movement preached what the Depression had previously taught—the need for substitution and economy. This attack on waste had actually started before the war with a declared "War Against Waste Day" in November 1941, for which food columnist Wilma Phillips Stewart of the *Des Moines Register* offered thirty suggestions on how to conserve food. Most small-town newspapers also encouraged conservation, as did the *Winterset News* with its prescription: "The patriot in the kitchen, who wants to serve her country as well as her family, may do both by caring [*sic*] on her own campaign against waste."[84]

Conservation, though, was an endless task, with something new to save being added all the time, and scrap salvaging became yet another area of effort for women on the kitchen front. These salvage efforts started with aluminum. Aluminum cookware had first been introduced in the 1890s, but was costly compared to graniteware. Still, aluminum is a nice cooking medium as well as attractive, so it had become popular by the 1940s. Hardly "scraps," aluminum cookware and utensils were still included in the drives, and women considered contributions of them to the initial aluminum drives indeed a sacrifice. The Iowa Legionnaires conducted an aluminum drive sponsored by the Office of Civilian Defense as early as July 1941, with participation in all ninety-nine counties. The collectors stored the cookware in twelve Iowa cities, then it went on to smelters. *American Cookery* recognized the sacrifice: "Patriot that you are, you've given your metal utensils to the scrap drive."[85]

Tin, collected in the second drive, became the "neglected stepchild" of the metal family because its sources—tin cans—did not shine as attractively as aluminum or as dramatically as iron, but the government encouraged everyone to be "tin-can-minded." Leslie C. Merrell, deputy chief of the tin-can unit from the War Production Board, came to Des Moines to promote the new drive. Merrell called Iowa's housewives "the kitchen commandos on the home front" and explained the tin-can process as "Save 'Em—Wash 'Em—Clean 'Em—Squash 'Em."[86]

"Win with Tin" and "Tie a Can to the Axis," chimed the new slogans. Children also helped with this salvage drive, and in just one collection, the Burlington Boy Scouts collected nineteen tons of tin cans on a Saturday, making seven drippy trips in the rain. Unfortunately, some of the tin from this drive ended up going to brewers and bottlers who had bid the price up on scrap collected by the community to three times as much as the War Production Board's offer. As Drew Pearson editorialized in the *Des Moines Register,* "Local salvage committees, which have accomplished a tough, patriotic job, are beginning to get sore. And the tragedy is that the next time a call comes to collect and save a vital war material, it may not be so easy."[87]

Though a seemingly insignificant waste material, kitchen fats became a vital resource for war taken directly from America's kitchen front, as the collection of fats helped in the manufacture of nearly everything from soap to explosives. The United States normally imported 2.5 billion pounds of fats, half from areas under Japanese control during the war, plus the Allies required an additional 1.5 billion pounds. Officials estimated the total waste of fats in American kitchens at 2 billion pounds, predicting that one-fourth of that could be recovered and hoping to get the rest of the fat supply from soybeans, cottonseed, and peanuts. First Lady Eleanor Roosevelt stressed in her column "My Day" the urgency of household-fat collections: "I have heard many a woman ask how she could do her bit when her days were filled to overflowing with housework and the care of the family. Here is one important way, and don't let's forget it."[88] Although many housewives had already been saving fat to reuse in various ways, the collection of it became a concentrated war effort.

Over and over, government advertisements reminded housewives to save at least one tablespoon of fat per day for use in the war, since billions of pounds of fat contributed to thousands of essential products, from munitions to medicines. Just one spoonful of fat could make almost anything: bullets, sulfa salve, or even synthetic rubber for jeep tires. The advice column "The Home Front" one day explained that a pound of waste kitchen fats contained enough glycerin to make one and a third pounds of gunpowder and almost demanded participation: "That's why we want every Iowa housewife to save every spoonful of grease, strain it into a wide-mouthed can, keep it in the refrigerator, and sell it to her meat market when she has collected a pound or more."[89]

The steps in the process of saving kitchen fats were relatively easy, but tedious. Housewives should save bits of fat from cuts of meat and melt this down. They should scrape the roaster, fryer, and broiling pans; skim grease off the tops of soups, stews, and gravies; and even save water from boiled hot dogs, chilling and scooping off the fat left on top. Fat could also be saved from frying fish or onions. Other tricks included using smaller amounts of fat in milk gravy and saving grease from deep-fat frying. All of this salvaged fat should be stored in a tin can for the butcher and redeemed for two free red points (which were used to purchase meats, fats, and some dairy products) and several cents for every pound. The collected grease then went to rendering plants, where it was boiled for several hours, filtered, then mixed with lye to create its end products of soap and glycerine. Chester Bowles, administrator of the Office of Price Administration and Civilian Supply, pointed out, "If all the 31,000,000 American housewives living in private dwellings saved even one tablespoon of used fat every day, this would add up to 353 million pounds in a year."[90]

Information concerning fat salvaging ranged from the technical to the glitzy. Technical information included displays of the chemical formulas as fats were converted to glycerine. Glitzy messages pictured glamorous stars eagerly working at this unglamorous task. For example, in one advertisement actress Helen Hayes pours fat from her skillet while two sailors smile approvingly, all under the headline "Bullets for Berlin—TNT for Tokio." In another, orchestra leader Guy Lombardo smiles lovingly at "the sizzling sound of the used cooking fat his wife pours into the salvage container—Sweet music!" In yet another ad, singer Kate Smith is pictured saying, "The help of every woman is needed in saving used fats for hundreds of battle field and homefront essentials. If you save every bit of fat you possibly can, you're doing a job to be proud of."[91]

The need for fats grew even greater in the fighting against the Japanese during 1945, when the U.S. government needed almost 100 million more pounds than the previous year, but fat-salvage collections mysteriously dropped. Each housewife's collection may have seemed insignificant, but the federal government advertisements continually pointed out the cumulative contribution of millions of pounds by millions of homemakers enlisted in the campaign.[92] Just a tablespoon a day.

Government pleas for fat salvage carried on even after the war, but people were told then that the material would be used for soap rather than ammunition production. Butchers continued to give small amounts of money for this salvage, but no added ration points could be offered since rationing ended with the war. Even the secretary of agriculture joined in with his request, which added respectability to fat salvaging, but some ads took on a negative tone, calling noncontributing women derogatory names, such as *Suspicious Sarah, Worrying Winnie,* and *Flighty Flo.* The advertisements had lost not only their patriotic tone but also their catchy wartime slogans. Postwar calls for fats were quite plain: "Where's there fat, there's soap."[93]

Throughout the war, the various salvage campaigns continued and continued. The war years grew increasingly stressful for homemakers, who tried not only to cook, create, economize, and salvage, but also to somehow remain cheerful, motivated, and efficient. Propaganda reminded homemakers on the kitchen front that this was the front every other war worker depended on. Columnist Stewart advised her Iowa readers to resolve themselves to their duty: "Let us smile as we do prepare those three meals a day, and make cooking a pleasure and not something that has to be done." The Madison County home extension agent reminded homemakers that despite the added stress of constant duties, these contributions were essential for victory. She offered hope: "The feeling of accomplishment that she will have at the end of a long day and the knowledge that she's aiding in the war effort will make her work worthwhile."[94]

Mrs. Eli Espe of Radcliffe offered a kitchen solution for many women's wartime stress and depression as she approached the situation more directly and less professionally. She began her essay "Live Calmly" in *Kitchen-Klatter* by identifying with women: "There may be times when you feel in order to retain your sanity you must do one of two things—either smash dishes or scream!" Since most women could not afford the first and worried what the neighbors would think if they tried the second suggestion, the author advised that one could "always compromise by taking one's spite out on the tinware in the kitchen and the glorious hullabaloo that can be raised with that should be enough to relieve even the nerve tension of the Axis Powers these days!"[95]

With all of these wartime sacrifices came the promise of a material reward. This motivation for all the war work was the dream of a designed postwar kitchen financed through war-bond savings. Ellen Plante, in her study *The American Kitchen,* maintains that by the 1930s the kitchen had become "the darling" of the middle-class home, with considerable time, thought, and money invested in its form and function. By the 1940s, designs shaped kitchens into *L* or *U* shapes with standardized built-ins, transforming this area from a utilitarian work room into the "kitchens of today."[96]

Kitchens became in the postwar era more and more a measure of success, and three considerations for ideal kitchen designs and appliances led the list: economy of effort, quality, and convenience. The Extension Service sponsored kitchen-planning meetings in Webster, Cedar, and Story counties, among others, and these programs continued into 1946. As *American Cookery* commented, "For many women their accelerated duties in war time have made awkward and inconvenient kitchens a bad headache."[97]

Economy of effort in the kitchen would be the major change for the postwar decades. The United States never did consider community kitchens an option during the war, as Great Britain did; the American focus remained on the privacy of family homes. The postwar emphasis for new kitchens focused on freedom as a reward for the years of extra hard work through the Depression and war years. Many homemakers had finally saved the money, especially through higher family wages and war bonds, to begin to purchase the modern kitchen cupboards and appliances. If extensive planning could make kitchens much more efficient, perhaps this hoped-for reallocation of work and energy in the home could finally be accomplished. What many American homemakers wanted out of the postwar prosperity was to be able to finally leave the kitchen for more of the day and focus on other areas of the home and family. As writer Gertrude Dieken promised homemakers during the war years, "Today's work hours are leisure hours tomorrow."[98]

The new model kitchen claimed to eliminate the drudgery in what was considered the most neglected room in the American home. Well-planned kitchens should be white and bright, perhaps with small desks and children's nooks included, and prefabricated steel or wooden cabinets helped to keep some of the remodeling costs down. High-quality new kitchen appliances represented the most dramatic and seductive of the postwar promises of freedom from kitchen work. The appliance that promised the most freedom was a new range. One advertising theme for stoves promised "Less Work for Housewives in American Kitchens." And as the American Gas Association joined in, "More fun, more freedom for every woman who cooks!" Home freezers were one of the new conveniences that promised to relieve some of the canning work or trips to the meat locker. Utility companies, of course, encouraged these purchases, and perhaps the catchiest postwar slogan was Iowa Power and Light's: "Bring on the Pie!"[99]

The other ideal in postwar kitchen design was remodeling for efficiency and step-saving. The *Red Oak Sun* noted of the postwar planning, "With an eye to postwar remodeling, the average Mrs. Homemaker casts the other eye upon her kitchen as the first room for improvements." Large country kitchens seemed no longer fashionable, and numerous published models for kitchens promised to streamline and lessen "stepping" (the amount of walking while preparing meals). These designs centered around a triangle of three work centers—cooking, dishwashing, and food storage.[100]

This planning for better organization, use of technology, and efficiency would shorten the time needed for cooking meals and washing dishes, thus somewhat removing women from the kitchen in the postwar years. Wartime homemakers, home economists, and kitchen-appliance advertisers had never expressed the idea that women would want to stay in the kitchen in the postwar years because homemakers had spent too many long hours in the kitchen during the war. Rather, the promise of modern postwar kitchen designs was to lessen the amount of time women spent on family meal preparation and cleanup. Homemakers planned on spending much of their time and energy in other rooms of the house during the hoped-for postwar prosperity.[101] The wartime aprons began coming off . . .

No longer in the postwar era was the kitchen and all its work based on production and preservation with a sharp concern about shortages. Instead, the new domestic emphasis was on freedom from drudgery—being able to place more energy on a family's psychological needs rather than sheer survival concerns. The promise of remodeled kitchens and new appliances seemed a possibility for many homemakers after the war.[102]

During the postwar period, the secretary of agriculture pleaded with Americans to consume less food: "Produced, preserved, and conserved at home, food will stretch farther around the world today." This was part of President Truman's formal urging of American citizens to eat less food as they remembered the millions of hungry people worldwide. Despite their experiences of shortages, rationing, and salvaging, American citizens had never really witnessed this war's starvation and possessed no deep empathy for the tragedy.[103] The kitchen front, with its emphasis on home canning, gardening, recycling, and conserving resources, had created an extremely successful environmental consciousness. Sadly, without the wartime incentives to produce, preserve, and conserve America's food resources, this "green" movement could not last without the "red" reasons of war.

Blueberry Pie and Home

The boys in the armed services also dreamed about kitchens, but their dream kitchens remained essentially the same, complete with the images and smells of their increasingly fond memories of food and comfort that home represented. This homeward gaze was to the American woman, whom John Blum describes as the person "who embodied the virtues of American civilization and the personal obligation to defend them." As revealed in their answers to GI surveys, soldiers and sailors did not dream of "Rosie the Riveter," but rather a woman like Mrs. Miniver, Hollywood's idealized middle-class housewife. What veterans wanted in a wife, according to the pollsters, was "a young, only slightly updated version of Mom" whose specialty was homemaking. As war correspondent Ernie Pyle would find in his countless discussions with battle-weary and lonely soldiers, one profound goal was to be home.[104]

Homemade items represented the symbol of home and security. Nestle's advertised the importance of home-baked food to all soldier and sailor sons with its slogan "Send C-Mail to the Wounded Over Here!" C-Mail was "Cheer Mail": cookies, cakes, chocolate. But ultimately it was blueberry pie, rather than apple, that became that material symbol of home during the Second World War. Pie, a favorite dessert which could not be sent through the mail or well prepared by the military mess hall, was first among many longed-for foods by home-starved young men. George Sullivan, of the famed Sullivan brothers, wrote to his mother at one point in the war about his food memories: "The chow is nothing like home though. Your five wandering boys would sure like to tie into one of your pot roasts." Don Thomas of Winterset wrote several postcards from a Philippine prison camp to his mother. Although the postcards had a fifty-word limit imposed by Japanese prison officials, Don still used some words to mention his longed-for food: "I think of you all and those pancakes," he wrote, and "Think of your pancakes, Mother."[105]

Eric Larrabee makes the point in *Commander in Chief: Franklin Delano Roosevelt, His Lieutenants, and Their War* that the shortage of food from the earliest days in Bataan demanded almost as much attention from the soldiers as the advancing Japanese.[106] One Iowa woman expressed desperation for her son to be safely home when she wrote anonymously to the *Farmer's Wife* section of *Farm Journal* about his captivity by the Japanese. "We have not had direct word from our son since March, 1942, when he was on Bataan," she wrote, "but I have his prison address and write to him at least once each week." She then explained her hopes and fears: "What do I write about? . . . Do I write about food? Hardly, when I know he probably doesn't get enough to eat. I'll certainly not remind him of the good things we still have back home. Neither do I dwell upon deaths, accidents or sickness. I write as often as I can, for I know that some of these letters will go the bottom of the sea. I only hope that precious Christmas box gets through!" She signed her letter simply—"Iowa Mother."

Reunions of soldiers and their families often centered on the emotional importance of the kitchen, sometimes the first room a returning soldier went to when he arrived home. Hospitality and love were found at last in a chaotic world finished with war, for now. In her book about her southwest Iowa family, Lucile Driftmier, daughter of the *Kitchen-Klatter* editor, described her brother's homecoming. "I heard later," she wistfully recalled, "that he ate mince pie and drank a gallon of milk when he finally reached home—he told Mother that those were the two things he'd thought about the most while he was in the Pacific."[107]

Finally, home.

Conclusion

War hurts everybody.

—John Wayne in *Back to Bataan* (1945)

On January 20, 1945, President Roosevelt delivered his fourth inaugural speech on a cold and overcast winter day in Washington, DC. Roosevelt's speech would be one of only three inaugural addresses ever in the United States during a war, and his was the shortest. To some Americans, it seemed almost a prayer. "We have learned lessons at a painful cost, and we shall profit by them," Roosevelt began. "We have learned that we cannot live alone, at peace; that our well-being is dependent on the well-being of other nations, far away. We have learned to be citizens of the world." A few hours later the president departed for the Yalta Conference. Roosevelt did not live to see an end to the terrible conflict, but in a draft for an April 11 speech, he called for an end to all wars. He wrote, "The work, my friends, is peace."[1]

Franklin Delano Roosevelt suffered a massive stroke on April 12, 1945. America's greatest soldier of the war was dead. A ten-year-old Iowa boy with the same birthday as President Roosevelt constructed a scrapbook of newspaper clippings about the president's death because Roosevelt had served as president for this young boy's entire life. The newspaper photos with their ragged edges were carefully arranged and pasted, telling the story of a grieving nation in the following days. One photo caption expressed some of Iowa's grief: "Sober faced women pause before

The Register and *Tribune* bulletin board Thursday afternoon to read the news of the president's death, which shocked a nation already burdened by war." One woman blankly stared at the bulletin, another dabbed her eyes with a handkerchief, and the third clutched her little boy's hand.[2]

President Roosevelt had initially defined American citizens' future involvement in World War II in a radio address two days after Pearl Harbor calling on all citizens to "cheerfully give up" for the war effort. "I am sure that the people in every part of the nation," he had continued, "are prepared in their individual living to win this war."[3]

Victory in Europe would be officially announced on May 8, 1945. Other than New York City's celebration, however, communities in the rest of the United States quietly observed V-E Day. Red Oak celebrated respectfully with a meeting at the Methodist Church after many residents listened to President Truman's radio address. The town paper tried to capture the day's events: "The fire whistle and siren sounded a prolonged blast, which also was the signal for the cessation of business activities. People gradually disappeared from the streets and soon the business district was almost completely deserted." Winterset residents reacted in a similar fashion: "The news of the war's end was received with restrained rejoicing. Whistles blew, and bells rang, but the sacrifices had been too great for any boisterous or unrestrained celebrating here."[4]

Victory in Europe represented a "half victory," as the *Des Moines Register* explained, because the fighting still continued on the Pacific front. For that reason, the reaction in Des Moines was extremely quiet on V-E Day as compared to Armistice Day, the end of World War I. A reporter rhythmically described the contrast, "People who had expected to sing said prayers. People who had expected to dance in taverns worked in victory gardens. People who had expected to tell the boss what to do on VE-day hurried back to a machine at the arms plant."[5]

Although the Second World War was not over yet, America's home front still had much to be thankful for, mostly that it did not resemble the ravaged European home front. When President Truman toured Berlin during the Potsdam Conference in July, he noted in his diary the long lines for essentials and the absolute devastation. Many homeless people were "scavenging to survive" among rubble and trash. "The destruction is a terrible thing," Truman later commented, "but they brought it on themselves. It just demonstrates what Man can do when he overreaches himself." On a more sympathetic note, he later reflected, "I fear that machines are ahead of morals by some centuries."[6]

Summer's End, 1945

Later that fateful summer, after the absolute devastation of the atomic bombs on August 6 and 9, President Truman announced on August 14 that the war was finally over. He declared a two-day holiday. Dorothy Thompson, a nationally syndicated editorialist, described "the first feeling of peace" as relief and joy but also emptiness. She portrayed the actions of her fellow residents as a bell began to toll: "Only some did not sing; they came, and joined in the celebration, too, but their faces looked drawn and there were tears in their eyes for the seven gold stars in the banner that flies over Main street. Everyone noticed, but pretended not to, happy that there will be no more gold stars, and sad, too."[7]

With the complete ending of the global war, most Americans celebrated Japan's defeat, unlike V-E Day's partial victory. Many Iowans simply wept or prayed, but others in Iowa celebrated V-J Day wildly. In Winterset, townspeople organized thanksgiving services after they heard the official radio announcement at 6 p.m. of Japan's surrender. Whistles blew and car horns blared and bells rang throughout the community, and some people even started a spontaneous bonfire in the square. In Red Oak, the sudden end of gas rationing meant a rush for stations to open with the sweet words "Fill 'er up," but most residents from this town stayed more solemn as nine hundred people there attended a memorial church service.[8]

Emotions had been pent up for far too long, so Sibley let off steam with an old-fashioned fireworks display; Spencer's cars ran bumper to bumper, honking; Waterloo went mad with air-raid sirens and factory whistles; Creston also had whistles and horns blaring, along with three men on a roof discharging shotguns in the air. Audubon ran out their fire truck; Fort Dodge created an impromptu snake dance; Marshalltown threw a victory dance in its coliseum; Algona burned Tojo in effigy; and Charles City tossed toilet paper (though it had been hard to buy during wartime) as confetti. Cedar Rapids went "haywire" with thousands of celebrating people swarming the loop with ticker tape flying; Newton held a parade with Company E, an Iowa division of the National Guard, marching, along with Maytag employees; Ottumwa fired its World War I cannon; Grinnell had impromptu parades and also started a huge bonfire; and Muscatine's business section filled with "happy, laughing, backslapping humanity" along with streaming confetti immediately after the surrender announcement.[9]

But not everyone in Iowa celebrated wildly. As a *Des Moines Register* writer pointed out, "The cacophony of auto horns, the town fire siren, church bells, occasional pistol and rifle shots, car backfires and screams and cheers, contrasted with the solemn march of the more devout to church." Des Moines residents organized a large ceremony for the next day at the Shrine Auditorium entitled "Community Service of Thanksgiving on the Occasion of the Termination of World War II." The program included well-known patriotic songs such as "My Country 'Tis of Thee" and "America the Beautiful."[10]

The Japanese were certainly not singing such songs, and most Americans did not even consider Japan's destruction. James Boyington, an Iowa soldier, was one exception, but he was in Japan to see what the bombs had wrought. He wrote home to his parents and described Yokohama looking as if it had been "scorched by a raging grass fire." He continued, "Wrecked by bombs dropped from B-29's the city stands as mute evidence of the power of modern aerial warfare, with only a few buildings left standing of a once modern Japanese city."[11] The retaliation for Pearl Harbor seemed over.

After the praying and the celebrating, many American citizens began to ask themselves about the immediate postwar period. How would peace change their lives? *Life* magazine described the hesitant and cautious nation with "a mood compounded partly of relaxation after the strenuous war years and partly of uncertain plans for the peace years ahead."[12]

"The Good War"?

World War II, as Archie Satterfield points out in the introduction to his history *The Home Front,* seemed almost like a popular short story: it had "a dramatic beginning, a middle fraught with conflict, and a happy ending." It never became a war, Satterfield concludes, "fogged by gray areas of morality."[13]

Three patterns have emerged that explain the remembrance of World War II as "the good war": the constant and strong emotions associated with the war years, the sense of urgency and purpose associated with the democratic version of war, and the sheer distance and thus romanticism associated with most Americans' roles for the war effort. Journalist Studs Terkel, who purposefully gave his oral history the ironic title *"The Good War,"* later wrote that most people remained profoundly affected by World War II yet never understood it. "The obscenity of war itself had never really been visited upon us," Terkel explains. "World War Two has warped our view of how we look at things today. We see things in terms of that war, which in a sense was a good war. But the twisted memory of it encourages the men of my generation to be willing, almost eager, to use military force anywhere in the world."[14] Perhaps Geoffrey Perret's title *Days of Sadness, Years of Triumph* most accurately depicts the continuing nostalgia of the war years, as the personal days of grief have faded into distant memories while what remains are the political and military triumphs.

Historians have disagreed on the following question: did the nostalgic view of World War II help Americans heal their war wounds, or did it fatally predispose this country to future wars? The personal and political fears remained a continual presence throughout the war years: the deep fear of social change after a decade-long depression, the racial and cultural fears of Eastern peoples and European governments, the fears concerning the condition and survival of American democracy, and the constant fear of death—whether abstract or extremely personal.[15]

Fears had heightened the intensity of the war years for everybody at home—children, youth, adults, the elderly. For Iowans, the war seemed all around and yet remained extremely distant since war conditions never became immediate, only imagined. This too carried an emotional toll. Afterward, in the confusing immediate postwar period and new atomic age, many public officials and private citizens did not want to admit those fears and vulnerabilities. We had won the war, and the war emotions immediately turned to nostalgia. Silence too became a way to heal. The war seemed just; the home-front effort, united and prosperous.[16] But World War II remained the most devastating total war ever; it never could be a "good war."

Iowans as Americans were proud of their soldierly efforts on the farm, production, community, and kitchen fronts. The United States government had desperately needed this wartime participation, production, and conservation to win the war on its battlefronts, and these urgent military needs transformed the war into an all-out effort. Each citizen felt needed as a soldier; thus, this war became the people's war. Because of their participation, the war seemed good. It had to, because everyone had battled in it and sacrificed for it.

Combat veterans, of course, deeply remembered the actual battlefront war. Some of their lives were transformed completely, such as the lives of soldiers Luellen Hastie, twenty years old at war's end, who had a shattered right leg; Martin Hintz, twenty-nine, who lost both legs; Everett Hagerdorn, thirty, left paralyzed; Wally Martin, twenty-five, wounded in both legs and arms; Walter Dunlop, twenty-six, who lost both legs; and Maynard Hugen, thirty-two, who suffered a smashed ankle. All six veterans certainly remembered Pearl Harbor on its fifth anniversary in 1946. "Yes, I remember December 7, 1941," Hugen said. "We were eating Sunday dinner at home and listening to a radio program called the Sunday afternoon serenade." Their futures had changed at that moment.[17]

Soldiers and soldierly citizens in Iowa had both contributed to this war, and many Iowans had sacrificed their lives. A total of 7,213 Iowa servicemen died, twice the number killed in the First World War. A later estimate placed the number of deaths at 8,398 of the 286,000 Iowa men who had served. Melvin Laskowski, nineteen, of Sheffield, was the first Iowan killed on duty at Pearl Harbor. In the first four months of war, 98 Iowa men had died, and by the end of the war, approximately 3 soldiers had given their lives for every 1,000 Iowa citizens. Nine Iowa servicemen were ultimately awarded the Congressional Medal of Honor.[18]

Yet accidents on the home fronts had actually taken a larger number of lives than the battlefronts: from December 7, 1941, to October 31, 1945, the number of Iowans who lost their lives in accidents totaled 8,639. Farming accidents accounted for half of these deaths.[19] The Second World War took its death toll in far, far too many ways to ever be considered a "good war."

Bessie Caudle's War

On August 16, 1940, Bessie Caudle thought of her only child and his future as she wrote: "This is the Day all men from 21 to 35 had to Register in Draft. Clark's No. 45." Caudle, a middle-aged housewife from Winterset, had begun writing her daily diary the day her son first left for college in 1932, and she never missed a day's entry for the next forty years.[20]

After draft registration, Caudle's son and his friend John decided to become part of the outward defense migration, the movement of people from the Midwest to the coasts for military jobs; she would write in early December that Clark was "Still talking Calif." On Wednesday, December 18, she sadly commented, "Well John and Clark left for Calif this morning. 5:45. I didn't do much all day." Her son later found work at the Douglas Aircraft Company in California.

After the many personal and national events that year related to the approaching storm of world war, on the last day of 1940 Caudle began her daily entry with the usual comment on the weather: "Another dark and gloomy day." She then continued, "Mrs. Sawyer called me at noon about John's letter in regard to Clark getting a job. . . . I listened at Midnight Program and we told her [Mildred, his girlfriend] about Clark's job." And so ended her 1940: listening to the radio, sadly thinking of her son's leaving for a California defense job, wondering about him in these days and months before war.

During a ride to see the new Ankeny ordnance plant construction on December 7, 1941, Caudle's life completely changed when news of Pearl Harbor came over the car radio. She seemed stunned, and later at home she listened until midnight to war news. The next day she heard that President Roosevelt had declared war on Japan. Caudle was now a soldier on Iowa's home front.

On December 10, Caudle received a letter from Clark and his new fiancée in California telling her they were safe despite the recent attack on Hawaii, and this lightened her mood. She bought a $5.90 sack of sugar that day, perhaps in preparation for war shortages. Although she spent the rest of the month doing the routine tasks of shopping, ironing, cooking, and cleaning, with occasional outings to movies starring Bob Hope or Jack Benny, her daily routine started to change as she participated more and more in the war effort.

Caudle bought a flashlight for her son and sent it to him for the blackouts in California. She started to keep meticulous records of each letter she received from him and his fiancée. She also began to worry and did not know how to stop. She gave the Red Cross a dollar donation; and she went to the site of a military plane accident that had occurred outside of Winterset on Christmas morning to see the wreckage. On New Year's Eve 1941 she recorded, "There has been the most happenings in this year for our Family. And hope everything works out for the best."

Although Caudle's participation was tied most directly to the kitchen front, she was not isolated from either the agricultural or production fronts. She regularly visited a neighboring farm for eggs, cream, butter, milk, peas, pork chops, sausage, and even a beef heart. She also gathered gooseberries and strawberries and even illegally accepted "a lot of points" (ration points) from the farm wife. Caudle also witnessed some farm dangers; she expressed concern in her diary for the farmer's son, who sustained injuries by a cow.

Caudle and her husband, Gean, visited the Ankeny ordnance plant site again on May 31, 1942. She wrote, "Well we took dinner and went to Camp Dodge and Ankeny defense plant." When the Caudles traveled to Kentucky to visit their son's training base after he was drafted, they also visited a nearby airplane plant. Clark Caudle never served overseas, but his mother still worried constantly about his safety, adding to her own stress during the war years.

Bessie Caudle also participated in some of the community-front activities and purchased at least ten war bonds. Although she did not state the amount of each bond she purchased, by war's end the Caudles had accumulated at least $800 in bonds. Gean Caudle "hauled our junk away" over two days in April 1943, but Caudle did not mention any other activities regarding scrap drives, perhaps because this couple had no young children at home to encourage these efforts. Rationing affected such items for Caudle as tires, gas, and silk hose. She continuously mentioned ration points and costs of products throughout her diary, along with the number of letters exchanged with her son working at his California defense job.

On the day President Roosevelt died, Caudle recorded her thoughts: "At 5 P.M. the News came over Radio Roosevelt's death in Warm Springs Georgia at 4:35. Such a shock." The following day she wrote, "I just listened at radio All day." She also listened on the third day to the news of his funeral, and her words, "very sad," seemed to capture the immediate sentiment of so many Americans.

As a small-town housewife, Caudle became most active in kitchen-front activities. Of the shortage items, meat rationing captured the most space in her diary, with notes about getting meat from the nearby farm and such comments as one about a friend visiting with "a nice Swiss steak," or one about "having a nice mess of liver for supper." Shopping sometimes seemed a noteworthy accomplishment: "I was lucky and got lb. of Bacon" or "70 cents for Beefsteak." She even mentioned, briefly, trading for meat points, an action not endorsed by the local ration board.

Bessie and Gean Caudle worked together on their victory garden each summer, but this was nothing new, since they had traditionally planted large gardens, with potatoes, onions, beets, tomatoes, corn, peas, and beans. Sometimes she found herself "very tired" after a day of gardening. Besides growing the victory vegetables, Caudle still managed to find the time each summer to admire and count each hibiscus flower.

Canning, however, became Caudle's most noted accomplishment. In 1942, she canned 47 pints and 79 quarts of such produce as apples, mulberries, beans, beets, pickles, tomatoes, and even grape juice. In 1943, she canned 70 quarts, adding such items as dill pickles and plums. In the last year of the war, she canned 49 pints and 103 quarts of food, adding such items to her canning list as peaches, corn, catsup, and green-tomato relish. Often the days in the kitchen were sweltering hot, but still she canned, even on days when her mother-in-law visited. A July 1945 entry was typical: "I done ironing and canned 4 qts., beet pickles. A terrible hot day."

During the hot days of August 1945, however, it is surprising that she did not note the bombing of either Hiroshima or Nagasaki. On August 9, however, she stated, "Heard about Japan considering surrendering." Each day after that, she expected the arrival of "good war news," which finally came on August 14: "And at six o'clock the news came Japan had surrendered. We went uptown and stopped at Sawyers till 9:30." The next day she especially noted that gas was no longer rationed.

Bessie Caudle, as one individual soldier citizen, performed her war duties on the home fronts of Iowa without hesitation or complaint. She worried about the effects of war on her son's life, but she never once questioned the country's participation in the Second World War.

Despite the changes Iowans had witnessed during the war, not everything had changed in what was, after all, slightly less than four years. Iowans still worked and celebrated together in their own particular style.

On December 7, 1945, Bessie Caudle entertained friends: "Well I had a waffle supper and had Carl Parkers in. We all had a nice visit."

And a year later, on December 7, 1946, members of the Evangelical United Brethren Church at Lundgren, Iowa, gathered for their traditional "God's Acre." Rural members contributed the produce from each farm's donated acre as a church donation to God. After shelling corn for most of the afternoon with fellow church members and other community people, the congregation and guests gathered for the Ladies' Aid Society dinner in the church basement. The menu consisted of chicken, potatoes, coleslaw, beans, and, of course, pie.[21]

Notes

~ Introduction

1. *Des Moines Register,* March 1, 1940, 1, 4.

2. Phil Stong, *Hawkeyes: A Biography of the State of Iowa,* vii, 4, 11.

3. Susan M. Hartmann, *The Home Front and Beyond: American Women in the 1940s,* 204.

4. T. A. Larson, *Wyoming's War Years, 1941–1945* (1954), xiii; Richard M. Ketchum, *The Borrowed Years, 1938–1941: America on the Way to War* (1993), 369; Henry A. Wallace, *The American Choice* (1943), 143.

5. *Des Moines Tribune,* November 11, 1940, 3; *Odebolt Chronicle,* April 1, 1940, 1; *Des Moines Tribune,* January 3, 1942, 1; *Des Moines Register,* December 6, 2006, 1.

6. *Des Moines Register,* August 28, 1939, 4.

7. Ibid., September 1, 1939, 1; September 2, 1939, 1; and September 3, 1939, Iowa News sec., 7.

8. *Des Moines Tribune,* September 1, 1939, sec. A, 1.

9. Roosevelt quoted in David M. Kennedy, *Freedom from Fear: The American People in Depression and War, 1929–1945* (1999), 427.

10. *Des Moines Register,* September 10, 1939, sec. 6, 1.

11. Ibid., October 8, 1939, General sec., 7; *Des Moines Tribune,* October 12, 1939, 10; and October 16, 1939, sec. A, 2.

12. *Des Moines Register,* August 10, 1940, 1; Richard Collier, *1940: The World in Flames* (1979), 63; *Winterset News,* August 8, 1940, 1.

13. Kennedy, *Freedom from Fear,* 386.

14. Manfred Jonas, *Isolationism in America, 1935–1941* (1966), vii, 99.

15. Robert A. Divine, *The Reluctant Belligerent: American Entry into*

World War II (1965), 87; *Des Moines Register,* June 11, 1940, 1, last page.

16. *Des Moines Register,* June 9, 1940, sec. 6, 1; *Des Moines Register,* June 23, 1940, Iowa News sec., 7.

17. *Des Moines Register,* June 14, 1940, 1, 6. In addition to Cosson, the men who signed the "plea" were J. N. (Ding) Darling, nationally syndicated cartoonist; Guy Logan, president of Standard Chemical Company; T. Henry Foster, president of John Morrell; B. F. Williams, president of Capital City Commercial College; and Horace Fosket, former president of the Des Moines Chamber of Commerce. For other interesting Iowa sidelights to the isolationism vs. war debate, see two articles in the *Annals of Iowa:* Justus Doenecke's "Verne Marshall's Leadership of the No Foreign War Committee, 1940" and Clayton Laurie's "Goebbels's Iowan: Frederick W. Kaltenback and Nazi Short-Wave Radio Broadcasts to America, 1939–1945."

18. Divine, *Reluctant Belligerent,* 99; Douglas Brinkley, ed., *The New York Times Living History: World War II, 1939–1942: The Axis Assault* (2003), 199; *Des Moines Register,* February 9, 1941, General sec., 11; and December 14, 1940, 6.

19. *Des Moines Register,* October 16, 1940, 1; and October 30, 1940, 8; *State of Iowa Official Register,* 1941–42, 365; Mike Wright, *What They Didn't Teach You about World War II* (1998), 2.

20. *Des Moines Tribune,* September 14, 1940, 1; and September 2, 1940, 1.

21. *Iowa Parent-Teacher,* November 1940, 2; "Here Is What Ten Des Moines Women Think of Conscription," *Des Moines Register,* August 11, 1940, 1.

22. 1940 Iowa Industrial and Defense Commission minutes, Folder 1940–1941, Commission Minutes and Related Materials, 1940–1954, State Historical Society of Iowa Archive, Des Moines.

23. *Des Moines Register,* October 11, 1940, 4; and October 27, 1940, Society sec., 11.

24. *Des Moines Tribune,* September 6, 1940, 8.

25. Ibid., October 9, 1939, 7.

26. Ibid., September 12, 1940, 14.

27. *Des Moines Register,* November 6, 1940, 1; November 27, 1940, 9; December 6, 1940, 8; and December 23, 1940, 3. The ten states that cast their electoral votes for Willkie were Vermont, Maine, North Da-

kota, South Dakota, Nebraska, Kansas, Colorado, Indiana, Michigan, and Iowa.

28. *Des Moines Tribune,* July 26, 1940, 5.

29. *Des Moines Register,* December 10, 1940, 1; and October 5, 1940, 1.

30. Samuel Grafton, *An American Diary* (1943), December 1940; "What Editors of Iowa Have to Say about Marshall and 'No War Committee,'" *Des Moines Register,* January 19, 1941, Commercial sec., 10.

31. *Des Moines Register,* December 14, 1940, General sec., 9; and January 10, 1941, 12.

32. Brinkley, *World War II,* 193; *Des Moines Register,* January 15, 1941, 1; and January 24, 1941, 11.

33. *Des Moines Register,* February 1, 1941, 3.

34. Presidential Executive Order no. 8757, "Establishing the Office of Civilian Defense in the Office for Emergency Management," May 20, 1941, *Code of Federal Regulations,* title 3 (1938–1943 Compilation); letter dated August 18, 1941, County Defense Councils, State Historical Society of Iowa Archive.

35. Letters dated September 12, 1941; September 22, 1941; and September 19, 1941, County Defense Councils, Folder 1, State Historical Society of Iowa Archive.

36. Ibid., letter dated August 19, 1941.

37. Ibid., Folder 2, letters dated August 18, 1941; September 11, 1941; September 13, 1941; and January 9, 1942.

38. Ibid., Folder 2, letter dated August 26, 1941.

39. *Des Moines Register,* September 20, 1940, Iowa News sec., 1; October 16, 1940, sec. A, 1; January 3, 1941, 7; January 10, 1941, 1; January 19, 1941, Commercial sec., 11; and April 6, 1941, 2.

40. Letter dated August 23, 1941, County Defense Councils, State Historical Society of Iowa Archive.

41. Ibid., letter dated September 11, 1941.

42. Ibid., letter dated August 28, 1941.

43. *Des Moines Register,* March 8, 1978; and November 9, 1944; *New York Times,* March 4, 1973; all in Sen. Guy M. Gillette, Biographical Clippings File, State Historical Society of Iowa Archive.

44. *Des Moines Tribune,* September 2, 1939, 1; *Des Moines Register,* September 17, 1945, in Sen. Clyde Herring, Biographical Clippings File, State Historical Society of Iowa Archive.

45. *Time,* October 13, 1941, 15; and October 6, 1941, cover.

46. *Des Moines Register,* December 1, 1941, 3.

47. *Des Moines Tribune,* December 5, 1941, 8; *Des Moines Register,* December 2, 1941, 1.

48. *Des Moines Register,* December 6, 1941, 4; David L. Roll and Keith D. McFarland, *Louis Johnson and the Arming of America: The Roosevelt and Truman Years* (2005), 48.

49. *Des Moines Register,* December 8, 1941, 1, 7. In 1917, Montana Representative Jeanette Rankin's vote was one of fifty-six "no" votes cast in the House and the Senate on the declaration of war against Germany.

50. George William McDaniel, "World War II Comes to Davenport," 92.

51. Ibid., 94; Ross Gregory, *America in 1941: A Nation at the Crossroads* (1989), 279.

52. "*The Winterset Madisonian,* 100th Anniversary Edition, 1856–1956," 1, in World War II–Korea file, Madison County Historical Society, Winterset, Iowa; *Red Oak Sun,* February 19, 1942, 1; William J. Petersen, "Remember Pearl Harbor," 35.

53. *Winterset News,* January 22, 1942, 2; *Winterset Madisonian,* January 21, 1942, 1; *Des Moines Tribune,* January 13, 1942, 16.

54. Eric Larrabee, *Commander in Chief: Franklin Delano Roosevelt, His Lieutenants, and Their War* (1987), 4; Archie Satterfield, *The Home Front: An Oral History of the War Years in America, 1941–1945* (1981), 41; Petersen, "Remember Pearl Harbor," 46, 44.

55. *Des Moines Register,* June 8, 1942, 1.

Chapter 1. "Soldiers of the Soil: The Farm Front"

1. *Life,* August 11, 1941, 58–61.

2. Asher Hobson, "War Adjustments for American Agriculture"; John D. Black, "American Agriculture in the New War and Defense Situation," 28–36; *Iowa Bureau Farmer,* January 1942, 3.

3. Iowa State Department of Agriculture, *1943 Iowa Year Book of Agriculture,* 9.

4. *Life,* August 11, 1941, 58; *Prairie Farmer,* July 11, 1942.

5. *Wallaces' Farmer,* February 6, 1943, 1; Howard R. Tolley, *The Farmer Citizen at War* (1943), 272; *Winterset Madisonian,* October 22, 1941;

John J. Corson, *Manpower for Victory: Total Mobilization for Total War* (1943), 36; John B. Canning, "Foods for Defense," 701; David Hinshaw, *The Home Front* (1943), 233, 235.

6. Hinshaw, *The Home Front,* 29.

7. *Life,* May 25, 1942, 79, 84, 85.

8. *Prairie Farmer,* January 23, 1943, 15.

9. *Iowa Veterinarian,* January–February 1945, 30; *Iowa Farm Bureau Spokesman,* January 2, 1943, 7; *Iowa Veterinarian,* November–December 1942, 22; and September–October 1943, 36.

10. *Iowa Veterinarian,* November–December 1944, 20.

11. Alan L. Olmstead and Paul W. Rhode, "The Agricultural Mechanization Controversy of the Interwar Years," *Agricultural History* 68 (Summer 1994): 35–53; A. N. Johnson, "The Impact of Farm Machinery on the Farm Economy," 59; Iowa State Department of Agriculture, *1942 Iowa Year Book of Agriculture,* 187.

12. Robert E. Ankli, "Horses vs. Tractors on the Corn Belt," 134; Reynold Wik, "The American Farm Tractor as Father of the Military Tank," 126; Arthur G. Peterson, "Governmental Policy Relating to Farm Machinery in World War I"; *Burlington Hawk-Eye Gazette,* September 17, 1942, 1; *1943 Iowa Year Book of Agriculture,* 11.

13. *Red Oak Sun,* January 30, 1941, 7; *Des Moines Register,* April 25, 1943, Commercial sec., 7.

14. *Des Moines Register,* December 27, 1942; *Iowa Agriculturist,* March 1943, back cover.

15. *Successful Farming,* January 1941, 64; Richard Overy, "A War of Engines, Technology and Military Power," in *Why the Allies Won* (1997); *Successful Farming,* February 1944, 11; and December 1942, 26; *Iowa Agriculturist,* March 1943, 4; and April 1943, 3; *Wallaces' Farmer,* January 11, 1941, 3; Frank W. Fox, *Madison Avenue Goes to War: The Strange Military Career of American Advertising, 1941–1945,* 96.

16. *Winterset Madisonian,* August 28, 1946, 4; *Palimpsest* 31 (March 1950): 116; *Des Moines Register,* June 30, 1946, sec. X, 10; and July 7, 1946, sec. H, 21. The total number of all farms had decreased from 213,318 in 1940 to 205,399 by January 1946, almost 8,000 fewer farms.

17. Graham Hutton, *Midwest at Noon* (1946); Hiram Drache, "Midwest Agriculture: Changing with Technology," 302; E. Bradford Burns, *Kinship with the Land: Regionalist Thought in Iowa, 1894–1942* (1996), 166.

18. *Des Moines Register,* November 24, 1943, sec. A, 34; *Wallaces' Farmer,* July 21, 1945, 21.

19. *Kossuth County Advance,* November 9, 1944, 1; and November 2, 1943, 1. The power take-off is a rapidly revolving attachment to many tractors that acted as a power source for farm implements but could prove very dangerous when the safety cover was removed.

20. *Better Iowa,* October 22, 1945, 1; *Prairie Farmer,* July 21, 1945, 18; *Successful Farming,* December 1942, 23.

21. *Wallaces' Farmer,* July 1, 1944, 5.

22. *Wallaces' Farmer,* July 21, 1945, 3; *Accident Facts,* 1946 ed. (Chicago: National Safety Council, Inc., 1946).

23. *Des Moines Register,* October 10, 1942, 5; *Des Moines Tribune,* October 28, 1942, 1; Gordon Marshall, "Hired Men: Iowa's Unsung Farm Resource," 152.

24. C. Calvin Smith, *War and Wartime Changes: The Transformation of Arkansas, 1940–1945* (1986), 122; Albert A. Blum, "The Farmer, the Army and the Draft," 41; Selden Menefee, *Assignment U.S.A.* (1943), 243; *1942 Iowa Year Book of Agriculture,* 10–11; Howard R. Tolley, *The Farmer Citizen at War,* 164; Richard Polenberg, ed., *America at War: The Home Front, 1941–1945* (1968), 58–59; Corson, *Manpower for Victory,* 57; *1943 Iowa Year Book of Agriculture,* 10.

25. Satterfield, *The Home Front,* 117; Robert C. Clark, "Fighting or Farm Front?" *Iowa Farm Economist,* January–February 1943, 14; Mark Jonathan Harris, Franklin D. Mitchell, and Steven J. Schechter, *The Homefront: America during World War II* (1984), 166.

26. Hugh Sidey, quoted in Roy Hoopes, *Americans Remember the Home Front: An Oral Narrative,* 263.

27. Harry Schwartz, "Hired Farm Labor in World War II," 828–29; Corson, *Manpower for Victory,* 39; *1943 Iowa Year Book of Agriculture,* 376; *Iowa Farm Bureau Spokesman,* February 26, 1944, 11. In late 1942, local draft boards considered four points before deciding whether to grant a farm deferment: the importance of the farm's products, the farm's contribution, the worker's skills, and the relative labor shortage in each particular region. See Blum, "The Farmer, the Army and the Draft," 34; Corson, *Manpower for Victory,* 39; and Schwartz, "Hired Farm Labor," 831. The Selective Training and Service Act of 1940 had forbidden group deferments, yet in the "Teen Age Draft Bill" of late

1942, Sen. Millard Tydings of Maryland introduced an amendment to provide for the deferment from military service of essential farm workers.

28. *Des Moines Register,* July 28, 1943, 6; *Iowa Farm Bureau Spokesman,* May 29, 1943, 1; and June 5, 1943, 3; *Des Moines Register,* August 14, 1945, 16.

29. *Wallaces' Farmer,* January 9, 1943, 1.

30. Ibid., 5.

31. Ibid., January 15, 1944, 1, 21.

32. Peter H. Curtis, "A Place of Peace in a World of War: The Scattergood Refugee Hostel, 1939–1943," 52.

33. *Des Moines Register,* October 11, 1943, 6.

34. V. R. Cardozier, *The Mobilization of the United States in World War II: How the Government, Military and Industry Prepared for War,* 61, 62; Cabell Phillips, *The 1940s: Decade of Triumph and Trouble* (1975), 113; *Des Moines Register,* May 24, 1988, World War II vertical file, Des Moines Public Library.

35. Wayne D. Rasmussen, *A History of the Emergency Farm Labor Supply Program, 1943–1947,* 226, 261; *Des Moines Register,* July 23, 1944, sec. 4, 1; sec. L, 5.

36. Judith M. Gansberg, *Stalag U.S.A.: The Remarkable Story of German POWs in America,* 5, 13, 20, 26, 34; *Kossuth County Advance,* April 6, 1944, 1; Rasmussen, *History of the Emergency Farm Labor Supply Program,* 98–99.

37. *Kossuth County Advance,* September 18, 1945, 1.

38. *Better Iowa,* February 7, 1944, 1; Iowa State Department of Agriculture, *1944 Iowa Year Book of Agriculture,* 350; W. H. Stacy, "Holding Their Own," *Iowa Farm Economist,* October 1943, 11; *Des Moines Register,* March 14, 1945, Iowa News sec., 4.

39. *Des Moines Register,* October 11, 1942, Iowa News sec., 7.

40. Sarah Elbert, "Farmer Takes a Wife: Women in America's Farming Families," in Lourdes Beneria and Catharine R. Stimpson, eds., *Women, Households, and the Economy* (1987), 181, 182.

41. *Prairie Farmer,* May 13, 1944, 3; *Iowa Farm Economist,* October 1943, 11; *Burlington Hawk-Eye Gazette,* March 17, 1943, 10.

42. *Winterset Madisonian,* November 25, 1942, 3; *Des Moines Tribune,* April 5, 1945, 12.

43. Barbara M. Tucker, "Agricultural Workers in World War II: The Reserve Army of Children, Black Americans, and Jamaicans," *Agricultural History* 68 (Winter 1994): 63; *Farm Journal,* September 1942, 14.

44. *Life,* May 25, 1942, cover; *Prairie Farmer,* February 6, 1943, 9.

45. *Iowa Farm Bureau Spokesman,* January 9, 1943, 1; August 21, 1943, 1; April 8, 1944, 1; and September 2, 1944, 1; *Burlington Hawk-Eye Gazette,* March 17, 1943, 10; *News for Homemakers* (radio show), WOI, Ames, Iowa, March 10, 1945; and October 4, 1944.

46. Rasmussen, *History of the Emergency Farm Labor Supply Program,* 120–30.

47. *News for Homemakers,* WOI, Ames, October 12, 1945.

48. Phyllis Elvira Gough, *Tasks Done by 100 Iowa State College Freshmen Women Living on Farms during 1942 in Iowa and Surrounding States,* 1, 32, 44, 19; *Wallaces' Farmer,* August 22, 1942, 15.

49. *Des Moines Tribune,* November 23, 1942, 7; and June 28, 1943, 11.

50. *Iowa Bureau Farmer,* May 1943, 7.

51. *Iowa Agriculturist,* April 1942, 15.

52. Deborah Montgomerie, "Men's Jobs and Women's Work: The New Zealand Women's Land Service in World War II," *Agricultural History* 63 (Summer 1989): 1; *Farm Journal,* September 1944, 48; *Prairie Farmer,* September 1, 1941, 23; and September 4, 1943, 1; *Wallaces' Farmer,* April 17, 1943, 1; Janet M. Labrie, "The Depiction of Women's Field Work in Rural Fiction," *Agricultural History* 67 (Spring 1993): 121; *Successful Farming,* May 1943, 70; August 1943, 79; and July 1944, 59.

53. *Wallaces' Farmer,* March 4, 1944, 6.

54. *Prairie Farmer,* September 6, 1941, 23; *Des Moines Register,* June 29, 1943, 9.

55. *Des Moines Register,* June 15, 1944, 4.

56. *Des Moines Register,* February 21, 1943, sec. H, 15.

57. *Red Oak Express,* October 30, 1941, 1; *Des Moines Register,* April 8, 1945, sec. S, 3; *Prairie Farmer,* March 20, 1943, 13; and June 12, 1943, 11.

58. Gilbert C. Fite, *American Farmers: The New Minority* (1981), 88, 238; David B. Danbom, *The Resisted Revolution: Urban America and the Industrialization of Agriculture, 1900–1930* (1979), vi; Ruth Milkman, *Gender at Work: The Dynamics of Job Segregation by Sex during World War II* (1987), 12; O. R. Johnson, "The Family Farm" (see especially "Adopting Industrial Methods May Be Necessary"), 533–35; Rich-

ard Polenberg, *War and Society: The United States, 1941–1945,* 242; *Life,* May 25, 1942, 84.

59. Louis Bromfield, *Pleasant Valley* (1943), 48; Louis Bromfield, *The World We Live In* ("The Pond") (1944), 11.

60. Bromfield, *Pleasant Valley,* 14; *Des Moines Tribune,* July 22, 1942, 1, 7; *Collier's,* June 12, 1943, 11, 62, 64; *Iowa Farm Bureau Spokesman,* June 12, 1943, 1.

61. Carey McWilliams, *Ill Fares the Land: Migrants and Migratory Labor in the United States* (1942), 318, 322, 323.

62. Paul Corey, *Acres of Antaeus* (1946), 38; Curtis K. Stadtfeld, *From the Land and Back* (1972), 28.

63. *1945 Iowa Year Book of Agriculture,* 12, 17, 31.

64. *Des Moines Register,* February 25, 1945, sec. H, 1; *1945 Iowa Year Book of Agriculture,* 582, 9.

65. Fite, *American Farmers,* 234, 243.

66. Harold Lee, *Roswell Garst—A Biography* (1984), 133; *Red Oak Sun,* July 3, 1941, 3; *Burlington Hawk-Eye Gazette,* November 30, 1942, 1; *Des Moines Register,* February 13, 1946, 15; John Dos Passos, *State of the Nation* (1944), 273.

67. Homer Croy, *Corn Country* (1947), 5; *Iowa Agriculturist,* March 1943, cover, 8, 9.

68. *Iowa Agriculturist,* March 1942, 12, 13, 16.

69. *Farm Science Reporter,* July 1944, 14; *Wallaces' Farmer,* July 11, 1942, 16; *1944 Iowa Year Book of Agriculture,* 12; Iowa State Department of Agriculture, *1945 Iowa Year Book of Agriculture,* 14, 15; *Better Iowa,* May 4, 1942, 1; *Iowa Poultry Association Year Book,* 1945, back cover; *News for Homemakers,* WOI, Ames, March 7, 1944; William L. Cavert, "The Technological Revolution in Agriculture, 1910–1955," 22; *Iowa Poultry Association Year Book,* 1943, 7.

70. Iowa State College, Members of the Staff and the Iowa Agricultural Experiment Station, *A Century of Farming in Iowa, 1846–1946* (1946), 64–65; *Wallaces' Farmer,* July 11, 1942, 9; *Farm Science Reporter,* July 1942, 3; *Iowa Farm Bureau Spokesman,* July 24, 1943, 1; and March 11, 1944, 6; *1944 Iowa Year Book of Agriculture,* 8; *1945 Iowa Year Book of Agriculture,* 8; *Better Iowa,* September 4, 1944, 1.

71. *Des Moines Register,* February 21, 1943, 13; *Wallaces' Farmer,* October 2, 1943, 22; *Farm Science Reporter,* January 1944, 16–19; *Iowa Farm*

Bureau Spokesman, January 23, 1943, 1.

72. *Algona Upper Des Moines* (newspaper), November 24, 1942, 1; and February 4, 1943, 6.

73. *Des Moines Tribune,* September 21, 1943, 1, 9; *Des Moines Register,* December 19, 1943, sec. L, 6.

74. *Iowa Farm Bureau Spokesman,* June 22, 1944, 10; *Des Moines Tribune,* February 12, 1946, 6.

75. *Iowa Farm Science,* October 1946, 8, 9; *Des Moines Register,* March 3, 1946, sec. H, 24.

76. *1945 Iowa Year Book of Agriculture,* 11; *Wallaces' Farmer,* March 16, 1946, 13.

77. John Morton Blum, *V Was for Victory: Politics and American Culture during World War II* (1976), 116.

78. Dos Passos, *State of the Nation,* 273.

79. Hilary St. George Saunders, *Pioneers! O Pioneers!* (1944), 106, 107.

80. J. Robert Moskin, *Mr. Truman's War: The Final Victories of World War II and the Birth of the Postwar World* (1996), 159; Allen J. Matusow, *Farm Policies and Politics in the Truman Years* (1967), 4–5; Alonzo L. Hamby, *Man of the People: A Life of Harry S. Truman* (1995), 370.

81. Barton J. Bernstein, "The Postwar Famine and Price Control, 1946," 235, 239–40; *Des Moines Register,* November 20, 1945, World War II Clippings File #2, State Historical Society of Iowa Archive; *Des Moines Tribune,* March 15, 1943, 1; David Fromkin, *In the Time of the Americans: FDR, Truman, Eisenhower, Marshall, MacArthur—The Generation That Changed America's Role in the World* (1995), 447; *Des Moines Tribune,* January 1, 1945, 1; Ralph Butterfield, ed., *Patton's GI Photographers* (1992), 79, 16; Moskin, *Mr. Truman's War,* 161.

82. Max Hastings, *Victory in Europe: D-Day to V-E Day* (1985), 170, 179–80; Martin Gilbert, *The Day the War Ended: May 8, 1945—Victory in Europe* (1995), 38.

83. Donald J. Willis, *The Incredible Year* (1988), 136–37.

84. Earl R. Beck in *The European Home Fronts, 1939–1945* makes the statement that no book "dealing with the trials of civilians during World War II can pass over the monstrous tragedy inflicted on the Jews of Europe" (p. 93). On October 3, 1945, photographs were printed in the *Des Moines Register* of prisoners' artwork of the torture inflicted.

85. *Des Moines Register,* March 16, 1945, 7; Saunders, *Pioneers! O Pioneers!* 102.

86. *Des Moines Register,* August 18, 1985, sec. A, 1.

87. Studs Terkel, *"The Good War": An Oral History of World War II* (1984), 9–10.

~ Chapter 2. "'E' Awards and WOWs: The Production Front"

1. *Iowa Taxpayer,* November 1941, Supplement, 5A; *American Business,* April 1941, 24; *Life,* March 31, 1941, 66, 67; *Iowa Business Digest,* April 1941, 3; and July 1942, 1; *Independent Woman,* April 1941, 109. Welch was the president of the University of Dubuque.

2. *Des Moines Register,* September 17, 1939, sec. 6, 1; *Iowa Business Digest,* March 1941, 2, 3; and July 1941, 2. In the two years before December 1941, Congress authorized $74.4 billion for defense production (Phillips, *The 1940s,* 67).

3. *Des Moines Register,* December 21, 1941, 3; January 8, 1942, 5; May 10, 1942, sec. 4, 3.

4. *Life,* July 7, 1941, 17; Cardozier, *Mobilization of the United States,* 72.

5. *Iowa Unionist,* July 16, 1943, 1.

6. *Burlington Hawk-Eye Gazette,* September 5, 1942, 10; *Burlington Hawk-Eye Gazette* clipping, March 5, 1942, in Iowa Army Ammunition Plant vertical file, Burlington Public Library. (No page numbers are noted on clippings in file.)

7. Max Lerner, *Public Journal: Marginal Notes on Wartime America* (1945), 158; Ernie Pyle, *Here Is Your War* (1943), 177.

8. *Iowa Business Digest,* February 1942, 4; *Life,* July 7, 1941, 17; Stephen J. Leonard, "Denver at War: The Home Front in World War II," 30; Francis Walton, *Miracle of World War II: How American Industry Made Victory Possible* (1956), chap. 1.

9. *Des Moines Register,* August 24, 1940, 5.

10. Cardozier, *Mobilization of the United States,* 122; Patricia Dooley, "Gopher Ordnance Works: Condemnation, Construction, and Community Response," 217; Joel Davidson, "Building for War, Preparing for Peace," in Donald Albrecht, ed., *World War II and the American Dream: How Wartime Building Changed a Nation* (1995), 209; Harry C.

Thomson and Lida Mayo, *The Ordnance Department: Procurement and Supply* (1960), 43.

11. Dooley, "Gopher Ordnance Works," 218; Robert Hungerford Dodds, *World War II Construction and Construction Problems at the Navy's Continental Ammunition Depots,* 53; Perry R. Duis and Scott LaFrance, *We've Got a Job to Do: Chicagoans and World War II* (1992), 95; Thomas Parrish, *Roosevelt and Marshall: Partners in Politics and War* (1989), 317; *American Business,* December 1941, 9.

12. Lowell Juilliard Carr and James Edson Stermer, *Willow Run: A Study of Industrialization and Cultural Inadequacy* (1952), xviii; George A. Larson, "Nebraska's World War II Bomber Plant: The Glenn L. Martin–Nebraska Company," 32; Francis E. Merrill, *Social Problems on the Home Front: A Study of War-Time Influences,* 9; Margaret Crawford, "Daily Life on the Home Front," in Albrecht, *World War II and the American Dream,* 119; Max Parvin Cavnes, *The Hoosier Community at War* (1961), 91, 92, 97.

13. *A Guide to Burlington, Iowa,* 7, 8; Iowa Centennial Des Moines County Committee, *Burlington—Then and Now,* no page numbers; *Burlington Hawk-Eye Gazette* clipping, 1968, in Burlington vertical file, State Historical Society of Iowa Archive.

14. *Burlington Hawk-Eye Gazette,* November 6, 1940, 1; and December 13, 1940, 1; *Burlington Hawk-Eye Gazette* clippings, November 9, 1940; November 10, 1940; November 23, 1940; and November 1940, Iowa Ordnance Plant Scrapbook (this scrapbook contains only *Burlington Hawk-Eye Gazette* articles; most dates are listed, but not page numbers), Burlington Public Library.

15. *Burlington Hawk-Eye Gazette* clippings, July 1941; March 19, 1941; February 1, 1941; November 8, 18, and 27, 1940; December 9 and 12, 1940, IOP Scrapbook, Burlington Public Library; *Iowa Farm Economist,* August 1941, 16; *Burlington Hawk-Eye Gazette,* December 2, 1940, 2.

16. *Burlington Hawk-Eye Gazette* clippings, December 12, 27, 30, and 31, 1940; January 4 and 11, 1941; and February 11, 1941, IOP Scrapbook, Burlington Public Library.

17. *Burlington Hawk-Eye Gazette* clippings, February 5, 1941; and March 25, 1941, IOP Scrapbook, Burlington Public Library.

18. *Burlington Hawk-Eye Gazette* clippings, June 1941; June 7, 10, and 14, 1941; July 12, 1941; August 14, 16, and 30, 1941, IOP Scrapbook, Bur-

lington Public Library.

19. *Burlington Hawk-Eye Gazette,* July 9, 1961, 20; *Burlington Hawk-Eye Gazette* clipping, February 13, 1941, IOP Scrapbook, Burlington Public Library.

20. *Burlington Hawk-Eye Gazette* clippings, February 13, 19, and 27, 1941; April 30, 1941; May 29, 1941; June 18, 1941; and June 1941, IOP Scrapbook, Burlington Public Library; *Burlington Hawk-Eye Gazette* clipping, July 1941 (Defense Day), 2, IAAP vertical file, Burlington Public Library.

21. *Burlington Hawk-Eye Gazette* clipping, July 31, 1941, IOP Scrapbook, Burlington Public Library.

22. *Burlington Hawk-Eye Gazette* clippings, November 7, 1941; and January 7, 1942, IOP Scrapbook, Burlington Public Library; *Burlington Hawk-Eye Gazette,* June 3, 1991, 1.

23. *Burlington Hawk-Eye Gazette* clippings, July 9, 1941; July 10, 1941; and December 31, 1941, IOP Scrapbook, Burlington Public Library.

24. *Des Moines Register,* July 30, 1941, 14; *Burlington Hawk-Eye Gazette* clippings, July 11, 25, and 31, 1941; and August 1, 1941, IOP Scrapbook, Burlington Public Library.

25. *Burlington Hawk-Eye Gazette* clippings, July 28 and 29, 1941; and August 1, 1941, IOP Scrapbook, Burlington Public Library; *Des Moines Tribune,* August 1, 1941, 5.

26. *Burlington Hawk-Eye Gazette* clipping, August 1, 1941, IOP Scrapbook, Burlington Public Library.

27. Editorial, *Cedar Rapids Gazette,* quoted in *Burlington Hawk-Eye Gazette* clipping, August 2, 1941, IOP Scrapbook, Burlington Public Library.

28. *Des Moines Tribune,* July 31, 1941, 11.

29. *Burlington Hawk-Eye Gazette* clipping, August 4, 1942, IAAP vertical file, Burlington Public Library; *Burlington Hawk-Eye Gazette* clippings, July 30, 1941; October 18 and 19, 1941, IOP Scrapbook, Burlington Public Library.

30. *Burlington Hawk-Eye Gazette* clipping, July 17, 1942, IAAP vertical file, Burlington Public Library; *Iowa Legionnaire,* July 16, 1943, 6; *Burlington Hawk-Eye Gazette,* June 25, 1943, 1.

31. Thomson and Mayo, *The Ordnance Department,* 131; *Des Moines Register,* December 14, 1941, 1, 6.

32. *Des Moines Tribune,* December 12, 1941, 1; and December 13, 1941, 1; *Burlington Hawk-Eye Gazette,* December 12, 1941, 1.

33. *Burlington Hawk-Eye Gazette* clippings, December 13, 14, 15, 16, and 22, 1941; January 27 and 28, 1942; and March 6, 1942, IOP Scrapbook, Burlington Public Library. The first identified fatalities were Lyle M. Teal, 27, Keosauqua; E. C. Schillerstrom, 50, Agency; Pearly J. Pettit, 48, Lansing; John K. Cummings, 36, Bunch; Woodrow Wehrle, 26, Rome; and Wayne P. Hoefle, 36, Fort Madison. Added to the fatalities list were Dwight Strawhacker, Oakville; Tracy A. Perry, West Burlington; Virgil Hopkins, Middletown; Gora Gore, Bloomfield; R. I. McKay, Washington; and L. E. Robbins, Keosauqua.

34. *Burlington Hawk-Eye Gazette* clipping, December 26, 1942, IOP Scrapbook, Burlington Public Library; *Des Moines Register,* December 13, 1941, 1, 10; *Burlington Hawk-Eye Gazette* clippings, March 6, 7, 9, 13, and 27, 1942, IOP Scrapbook, Burlington Public Library; *Des Moines Register,* March 8, 1942, sec. 4, 1; *Burlington Hawk-Eye Gazette,* March 5, 1942, 4.

35. Harold Henry Klontz, 22, Packwood; Ralph Robert Carson, 23, West Point; Lawrence Greiner, 29, Keota; Pearl Clifford Carver, 27, Mount Pleasant; Harold R. Wyatt, 27, Keokuk; Archie S. Booth, 42, Colchester, Illinois; Ernest Strausbaugh, 28, Roseville, Illinois; Hartzell Popejoy, 36, Fairfield; Royal L. Murray, 41, East Moline, Illinois; Hershel M. Goddard, 30, Oskaloosa; Grover C. Kieth, 45, Cedar Rapids; Andrew Voorhees, 33, Raritan, Illinois; Bernard L. Melton, 29, London Mills, Illinois; Henry Hummel, 28, Monmouth, Illinois; William Buford England, 23, Colusa, Illinois; Harold Henry Klontz, 22, Ollie; Olyn Claire Rogers, 31, Sparksburg; Clyd Hughes, Cincinnati (Iowa); Clarence Wilson; and Kenneth Van Sickel (listed in *Burlington Hawk-Eye Gazette,* March 5, 1942).

36. *Burlington Hawk-Eye Gazette* clipping, March 5, 1942, IOP Scrapbook, Burlington Public Library.

37. *Burlington Hawk-Eye Gazette* clipping, March 24, 1942, IOP Scrapbook, Burlington Public Library.

38. *Des Moines Register,* March 6, 1942, 1, 5; *Burlington Hawk-Eye Gazette,* March 6, 1942, 1; *Burlington Hawk-Eye Gazette* clipping, March 7, 1942, IOP Scrapbook, Burlington Public Library.

39. *Burlington Hawk-Eye Gazette* clipping, March 27, 1942, IOP Scrapbook, Burlington Public Library.

40. *Red Oak Sun,* February 13, 1941, 7.

41. *Iowan,* January 1953, 8; "Burlington Gave Blood, Sweat, Tears to World War II Effort," in *The Hawk-Eye's History of Burlington, 125th Anniversary* (1962), Burlington file, State Historical Society of Iowa Archive.

42. *Business Week,* August 11, 1945, 44; *Des Moines Register* clipping, November 4, 1951, Burlington vertical file, State Historical Society of Iowa Archive.

43. Ann Arnold Lemert, *First You Take a Pick and Shovel—The Story of the Mason Companies* (1979), 160–67.

44. *Des Moines Register* clipping, November 4, 1951, Burlington vertical file, State Historical Society of Iowa Archive.

45. *Des Moines Register,* July 11, 1941, 1.

46. *Burlington Hawk-Eye Gazette* clipping, March 20, 1941, IOP Scrapbook, Burlington Public Library.

47. *Red Oak Sun,* May 29, 1941, 7; *Des Moines Register,* June 12, 1941, 1.

48. *Des Moines Tribune,* July 7, 1941, 1.

49. "A History of Ankeny," compiled by Art Hildreth, Ankeny vertical file, State Historical Society of Iowa Archive; *Des Moines Register,* July 3, 1941, 5.

50. *Des Moines Register* clipping, July 7, 1941, Des Moines Ordnance Plant (DMOP) vertical file, Des Moines Public Library.

51. *Des Moines Register,* July 3, 1941, 1, 5; *Des Moines Register* clippings, July 9, 1941; and July 4, 1941, 5, DMOP vertical file, Des Moines Public Library.

52. *Des Moines Register* clippings, July 26 and 30, 1941, DMOP vertical file, Des Moines Public Library.

53. *Des Moines Register,* July 31, 1941, 4; and July 30, 1941, 1; *Des Moines Tribune,* July 8, 1941, 1; *Des Moines Register* clipping, July 23, 1941, DMOP vertical file, Des Moines Public Library.

54. *Des Moines Tribune* clipping, August 13, 1941; and *Des Moines Register* clippings, July 18 and 28, 1941, all from DMOP vertical file, Des Moines Public Library; *Ankeny Times,* May 14, 1943, 1; *Des Moines Tribune,* November 4, 1941, 1A.

55. *Des Moines Register,* July 11, 1941, 1; and August 15, 1941, 5.

56. *Des Moines Tribune* clippings, August 13, 1941; July 2, 1941; *Des Moines Register* clippings, August 5 and 24, 1941, all from DMOP vertical

file, Des Moines Public Library; *Des Moines Tribune,* July 28, 1941, 1; *Des Moines Register,* July 29, 1941, 5; September 7, 1941, Iowa sec., 8.

57. *Des Moines Register,* September 21, 1941, Iowa sec., 3; *Des Moines Register,* October 19, 1941, Commercial sec., 12; DMOP vertical file, Des Moines Public Library: *Des Moines Tribune* clippings, October 17, 1941; and November 7, 28, and 30, 1941.

58. *Des Moines Tribune,* September 12, 1941, DMOP vertical file, Des Moines Public Library; *Des Moines Tribune,* September 1, 1941, 1; *Des Moines Register,* September 27, 1941, 1.

59. *Des Moines Register* clipping, March 4, 1942, DMOP vertical file, Des Moines Public Library; *Des Moines Register,* December 14, 1941, Commercial sec., 12.

60. *Iowa Bystander,* July 17, 1941, 1; and August 7, 1941, 1; Joel Seidman, *American Labor from Defense to Reconversion* (1953), 165; Karen Tucker Anderson, "Last Hired, First Fired: Black Women Workers during World War II," 82–85.

61. *Iowa Bystander,* April 9, 1942, 1.

62. *Des Moines Register,* April 13, 1942, 7; *Iowa Bystander,* June 17, 1943, 4; Daniel Nelson, *Farm and Factory: Workers in the Midwest, 1880–1990* (1995), 146.

63. *Iowa Bystander,* April 16, 1942, 1.

64. Ibid., February 15, 1945, 3.

65. Shelton Stromquist, *Solidarity and Survival: An Oral History of Iowa Labor in the Twentieth Century* (1993), 246, 248, 249.

66. *Des Moines Tribune* clippings, August 19, 1943; and June 1, 1944, both from DMOP vertical file, Des Moines Public Library; *Des Moines Register,* November 25, 1944, 1.

67. *Iowa Bystander,* February 15, 1945, 3.

68. Stephen E. Ambrose, *Citizen Soldiers: The U.S. Army from the Normandy Beaches to the Bulge to the Surrender of Germany, June 7, 1944–May 7, 1945* (1997), 52, 72, 371; *Iowa Bystander,* May 17, 1945, 2.

69. *Des Moines Register,* September 9, 1945, sec. 4, 1, 4.

70. *Des Moines Register,* June 28, 1945, 4; *Des Moines Tribune,* February 15, 1944, 6.

71. *Des Moines Register,* June 28, 1945, 1; and August 5, 1945, sec. L, 3; *Des Moines Tribune,* August 21, 1945, 7; July 31, 1945, 1, 6; and August 23, 1945, 1.

72. *Des Moines Tribune* clippings, January 15, 1946; and December 17,

1945, DMOP vertical file, Des Moines Public Library; *Des Moines Register,* January 13, 1946, sec. L, 5.

73. Advertisement for *U.S. News,* January 10, 1947, DMOP vertical file, Des Moines Public Library; list of DMOP statistics, World War II vertical file, Ankeny Public Library; *Ankeny: First 100 Years* (advertising insert), 89, Ankeny Public Library.

74. *Des Moines Tribune,* August 11, 1942, 16.

75. Duis and LaFrance, *We've Got a Job to Do,* 93; John F. Zwicky, *A State at War: The Home Front in Illinois during the Second World War,* 87–88.

76. *American Business,* December 1941, 10; *Business Week,* August 14, 1943, 59.

77. *Des Moines Tribune,* September 5, 1945, 7; and December 9, 1942, 15; *Des Moines Register,* February 8, 1943, 1; and May 14, 1944, sec. X, 8.

78. *Des Moines Register,* August 11, 1942, 7; and August 27, 1942, 1, 7.

79. *Iowa Bystander,* December 23, 1943, 1; *Des Moines Register,* March 28, 1943, Commercial sec., 8; and September 24, 1944, sec. X, 8.

80. *Des Moines Register,* November 12, 1942, 1.

81. *Des Moines Tribune,* December 3, 1942, 14.

82. *Des Moines Register,* December 13, 1942, Iowa sec., 5; December 16, 1942, 1, 8; and July 23, 1944, sec. X, 8; *Des Moines Tribune,* January 22, 1945, 9.

83. *Charles City Press,* December 29, 1942, 1; *Des Moines Register,* January 21, 1943, 3; and January 22, 1943, 8.

84. *Des Moines Register,* March 16, 1943, 1; *Sioux City Journal-Tribune,* March 15, 1943, 1, 14.

85. *Davenport Democrat and Leader,* March 30, 1943, 15, 16, 17, 18, 21, and sec. 2, 16.

86. *Davenport Democrat and Leader,* April 1, 1943, 1, 6.

87. *Des Moines Register,* July 24, 1943, 1, 5; *Burlington Hawk-Eye Gazette,* August 1, 1942, 7; *Clarinda Herald-Journal,* July 26, 1943, 1.

88. *Des Moines Tribune,* April 13, 1943, 15; *Clinton Herald,* May 7, 1943, sec. A, 1, 3, 8; *Davenport Democrat and Leader,* June 23, 1943, 2; and June 27, 1943, 10.

89. *Des Moines Register,* July 15, 1943, 3; and September 16, 1944, 1, 12.

90. Albert W. Palmer, Frank W. McCulloch, and Stoddard Lane, *Social Action: Labor Troubles and the Local Church,* 4.

91. *Iowan,* October–November 1955, 37.

92. Maytag Company, *Yesterday, Today, and Tomorrow* (1945), 4, 12, 15, 16, 21; A. B. Funk, *Fred L. Maytag: A Biography* (1936), 54, 68, 69.

93. *Jasper County Review,* May 14, 1941, 1; Palmer, McCulloch, and Lane, *Social Action,* 5, 6, 17, 18; *Jasper County Review,* August 7, 1941, 1.

94. Maytag Company, *Yesterday, Today, and Tomorrow,* 10, 12, 18; Palmer, McCulloch, and Lane, *Social Action,* 13; *Jasper County News,* October 24, 1940, 6; *Newton Daily,* May 14, 1941, 6.

95. Lee Kennett, *For the Duration . . . The United States Goes to War, Pearl Harbor–1942* (1985), 108; *Des Moines Register,* April 15, 1942, 14.

96. Maytag Company, *Yesterday, Today, and Tomorrow,* 28, 29; Robert Hoover and John Hoover, *An American Quality Legend: How Maytag Saved Our Moms, Vexed the Competition, and Presaged America's Quality Revolution* (1993), 156.

97. Maytag Company, *Yesterday, Today, and Tomorrow,* 30, 34, 36, 37; Hoover and Hoover, *An American Quality Legend,* 157.

98. *Mason City Globe Gazette,* July 13, 1943, 1; and July 14, 1943, 18; *Des Moines Register,* July 24, 1943, 5.

99. *Des Moines Register,* March 6, 1940, 15; and March 31, 1940, 1.

100. Stromquist, *Solidarity and Survival,* 125.

101. William L. O'Neill, *A Democracy at War: America's Fight at Home and Abroad in World War II* (1993), 214; Hinshaw, *The Home Front,* 185–86; Nelson Lichtenstein, *Labor's War at Home: The CIO in World War II* (1982), 5–6.

102. *Iowa Business,* October 1946, 22; *Des Moines Tribune,* January 8, 1944, 1; Seidman, *American Labor,* 153.

103. Natsuki Aruga, "'An' Finish School': Child Labor during World War II," 498, 517; *Burlington Hawk-Eye Gazette,* November 17, 1942, 2; Polenberg, *War and Society,* 79.

104. *Collier's,* April 24, 1943, 18, 19, 56.

105. *Iowa Farm Bureau Spokesman,* August 26, 1944, 4.

106. D'Ann Campbell, *Women at War with America: Private Lives in a Patriotic Era* (1984), 154; Deborah Fink, "World War II and Rural Women," in Marvin Bergman, ed., *Iowa History Reader* (1996), 351; Karen Anderson, *Wartime Women: Sex Roles, Family Relationships, and the Status of Women during World War II* (1981), 177; Milkman, *Gender at Work,* 61, 40, 19, 13; O'Neill, *A Democracy at War,* 332.

107. *Independent Woman,* June 1943, 166; Allan M. Winkler, *Home Front U.S.A.* (1986), 49, 54.

108. Neil Wynn, "The United States," in Jeremy Noakes, ed., *The Civilian in War: The Home Front in Europe, Japan, and the USA in World War II* (1992), 86; Maureen Honey, "Remembering Rosie: Advertising Images of Women in World War II," in Kenneth Paul O'Brien and Lynn Hudson Parsons, eds., *The Home-Front War: World War II and American Society* (1995), 83; Gulielma Fell Alsop and Mary F. McBride, "Arms and the Girl," in Judy Barrett Litoff and David C. Smith, eds., *American Women in a World at War: Contemporary Accounts from World War II* (1997), 168; Evelyn Steele, *Wartime Opportunities for Women* (1943), 1; Olga Gruhzit-Hoyt, *They Also Served: American Women in World War II* (1995), 135; *Time,* March 2, 1942, 61.

109. Nelson Lichtenstein, "The Making of the Postwar Working Class: Cultural Pluralism and Social Structure in World War II," 54; *Burlington Hawk-Eye Gazette,* January 9, 1943, 1; *Iowa Bystander,* July 1, 1943, 1.

110. *Des Moines Register,* March 5, 1943, 1; *Des Moines Tribune,* October 2, 1943, 2; Nancy Baker Wise and Christy Wise, *A Mouthful of Rivets: Women at Work in World War II* (1994), 200–201.

111. *Time,* May 11, 1942, 63; Donna Marie Sciancalepore, *The Contribution of Working Women of Waterloo during World War II,* 42, 44.

112. Jacqueline Smetak, "Women on the Home Front: The Iowa WIPEs," 180; *Waterloo Democrat* clipping, March 2, 1943, World War II vertical file, Grout Museum, Waterloo, Iowa.

113. Chester W. Gregory, *Women in Defense Work during World War II: An Analysis of the Labor Problem and Women's Rights* (1974), xvii; Elizabeth Gurley Flynn, *Women in the War,* 23; Doris Weatherford, *American Women and World War II* (1990), 158.

114. Jacqueline Jones, *Labor of Love, Labor of Sorrow: Black Women, Work, and the Family, from Slavery to the Present* (1985), 254; *Iowa Farm Economist,* October 1943, 11.

115. *Des Moines Tribune,* September 10, 1943, 11; and September 16, 1943, 1, 17; *Iowa Bystander,* October 28, 1943, 2; *Des Moines Register,* March 15, 1942, sec. 4, 1; *Des Moines Tribune,* October 2, 1943, 1.

116. *Des Moines Register,* April 21, 1943, 4; *Iowa Parent-Teacher,* December 1942, 5–6; and January 1943, 3.

117. *Des Moines Tribune,* July 4, 1945, 1, 3.

118. *Des Moines Register,* November 10, 1945, 4; Wise and Wise, *A Mouthful of Rivets,* 202.

119. *Des Moines Tribune,* July 18, 1945, 1; *Des Moines Register,* August 1, 1945, 1.

120. *Red Oak Sun,* November 29, 1945, 3.

121. *Winterset Madisonian,* September 4, 1946, 4.

122. John Hershey, *Hiroshima* (1946), 3; Lester Brooks, *Behind Japan's Surrender: The Secret Struggle That Ended an Empire* (1968), 164; *Des Moines Register,* June 3, 1946, 1; Robert Jay Lifton and Greg Mitchell, *Hiroshima in America: Fifty Years of Denial* (1995), 5.

123. Brooks, *Behind Japan's Surrender,* 356–57.

124. William L. Shirer, *An August to Remember: A Historian Remembers the Last Days of World War II and the End of the World That Was* (1986), 12, 13.

125. Robert Westbrook, "Horrors—Theirs and Ours: The *Politics* Circle and the Good War," 10; Richard Rhodes, *The Making of the Atomic Bomb* (1986), 325, 475; Moskin, *Mr. Truman's War,* 288; Winston S. Churchill, *Memoirs of the Second World War: An Abridgement of the Six Volumes of "The Second World War"* (1991), 582; Lifton and Mitchell, *Hiroshima in America,* 239; Terkel, *"The Good War,"* 137.

126. Jim Skahill, *Way Back When! 1924–1944. Hundreds of Characters Stumbling through the Great Depression,* 201, 202.

127. Robert Edson Lee, *To the War* (1968), 109, 112.

128. Moskin, *Mr. Truman's War,* 299; Ned Disque, "The Atom at Ames," *Iowan,* September 1956, 11; *Des Moines Register,* October 13, 1945, 10; Rhodes, *The Making of the Atomic Bomb,* 435.

129. *Iowa Bystander,* November 22, 1945, 1.

130. *Des Moines Tribune,* August 8, 1945; *Des Moines Register,* August 11, 1946, sec. 9, 5.

131. Disque, "The Atom at Ames," 12.

Chapter 3. "Bonds, Scrap, and Boys: The Community Front"

1. *Des Moines Register,* February 11, 1942, 13.

2. U.S. Office of War Information, *Small Town U.S.A.,* 3, 4, 8, 20, 36; *Saturday Evening Post,* May 22, 1943, 57; and September 9, 1944, 90.

3. *Des Moines Register,* June 3, 1945, sec. 9, 2; May 13, 1945, sec. 9, 2; January 28, 1945, sec. 9, 2; July 16, 1944, sec. 4, 1; February 14, 1943, 1; and July 9, 1944, sec. 9, 2.

4. *Des Moines Register,* July 3, 1944, 6; *Better Iowa,* February 9, 1942, 1.

5. *Iowa Parent-Teacher,* January 1942, 4; and April 1942, 3.

6. *Red Oak Express,* August 13, 1942, 5; *Winterset Madisonian,* August 26, 1942, 1; *Clarinda Herald-Journal,* August 13, 1942, 4.

7. James L. Abrahamson, *The American Home Front: Revolutionary War, Civil War, World War I, World War II* (1983), 140; Mary Watters, *Illinois in the Second World War: Operation Home Front,* 292, 255, 256; Polenberg, *America at War,* 11.

8. Polenberg, *War and Society,* 52, 136; Nancy Ruth Derr, *Iowans during World War I: A Study of Change under Stress,* 352–54, 182–83, 374, 414–15.

9. Duis and LaFrance, *We've Got a Job to Do,* 17; Robert K. Merton, *Mass Persuasion: The Social Psychology of a War Bond Drive* (1946), 45, 46, 49, 50, 51, 57.

10. Allan M. Winkler, *The Politics of Propaganda: The Office of War Information, 1942–1945,* 2, 3; Fox, *Madison Avenue Goes to War,* 15, 55, 62, and chap. 5, "The Ad Behind the Ad."

11. *Red Oak Sun,* January 14, 1942, 2; *Red Oak Express,* April 6, 1942, 2; June 15, 1942, 8; and October 25, 1943, 6; *Saturday Evening Post,* July 1, 1944, cover.

12. Dana Polan, *Power and Paranoia: History, Narrative, and the American Cinema, 1940–1950,* 74, 165; Richard Overy, *Why the Allies Won* (1995), 286; John W. Dower, "Race, Language, and War in Two Cultures: World War II in Asia," in Lewis A. Erenberg and Susan E. Hirsch, eds., *The War in American Culture: Society and Consciousness during World War II* (1996), 169, 170, 173; Geoffrey Perret, *There's a War to Be Won: The United States Army in World War II* (1991), 272.

13. *Newsweek,* July 6, 1942; *Red Oak Sun,* May 1, 1941, 1; *Des Moines Register,* April 10, 1942, 5; *Iowa Business Digest,* July 31, 1942, 2; *Winterset News,* June 11, 1942, 4.

14. *Life,* May 25, 1942, 37–40; William J. Petersen, "Beginnings of Davenport: Then and Now."

15. *Des Moines Tribune,* July 1, 1942, 1, 5, 20; *Des Moines Register,* July 2, 1942, 7.

16. *Des Moines Tribune,* July 1, 1942, 13.

17. *Clarinda Herald-Journal,* December 7, 1942, 3; and December 14, 1942, 3; *Des Moines Tribune,* December 29, 1942, 1, 7.

18. *Red Oak Express,* April 19, 1943, 3; *Iowa Bystander,* April 15, 1943, 2; *Des Moines Register,* June 8, 1943, 1.

19. *Des Moines Tribune,* October 29, 1942, 14; *Burlington Hawk-Eye Gazette,* September 29, 1942, 7; *Des Moines Tribune,* February 12, 1943, 11; *Mason City Globe Gazette,* April 22, 1943, 17.

20. *Children's Activities—for Home and School* (magazine), October 1942, 1; Kennett, *For the Duration,* 186; *Iowa Parent-Teacher,* June–July 1945, 15; *Iowa Farm Bureau Spokesman,* July 22, 1944, 9.

21. *Des Moines Tribune* clipping, May 19, 1943, Des Moines Public Library, World War II vertical file; *Winterset News,* September 9, 1943, 3.

22. *Red Oak Sun,* November 12, 1942, 3; *Des Moines Tribune,* November 10, 1942, 12; *Des Moines Register,* September 26, 1943, sec. S, 4; *Winterset Madisonian,* November 18, 1942, 1.

23. *Iowa Bystander,* September 9, 1943, 2; *Des Moines Tribune,* September 13, 1943, 3; and September 15, 1943, 3; *Des Moines Register,* October 10, 1943, 1; and October 19, 1943, 4.

24. *Des Moines Tribune,* January 10, 1944, 4; and January 18, 1944, 1; *Des Moines Register,* February 15, 1944, 1, 4.

25. *Mason City Globe Gazette,* March 17, 1943, 3; *Creston News Advertiser,* February 14, 1944, 1; Henrietta Zagel, "The Iowa BPW—1919–1970," 136; *News for Homemakers,* WOI, Ames, October 12, 1945; *Iowa Clubwoman,* January–February 1943, 5; Hazel P. Buffum, "Iowa Federation of Women's Clubs—Ideas and Achievements," 249.

26. *Des Moines Register,* April 8, 1944, 4; and June 11, 1944, sec. 9, 2; *Red Oak Express,* May 15, 1944, 1; *Des Moines Register,* June 18, 1944, 5; Russel D. Buhite and David W. Levy, *FDR's Fireside Chats,* June 12, 1944.

27. *Des Moines Register,* June 18, 1944, sec. E, 2; and June 11, 1944, sec. 6, 1.

28. *Des Moines Register,* July 15, 1944, 4; *Red Oak Sun,* July 6, 1944, 1; *Winterset News,* July 6, 1944, 1.

29. *Des Moines Tribune,* November 20, 1944, 1; and November 21, 1944, 12; *Red Oak Sun,* December 28, 1944, 8; *Clarinda Herald-Journal,* December 4, 1944, 6; *Des Moines Register,* November 19, 1944, sec.

G, 8; November 26, 1944, sec. G, 8; and December 2, 1944, 6; *Winterset News,* November 23, 1944, 6; and December 7, 1944, 6; *Red Oak Express,* December 4, 1944, 4; *Winterset Madisonian,* November 22, 1944, 3; and November 29, 1944, 8.

30. *Red Oak Express,* November 13, 1944, 1; November 16, 1944, 1; December 18, 1944, 1; and January 11, 1945, 1; *Red Oak Sun,* December 7, 1944, 1; *Iowa Parent-Teacher,* November 1944, 16.

31. *Red Oak Sun,* May 10, 1945, 1; *Clarinda Herald-Journal,* May 10, 1945, 4; *Des Moines Register,* May 13, 1945, sec. E, 9; *Red Oak Sun,* June 28, 1945, 8.

32. *Des Moines Tribune,* June 7, 1945, 17; *Red Oak Sun,* July 19, 1945, 1; *Des Moines Register,* May 14, 1945, 1; July 8, 1945, sec. 4, 1; and July 13, 1945, 1.

33. *Business Week,* August 25, 1945, 74; *Red Oak Express,* October 22, 1945, 3; *Winterset Madisonian,* November 14, 1945, 1.

34. *Business Week,* September 1, 1945, 83; *Red Oak Sun,* October 25, 1945, 1; *Des Moines Register,* August 27, 1945, 10; and November 13, 1945, 5; *Iowa Bystander,* September 13, 1945, 2; and November 8, 1945, 3; *Des Moines Tribune,* November 1, 1945, 12.

35. *Des Moines Tribune,* November 7, 1945, 6; and November 12, 1945, 8; *Perry Daily Chief,* January 7, 1946, 1.

36. *Des Moines Register,* March 3, 1946, sec. 4, 4; *Des Moines Tribune,* January 9, 1946, 9; March 13, 1946, 6; May 22, 1946, 6; August 7, 1946, 10; September 18, 1946, 12; and October 16, 1946, 12.

37. *Des Moines Register,* October 3, 1946, 5; and April 1, 1946, 1.

38. *Life,* January 12, 1942, 96; and March 23, 1942, 124; *Des Moines Register,* October 1, 1942, 1, 9.

39. Watters, *Illinois in the Second World War,* 263; *Saturday Evening Post,* June 27, 1942, 29, 80.

40. *Des Moines Register,* October 31, 1942, 4; and June 27, 1943, Society sec., 3.

41. Watters, *Illinois in the Second World War,* 271, 273; Jordan Braverman, *To Hasten the Homecoming: How Americans Fought World War II through the Media* (1996), 226.

42. *Saturday Evening Post,* September 26, 1942, 15.

43. Ibid.; *Winterset Madisonian,* October 14, 1942, 1; Marc Scott Miller, *The Irony of Victory: World War II and Lowell, Massachusetts* (1988), 187.

44. *Winterset Madisonian,* September 30, 1942, 1; *Burlington Hawk-Eye Gazette,* September 23, 1942, 12; and October 8, 1942, 14; *Des Moines Register,* September 24, 1942, 9.

45. *Winterset Madisonian,* September 30, 1942, 1; *Des Moines Register,* September 27, 1942, sec. 4, 1; *Winterset Madisonian,* September 2, 1942, 1.

46. *Winterset Madisonian,* December 23, 1942, 6; *1943 Winterset Boomerang* (high school yearbook), no page numbers.

47. *Clarinda Herald-Journal,* August 27, 1942, 1; September 3, 1942, 1; October 15, 1942, 1; and October 19, 1942, 1.

48. *Red Oak Sun,* August 28, 1942, 1; September 3, 1942, 1; September 10, 1942, 1; and October 1, 1942, 4; *Red Oak Express,* August 17, 1942, 1; August 31, 1942, 1; and September 14, 1942, 1.

49. *Des Moines Tribune,* April 20, 1943, 9; and June 10, 1943, 6; *Red Oak Sun,* February 18, 1943, 6.

50. *Iowa Legionnaire,* September 18, 1942, 1, 3; October 16, 1942, 1; November 6, 1942, 1; December 18, 1942, 1; January 15, 1943, 1; March 19, 1943, 6; April 16, 1943, 1; and November 19, 1943, 1.

51. *Des Moines Tribune,* October 1, 1942, 28; Margaret Bourke-White, "*Purple Heart Valley*": *A Combat Chronicle of the War in Italy* (1944), photo caption after p. 168; *Des Moines Register,* October 22, 1942, 6; Harris, Mitchell, and Schechter, *The Homefront,* 77; *Washington Evening Journal,* July 24, 1945, 1.

52. *Des Moines Tribune,* December 9, 1943, 10.

53. *Life,* June 5, 1944, 67, 68; *Burlington Hawk-Eye Gazette,* May 8, 1942, 2; *Winterset News,* January 20, 1944, 1; *Kossuth County Advance,* April 10, 1945, 1.

54. *Iowa Business,* June 1941; *Winterset Madisonian,* June 17, 1942, 1; *Collier's,* February 28, 1942, 37.

55. *Oelwein Daily Register,* July 22, 1942, 1; *Des Moines Register,* June 30, 1942, 6; *Burlington Hawk-Eye Gazette,* June 18, 1942, 2.

56. *Des Moines Register,* January 31, 1943, General sec., 5; *Iowa Clubwoman,* November–December 1943, 8; *Independent Woman,* November 1942, 340.

57. *Collier's,* January 24, 1942, 42; *Iowa Library Quarterly,* January 1944, 205.

58. *Red Oak Sun,* September 28, 1944, 1; *Iowa Farm Bureau Spokesman,* January 13, 1945, 1; *Kossuth County Advance,* December 14, 1944, 1.

59. *Des Moines Tribune,* March 20, 1942, 16.

60. Kenny A. Franks, "'Goodbye, Dear, I'll Be Back in a Year': The Mobilization of the Oklahoma National Guard for World War II," 347; *Red Oak Sun,* February 6, 1941, 1; February 27, 1941, 1; March 6, 1941, 1; and March 13, 1941, 1; Thomas Parrish, *Roosevelt and Marshall: Partners in Politics and War,* 177.

61. *Red Oak Express,* January 25, 1943, 1; and December 14, 1942, 1.

62. *Burlington Hawk-Eye Gazette,* March 30, 1943, 1; *Life,* May 3, 1943, 26, 27; Business and Professional Women's Club, *Cavalcade of a Century* (self-published, 1953), 53.

63. *Red Oak Express,* March 11, 1943, 1; *Red Oak Sun,* March 8, 1943, 1; and April 1, 1943, 1; *Red Oak Express,* March 15, 1943, 1.

64. *Red Oak Express,* April 19, 1943, 1; May 27, 1943, 1; and July 22, 1943, 1; *Burlington Hawk-Eye Gazette,* July 10, 1943, 7.

65. *Life,* September 13, 1943, as quoted in the *Red Oak Express,* September 13, 1943, 1; *Red Oak Express,* December 6, 1945, 1; December 13, 1945, 1; and December 20, 1945, 1.

66. *Red Oak Express,* September 28, 1944, 1.

67. *Des Moines Register,* December 16, 1945, sec. 9, 7.

68. Matthew Parker, *Monte Cassino: The Hardest-Fought Battle of World War II* (2004), 63, 64, 66 (Pyle quote).

69. *Saturday Evening Post,* August 17, 1946, 14.

70. *Life,* July 26, 1943, 34, 35; *Look,* May 16, 1944, 55; *Time,* July 26, 1943, 26; *Newsweek,* July 26, 1943, 42; *Prologue: Quarterly of the National Archives and Records Administration* 36, no. 4 (Winter 2004): 41; *Burlington Hawk-Eye Gazette,* July 15, 1943, 1. Lt. Col. Moore had been scheduled to arrive at the Omaha airport a day earlier, and his wife and daughter had waited seven hours for his plane to arrive. His plane had complications, so Moore arrived the next day by train.

71. Unidentified newspaper clipping, World War II vertical file, Red Oak Public Library.

72. Unidentified newspaper clipping, World War II miscellaneous papers, Montgomery County Historical Society, Red Oak, Iowa.

73. Alan B. Spitzer, "A Historian's Memory of the Second World War," 170; *Des Moines Register,* October 14, 1998, sec. M, 1.

74. Lloyd G. Dunn, "We Were in the Infantry, 103rd Division, WWII," World War II vertical file, Clarinda Public Library; Kenneth E. Colton,

"That Our Memory May Be Green: The Iowa War Records Commission," 95.

75. *Des Moines Register,* September 10, 1941, 1.

76. *Des Moines Tribune,* June 30, 1942, 1; and June 24, 1942, 1; *Des Moines Register,* July 1, 1942, 3.

77. *Davenport Democrat and Leader,* March 11, 1945, sec. 3, 1; *Webster City Daily Freeman Journal,* June 17, 1943, 1; *Des Moines Register,* February 21, 1943, sec. 4, 3.

78. *Des Moines Tribune,* October 5, 1943, 1, 7.

79. *Des Moines Register,* March 27, 1943, 2; *Iowa Bureau Farmer,* March 1945, 9; *Davenport Democrat and Leader,* September 10, 1943, 8.

80. *Des Moines Tribune,* January 3, 1942, 1; John R. Satterfield, *We Band of Brothers: The Sullivans and World War II* (1995), 176, 67.

81. *Des Moines Tribune,* January 3, 1942, 1; *Des Moines Register,* February 15, 1942, 1; *Des Moines Tribune,* January 12, 1943, 1; *Des Moines Register,* January 15, 1943, 1; *Life,* January 25, 1943, 37.

82. *Life,* February 15, 1943, 4.

83. *Des Moines Register,* July 11, 1943, Society sec., 10; Kennedy, *Freedom from Fear,* 559. For this more realistic interpretation, see Dan Kurzman's *Left to Die: The Tragedy of the* U.S.S. Juneau (1994), in which Kurzman tells the story of how nearly seven hundred men—including the five Sullivan brothers—died in torpedo and shark attacks in one of World War II's most secret scandals.

84. *Dubuque Telegraph-Herald,* February 10, 1943, 1, 3. 87. Satterfield, *We Band of Brothers,* 172, 179.

85. Satterfield, *We Band of Brothers,* 179.

86. *Newsweek,* February 15, 1943, 36.

87. Weatherford, *American Women and World War II,* 298–99.

88. Satterfield, *We Band of Brothers,* 184, 185; *Iowan,* Spring 1967, 8.

89. *Waterloo Daily Courier,* August 6, 1943, 1; *Iowan,* Winter 1988, 28.

90. Satterfield, *We Band of Brothers,* 164.

91. Bernard F. Dick, *The Star-Spangled Screen: The American World War II Film* (1985), 185.

92. Satterfield, *We Band of Brothers,* 199.

93. William M. Tuttle Jr., *"Daddy's Gone to War": The Second World War in the Lives of America's Children* (1993), 45.

94. *Des Moines Tribune,* January 7, 1946, 9.

95. Blum, *V Was for Victory,* 70.

96. *Time,* December 13, 1943, 92. The movie set for this typical Iowa town was actually in California.

97. Stephen E. Ambrose, *The Supreme Commander: The War Years of General Dwight D. Eisenhower* (1970), 323; Stephen E. Ambrose, *Eisenhower: Soldier and President* (1983–1984), 130, 128.

98. *1943 Winterset Boomerang* (yearbook), no page numbers.

99. *Iowa Legionnaire,* April 6, 1945, 5; Ambrose, *Citizen Soldiers,* 159. The information in this paragraph and the following are from miscellaneous documents in the Harry H. Smith and Harold L. Smith scrapbook in the Madison County Historical Society.

100. George L. from "the West Coast" to Mrs. Smith, letter on Thunderbird Motor Inn stationery from Washington, October 24, 1984, and clipping with photo dated July 11, 1951, Smith and Smith Scrapbook, Madison County Historical Society.

101. Iowa World War II Monument, pledge handout available at the site, near the Capitol Building in Des Moines, Iowa.

~ Chapter 4. "Mrs. America's Mission: The Kitchen Front"

1. *Des Moines Register,* January 25, 1942, sec. 3, 1.

2. *Des Moines Tribune,* March 30, 1943, 6.

3. *American Cookery,* March 1943, 316, 317.

4. Ibid., 292.

5. *Better Homes and Gardens,* February 1942, 5; *Practical Home Economics,* March 1943, 87; *Life,* November 24, 1941, 66, 67; Wright, "Soldier and His Food," in *What They Didn't Teach You about World War II,* 26–27; *Good Housekeeping,* April 1942, 4.

6. *Iowa Parent-Teacher,* November 1941, 30; *Life,* September 21, 1941, 78; *Independent Woman,* December 1942, 380.

7. Ann Oakley, *The Sociology of Housework* (1974), 29.

8. *Burlington Hawk-Eye Gazette,* July 27, 1943, 5.

9. *Kitchen-Klatter,* July 1941, 10; and October 1941, 12; *Good Housekeeping,* February 1942, 19; *Ladies' Home Journal,* April 1942, 109; *Red Oak Express,* November 8, 1943, 6; *Red Oak Sun,* July 2, 1942, 3.

10. *Kitchen-Klatter,* February 1943, 2; and August 1943, 2.

11. Evelyn Birkby, *Neighboring on the Air: Cooking with the KMA Radio Homemakers* (1991), 87, 97; Susan Puckett, *A Cook's Tour of Iowa* (1990), 11.

12. *Saturday Evening Post,* June 6, 1942, 91; "Victory Home Food Supply," Iowa State College pamphlet #23, Agricultural Extension Service, Iowa State University Archives, Ames.

13. Iowa State College Home Economics Extension Service Publications, vol. 12, pt. 1 (1911–1945), Iowa State University Archives; *Saturday Evening Post,* August 22, 1942, 77; June 13, 1942, 68; and June 6, 1942, 92, 93; *Practical Home Economics,* April 1942, 157; *Des Moines Register,* January 4, 1943, 7; *Independent Woman,* July 1942, 220; *News for Homemakers,* WOI, Ames, August 14, 1944.

14. Margot Murphy, *Wartime Meals: How to Plant Them, How to Buy Them, How to Cook Them,* 2; Terkel, *"The Good War,"* 224.

15. *Burlington Hawk-Eye Gazette,* August 4, 1942, 21; and July 8, 1942, 6.

16. Ibid., March 16, 1943, 6; March 15, 1943, 9; March 12, 1943, 9; March 13, 1943, 10; and May 7, 1943, 5, 7.

17. Duis and LaFrance, *We've Got a Job to Do,* 18; Anderson, *Wartime Women,* 155; M. Joyce Baker, *Images of Women in Film: The War Years, 1941–1945,* 4; Watters, *Illinois in the Second World War,* 346; Paul Fussell, *Wartime: Understanding and Behavior in the Second World War* (1989), 198, 195.

18. Richard Collier, *The Road to Pearl Harbor: 1941* (1981), 2, 3; Rayness Minns, *Bombers and Mash: The Domestic Front, 1939–1945* (1980), 86; Robert Kee, *1945: The World We Fought For* (1985), 37; Watters, *Illinois in the Second World War,* 331; Erenberg and Hirsch, *The War in American Culture,* 17.

19. Ann Starett, "Rationing Is Women's Job," *Independent Woman* (May 1942), 137–38; Duis and LaFrance, *We've Got a Job to Do,* 5; *Des Moines Register,* May 4, 1943, 7; *Time,* June 21, 1943, 64; Anderson, *Wartime Women,* 87; Weatherford, *American Women and World War II,* 206, 215, 216.

20. *Life,* February 7, 1944, 22; *Des Moines Tribune,* May 15, 1942, 17; February 22, 1943, 7; and February 23, 1944, 9.

21. Kennett, *For the Duration,* 183; *Des Moines Register,* February 21,

1943, sec. 3, 1; March 25, 1943, 1; and April 10, 1943, 1; *Des Moines Tribune,* November 25, 1942, sec. A, 35; and April 1, 1943, 4.

22. Paul Casdorph, *Let the Good Times Roll: Life at Home in America during World War II* (1989), 81; Mary Martha Thomas, *Riveting and Rationing in Dixie: Alabama Women and the Second World War* (1987), 96; *Des Moines Tribune,* January 1, 1943, 1; Phillips, *The 1940s,* 87, 104.

23. *Des Moines Register,* December 28, 1942, 1; and February 21, 1943, Iowa News sec., 5; *Winterset News,* February 18, 1943, 1; and April 22, 1943, 4; *Red Oak Express,* January 21, 1943, 1.

24. *Winterset News,* February 18, 1943, 3; ration book issued to Lena Moore, Montgomery County Historical Society, Red Oak, Iowa; collection of No. 2, 3, and 4 ration books, Madison County Historical Society; ration book issued to Lois J. Fitch, Military Box, Nodaway Valley Historical Museum, Clarinda, Iowa.

25. Sugar purchase certificate, World War II–Korea File, Madison County Historical Society; *Collier's,* April 11, 1942, 21; *Burlington Hawk-Eye Gazette,* February 4, 1942, 1; *Practical Home Economics,* May 1942, 188; *Independent Woman,* May 1942, 137.

26. *Prairie Farmer,* April 5, 1941, 39; *News for Homemakers,* WOI, Ames, October 28, 1944; *Farmer's Journal,* August 1945, 50; *Winterset News,* April 23, 1942, 4.

27. Frank E. Huggett, *"Goodnight Sweetheart": Songs and Memories of the Second World War* (1979), 128; *Winterset News,* September 11, 1941, 1; and March 11, 1943, 7; *Red Oak Sun,* July 12, 1945, 8; *Winterset Madisonian,* September 10, 1941, 1; and April 15, 1942, 5.

28. Martha Duncan, *On the Home Front* (radio show), WOI, Ames, Iowa, April 26, 1945, Script No. 275, Iowa State University Archives; Marion White, *Sweets without Sugar* (1942), 9.

29. Grover J. Sims, *Meat and Meat Animals in World War II* (1951), 11; Rae, *Cooking without Meat,* 11; *Burlington Hawk-Eye Gazette,* September 1, 1942, 1; *Winterset News,* March 4, 1943, 4.

30. *Red Oak Sun,* March 4, 1943, 6; and April 27, 1944, 6; *Winterset News,* March 4, 1943, 7.

31. Duis and LaFrance, *We've Got a Job to Do,* 23; Satterfield, *The Home Front,* 177; *Winterset News,* April 1, 1943, 4; and June 3, 1943, 6; *Iowa Farm Bureau Spokesman,* January 16, 1943, 1; January 9, 1943, 7; January 23, 1943, 7, 9; March 6, 1943, 8; February 27, 1943, 8; and January 30,

1943, 10.

32. Rae, *Cooking without Meat,* x.

33. *Des Moines Register,* June 18, 1945, World War II vertical file, Des Moines Public Library; Duncan, *On The Home Front* (radio show), "Stretching Fats and Oils," WOI, Ames, Iowa, Transcript No. 279, Iowa State University Archives; *Iowa Farm Bureau Spokesman,* November 18, 1944, 1; *American Cookery,* April 1945, 16, 17.

34. O. H. Brownlee, "Putting Dairying on a War Footing"; *Time,* October 11, 1943, 40; *Kossuth County Advance,* February 10, 1944, sec. A, 2.

35. Watters, *Illinois in the Second World War,* 334, 338; Elizabeth Clarkson Swart, "The Front Row," *Des Moines Tribune,* August 23, 1974, 13.

36. *Des Moines Tribune,* November 20, 1942, 4; *Des Moines Register,* April 12, 1942, sec. 9, 2.

37. *Business Week,* November 28, 1942, 62; *Burlington Hawk-Eye Gazette,* November 24, 1942, 14; *Business Week,* December 5, 1942, 32; *Winterset News,* January 21, 1943, 5.

38. *Red Oak Express,* June 28, 1943, 1; *Winterset News,* February 4, 1943, 3; *Burlington Hawk-Eye Gazette,* July 29, 1943, 2; *Red Oak Sun,* December 21, 1944, 6.

39. *Time,* March 8, 1943, 18; *New York Times,* February 23, 1943, 16; *Kitchen-Klatter,* January 1943, 1.

40. *Red Oak Express,* December 31, 1945, 1; Sims, *Meat and Meat Animals,* 13; *Des Moines Register,* January 7, 1946, 4; January 17, 1946, 1; and January 25, 1946, 7.

41. David M. Tucker, *Kitchen Gardening in America: A History* (1993), 175, 177; *Iowa Gardens,* 1941, 3.

42. *Prairie Farmer,* February 21, 1942, 5.

43. *Farm Journal,* February 1942, 26.

44. *Life,* March 30, 1942, 81; *Winterset News,* May 24, 1942, 2.

45. Kennett, *For the Duration,* 185; *Des Moines Register,* May 8, 1942, 7; *Iowa Gardens,* 1942, 46; *Farm Journal,* January 1943, 19; Bruce C. Smith, *The War Comes to Plum Street* (2005), 114.

46. Tucker, *Kitchen Gardening,* 134, 139, 136; *Independent Woman,* April 1944, 121.

47. *Iowa Farm Bureau Spokesman,* December 9, 1944, 6; Iowa State Department of Agriculture, *1943 Iowa Year Book of Agriculture,* 187.

48. *Prairie Farmer,* March 6, 1943, 1; *Newsweek,* February 14, 1944, 39;

Winterset News, April 1, 1943, 1.

49. *Burlington Hawk-Eye Gazette,* June 8, 1943, 2; *Iowa Agriculturist,* April 1943, 8, 9.

50. *Iowa Homemaker,* May 1942, 24; *News for Homemakers,* WOI, Ames, December 1, 1944.

51. *Independent Woman,* April 1944, 102; *Iowa Gardens,* 1943, 5.

52. Iowa State Department of Agriculture, *1944 Iowa Year Book of Agriculture,* 344; *Des Moines Tribune,* January 4, 1945, World War II vertical file, Des Moines Public Library; O'Neill, *A Democracy at War,* 137; Watters, *Illinois in the Second World War,* 278; *Iowa Gardens,* 1944, 3.

53. *Des Moines Register,* August 22, 1944, 3; *Iowa Parent-Teacher,* July–August 1943, 1.

54. *Kerr Canning Book,* introduction; Steve M. Barkin, "Fighting the Cartoon War: Information Strategies in World War II," *Journal of American Culture* 7 (Spring/Summer 1984): 113; Susan Strasser, *Never Done: A History of American Housework* (1982), 22, 23; *American Cookery,* August/September 1942, 46; *Better Homes and Gardens,* May 1943, 111; *Ladies' Home Journal,* August 1945, 64; *Farm Journal,* May 1944, 99.

55. *House and Garden's Wartime Manual for the Home* (1943), 94; *Better Homes and Gardens,* July 1944, 68; Demetria M. Taylor, *Complete Book of Home Canning* (1943), 1, 2; *Des Moines Register,* July 12, 1943, 6; September 26, 1943, sec. H, 19; and November 7, 1943, Iowa sec., 8.

56. *Winterset News,* May 20, 1943, 1; and June 3, 1943, 7; *News for Homemakers,* WOI, Ames, May 17, 1944; and May 28, 1944; *Prairie Farmer,* May 31, 1941, 13.

57. *Good Housekeeping,* June 1942, 111; *Iowa Bureau Farmer,* August 1943, 8; *News for Homemakers,* WOI, Ames, October 1, 1943.

58. *Winterset News,* May 28, 1942, 1; *Farm Journal,* August 1944, 42; *News for Homemakers,* WOI, Ames, May 6, 1944; May 10, 1944; and August 5, 1944.

59. *Winterset News,* July 29, 1943, 1; *Farm Science Reporter,* April 1944, 8; *Iowa Homemaker,* March 1944, 14; *Better Iowa Homes,* May 3, 1943, 1; *News for Homemakers,* WOI, Ames, August 16, 1943; and May 2, 1944.

60. *American Cookery,* March 1944, 30; William A. Lydgate, ed., *What Our People Think* (1944), 69; Duncan, *On the Home Front* (radio show), "A General Talk on Home Food Preservation," WOI, Ames, Iowa, Transcript No. 287, Iowa State University Archives; *Des Moines Register,*

December 31, 1944, World War II vertical file, Des Moines Public Library; *Business Week,* March 4, 1944, 24; *Des Moines Register,* July 17, 1946, 10; Duncan, *On the Home Front,* WOI, Ames, Iowa, Transcript No. 257, Iowa State University Archives.

61. Robert Heide and John Gilman, *Home Front America: Popular Culture of the World War II Era* (1995), 26; *House and Garden's Wartime Manual for the Home,* 91; Anne Pierce, ed., *Home Canning for Victory* (1942), xii.

62. *Farm Journal,* August 1945, cover; *Des Moines Tribune,* July 14, 1944, 6; Taylor, *Complete Book of Home Canning,* v; *Kitchen-Klatter,* October 1944, 2; Eleanor Arnold, ed., *Voices of American Homemakers* (1985), 145.

63. *Iowa Farm Bureau Spokesman,* April 13, 1946, 9; *Des Moines Register,* March 2, 1946, 7.

64. *Des Moines Tribune,* November 14, 1946, 17; and March 16, 1946, 1; *Winterset Madisonian,* April 24, 1946, 11.

65. *Wallaces' Farmer,* August 17, 1946, 28; Duncan, *On the Home Front,* WOI, Ames, Iowa, September 29, 1945, Script No. 311, Iowa State University Archives; *Winterset Madisonian,* July 31, 1946, 4, 5.

66. Alice B. Winn-Smith, *Thrifty Cooking for Wartime* (1942), viii, ix; *Good Housekeeping,* June 1943, 164; and October 1943, 147, 111.

67. Cardozier, *Mobilization of the United States,* 100; Nancy Shea, *The Waacs* (New York: Harper & Brothers, 1943); *Palimpsest* 28 (December 1947): 367; *Practical Home Economics,* May 1945, 261.

68. *Good Housekeeping,* April 1943, 165, 71.

69. *Better Homes and Gardens,* November 1943, 61; O'Neill, *A Democracy at War,* 134; *Ladies' Home Journal,* August 1943, 104.

70. *Ladies' Home Journal,* March 1943, 106; Helen Burke, *War-Time Kitchen* (1943), 9; *Burlington Hawk-Eye Gazette,* May 15, 1943, 7.

71. *Iowa Farm Bureau Spokesman,* February 6, 1943, 4; *News for Homemakers,* WOI, Ames, December 8, 1943.

72. Margaret Randolph Higonnet, Jane Jensen, Sonya Michel, and Margaret Collins Weitz, eds., *Behind the Lines: Gender and the Two World Wars* (1987), 1.

73. Baker, *Images of Women in Film,* 132, 133, 43; *Des Moines Tribune,* April 29, 1943, 19.

74. Fromkin, *In the Time of the Americans,* 381; Ellen M. Plante, *The*

American Kitchen, 1700 to the Present: From Hearth to Highrise (1995), 28.

75. Maureen Honey, *Creating Rosie the Riveter: Class, Gender, and Propaganda during World War II* (1984), 135; *Des Moines Tribune*, May 29, 1942, 4. For examples of the Avon advertisements, see *Ladies' Home Journal*, August 1943, 97; September 1943, 95; November 1943, 125; January 1944, 75; May 1944, 106; August 1944, 97; September 1944, 114; *Good Housekeeping*, June 1943, 105; December 1943, 154; February 1944, 166; April 1944, 113, 139; May 1944, 167; June 1944, 104; August 1944, 105; November 1944, 167; and *Better Homes and Gardens*, July 1943, 60; February 1944, 80; September 1944, 90; February 1945, 76.

76. Duis and LaFrance, *We've Got a Job to Do*, 18; *American Cookery*, March 1943, 294.

77. Ruth Schwartz Cowan, *More Work for Mother: The Ironies of Household Technology from the Open Hearth to the Microwave* (1983), 4, 7, 8; Ellen Malos, ed., *The Politics of Housework* (1980), 10, 29; Catherine Hall, "The History of the Housewife," in Malos, *The Politics of Housework*, 44–71; Campbell, *Women at War with America*, 165, 167; Thomas, *Riveting and Rationing in Dixie*, 99, and also chap. 6, "Housewives during Wartime."

78. *American Cookery*, October 1942, 108; *Business Week*, April 11, 1942, 37; and December 12, 1942, 56, 57.

79. Women's Interests Section, War Department, *The Soldier and His Housekeeping*, 6. The idea that housework is too trivial even to discuss, much less to write about, is recognized in Pat Mainardi's classic essay "The Politics of Housework," in Malos, ed., *The Politics of Housework*, 99–104.

80. Susan B. Anthony II, *Out of the Kitchen—Into the War: Women's Winning Role in the Nation's Drama* (1943), 206; Annette Chambers Noble, "Utah's Rosies: Women in the Utah War Industries during World War II," 130.

81. *Good Housekeeping*, June 1942, 107.

82. *Independent Woman*, October 1945, 279; *Farmers' Journal*, December 1945, 73; Susan M. Hartmann, "Prescriptions for Penelope: Literature on Women's Obligations to Returning World War II Veterans," 226, 224, 229; Amy Kesselman, *Fleeting Opportunities: Women Shipyard Workers in Portland and Vancouver during World War II and Reconversion*

(1990), 8; Leila J. Rupp, *Mobilizing Women for War: German and American Propaganda, 1939–1945* (1978), 156, 177–81.

83. *Kitchen-Klatter,* October 1943, 8; Campbell, *Women at War with America,* 181; *Kitchen-Klatter,* August 1943, 11; *Winterset News,* August 6, 1942, 8.

84. *Des Moines Register,* February 8, 1942, 1; *Des Moines Tribune,* June 13, 1942, 5; Duis and LaFrance, *We've Got a Job to Do,* 48; *Des Moines Register,* November 12, 1941, 10; *Winterset News,* April 30, 1942, 6.

85. Plante, *The American Kitchen,* 178; *Ladies' Home Journal,* September 1942, 60; *Iowa Legionnaire,* August 1, 1941, 3; Stan Cohen, *V for Victory: America's Home Front during World War II* (1991), 125; *American Cookery,* January 1943, 222.

86. *Des Moines Tribune,* August 6, 1942, 1, 5; and August 7, 1942, 1; *Burlington Hawk-Eye Gazette,* October 12, 1942, 2; and May 10, 1943, 2.

87. *Burlington Hawk-Eye Gazette,* May 17, 1943, 2; *Des Moines Register,* August 7, 1942, 8.

88. Hinshaw, *The Home Front,* 41; *Des Moines Tribune,* April 24, 1943, 4.

89. *Des Moines Tribune,* May 11, 1943, 2; January 17, 1944, 3; and February 19, 1945, 2; *Red Oak Express,* February 7, 1944, 4; March 3, 1944, 5; and June 19, 1944, 6; *Red Oak Sun,* May 3, 1945, 6; and January 21, 1943, 4.

90. *Des Moines Tribune,* May 29, 1944, 2; and April 5, 1944, 7; *Red Oak Sun,* August 23, 1945, 3; *Burlington Hawk-Eye Gazette,* July 2, 1942, 5.

91. *Winterset News,* August 6, 1942, 3; *Red Oak Sun,* April 5, 1945, 3; *Red Oak Express,* March 26, 1945, 3; *Red Oak Sun,* March 29, 1944, 2.

92. *Des Moines Register,* November 6, 1944, 7; *Red Oak Sun,* April 26, 1945, 6; May 17, 1945, 6; June 21, 1945, 3; and August 2, 1945, 7.

93. *Winterset Madisonian,* April 3, 1946, 11; and May 8, 1946, 3; *Des Moines Register,* January 1, 1946, 6; *Des Moines Tribune,* March 4, 1946, 4.

94. *Des Moines Register,* January 1, 1944, 5; *Winterset News,* September 10, 1942, 1.

95. *Kitchen-Klatter,* October 1942, 11.

96. *American Cookery,* May 1944, 77; Plante, *The American Kitchen,* 240, 260, 292.

97. *Good Housekeeping,* April 1943, 149; *Better Homes and Gardens,* June 1944, 51; *Saturday Evening Post,* May 6, 1944, 94; *Des Moines Register,* March 11, 1945, sec. X, 8; *Winterset News,* July 8, 1943, 6; *News for Homemakers,* WOI, Ames, November 8, 1945; *American Cookery,* February 1944, 27.

98. *Farm Journal,* July 1943, 49; *Successful Farming,* April 1943, 75.

99. *Wallaces' Farmer,* July 20, 1946, 22; and August 3, 1946, 44; *Successful Farming,* December 1943, 69; and March 1944, 85; *Better Homes and Gardens,* February 1944, 3; and April 1944, 3; *Saturday Evening Post,* May 27, 1944, 75; *Des Moines Register,* March 11, 1945, sec. 9, 6; *Life,* June 11, 1945, 105; *Winterset Madisonian,* September 25, 1946, 9.

100. *Red Oak Sun,* January 11, 1945, 7; *Farm Science Reporter,* April 1945, 11.

101. *Life,* February 19, 1945, 15; and June 11, 1945, 15.

102. *Des Moines Register,* August 25, 1946, sec. 9, 6; *Winterset Madisonian,* April 24, 1946, 10; *Wallaces' Farmer,* March 16, 1946, 32; and May 18, 1946, 30.

103. *Des Moines Tribune,* February 27, 1946, 1; *Iowa Farm Bureau Spokesman,* July 13, 1946, 10.

104. Blum, *V Was for Victory,* 301; *Better Homes and Gardens,* June 1943, 11; Honey, *Creating Rosie the Riveter,* 87; Erenberg and Hirsch, *The War in American Culture,* 155; Fox, *Madison Avenue Goes to War,* 78; Michael C. C. Adams, *The Best War Ever: America and World War II* (1994), 70; *Saturday Evening Post,* January 13, 1945, 65; Pyle, *Here Is Your War,* 15, 298.

105. Fox, *Madison Avenue Goes to War,* 75; *Good Housekeeping,* May 1945, 129; *American Cookery,* October 1944, 13; "The Wrigley Peace Pact of August 17, 1945," 3, Madison County Historical Society.

106. *Farm Journal,* December 1943, 48; Larrabee, *Commander in Chief,* 319.

107. Lucile Driftmier Verness, *The Story of an American Family* (1950), 70.

~ Conclusion

1. James MacGregor Burns, *Roosevelt: The Soldier of Freedom* (1970), 597.

2. Scrapbook purchased for the author's personal collection at the William F. and Blanche Easter Estate auction, Winterset, Iowa, January 11, 1997.

3. Annie Laurie Mohair and Doris Benardete, eds., *American Expression on the War and Peace* (1943), 10.

4. Earl R. Beck, *The European Home Fronts, 1939–1945* (1993), xii; *Clarinda Herald-Journal,* May 10, 1945, 1; *Red Oak Express,* May 10, 1945, 1; "*The Winterset Madisonian,* 100th Anniversary Edition, 1856–1956," 5, in World War II–Korea file, Madison County Historical Society.

5. *Des Moines Register,* September 10, 1944; and *Des Moines Tribune,* May 8, 1945, both in World War II vertical file, Des Moines Public Library.

6. Kee, *1945: The World We Fought For,* photo captions on 313 and 306; Moskin, *Mr. Truman's War,* 201.

7. *Des Moines Tribune,* August 20, 1945, 8.

8. *Winterset Madisonian,* August 15, 1945, 1; *Red Oak Express,* August 16, 1945, 1.

9. *Des Moines Tribune,* August 15, 1945, 11.

10. *Des Moines Register,* August 15, 1945, World War II Clippings File, State Historical Society of Iowa Archive; ceremony program, World War II vertical file, Des Moines Public Library.

11. *Red Oak Express,* December 13, 1945, 6.

12. *Life,* October 15, 1945, 29.

13. Satterfield, *The Home Front,* 3.

14. Terkel, quoted in Harris, Mitchell, and Schechter, *The Homefront,* 12.

15. Richard Polenberg, "The Good War? A Reappraisal of How World War II Affected American Society," 295, 296, 297.

16. For other insights, see Fussell's *Wartime,* 59, 142, 268; Albrecht's *World War II and the American Dream,* 250; both Warren F. Kimball's *Forged in War,* 9, and his *The Juggler: Franklin Roosevelt as Wartime Statesman,* 13; Norman Longmate's *The Home Front: An Anthology of Personal Experience, 1938–1945,* xiii; Kee's *1945: The World We Fought For,* xxvii; Miller's *The Irony of Victory,* 43; Erenberg and Hirsch's *The War in American Culture,* 105; Beck's *The European Home Fronts,* 133; Moskin's *Mr. Truman's War,* 128; Larrabee's *Commander in Chief,* 625, 627; O'Neill's *A Democracy at War,* 241; Martin Gilbert's *The Second World War: A Complete History,* 744; Winkler's *Home Front U.S.A.,* 2, 47; Casdorph's *Let the Good Times Roll,* 257; Fromkin's *In the Time of the Americans,* 313; Fox's *Madison Avenue Goes to War,* 3; Gerald F. Linderman's *The World within War: America's Combat Experience in World War II,* 302; Wynn's "The United States" in Noakes, ed., *The Civilian in*

War, 89; and Clayton James and Anne Sharp Wells's *From Pearl Harbor to V-J Day: The American Armed Forces in World War II,* 201.

17. *Des Moines Register,* December 8, 1946, sec. 4, 1; sec. L, 3.

18. *Des Moines Register,* January 2, 1946, 3; and June 23, 1946, sec. G, 9; *Iowa Legionnaire,* December 19, 1941, 5; and May 15, 1942, 8; "War, Conflict, or Campaign," *Palimpsest* 53 (April 1972); *Des Moines Register,* May 25, 1997, World War II vertical file, Ankeny Public Library.

19. *Iowa Farm Bureau Spokesman,* November 16, 1946, 1. Ten percent of Iowa's prewar population had served in the military.

20. Bessie Caudle, diary, 1940 volume, author's collection. Information in the following paragraphs is from the 1941, 1942, 1943, and 1945 volumes of Caudle's diary, also in author's collection. The volume for 1944 is missing from the collection. Caudle continued her daily entries until the late 1970s.

21. *Des Moines Register,* December 8, 1946, sec. 9, 2.

Bibliography

Wartime Sources

~ *Journal Articles*

Annals of Iowa Editorial Department. "Iowa Fighting Power Afloat." *Annals of Iowa* 24 (July 1942): 194–99.

Annals of Iowa Editorial Department. "War Memorial and Archives Building." *Annals of Iowa* 26 (April 1945): 307–11.

Annals of Iowa Editorial Department. "War Record Work in Iowa." *Annals of Iowa* 26 (July 1944): 61–63.

Bennett, M. K. "Essential Food Requirements in Wartime." *Journal of Farm Economics* 25 (November 1943): 835–47.

Black, John D. "American Agriculture in the New War and Defense Situation." *Journal of Farm Economics* 23 (1941): 28–36.

Brewster, John M. "Farm Technological Advance and Total Population Growth." *Journal of Farm Economics* 27 (August 1945): 509–25.

Canning, John B. "Foods for Defense." *Journal of Farm Economics* 23 (November 1941): 697–711.

Colton, Kenneth E. "Preserving War Records: The Iowa War Records Commission." *Annals of Iowa* 24 (July 1942): 84.

———. "That Our Memory May Be Green: The Iowa War Records Commission." *Annals of Iowa* 24 (July 1942): 91–104.

Deering, Charles C. "The Telephone in Iowa." *Annals of Iowa* 23 (April 1942): 287–308.

Gallaher, Ruth A. "Phil Stong's *Hawkeyes*." *Palimpsest* 21 (1940): 297–308.

Gallaher, Ruth A. "Pictures Are History." *Palimpsest* 27 (November 1946): 352–55.

Green, Constance. "The Role of Women as Production Workers in War Plants in Connecticut Valley." *Smith College Studies in History* 28 (1946): 1–78.

Hobson, Asher. "War Adjustments for American Agriculture." *Journal of Farm Economics* 22 (1940): 269–78.

Johnson, O. R. "The Family Farm." *Journal of Farm Economics* 26 (August 1944): 529–48.

Johnson, Sherman E. "Adapting Agricultural Programs for War Needs." *Journal of Farm Economics* 24 (February 1942): 1–16.

———. "Food Production Policies in Wartime." *Journal of Farm Economics* 25 (August 1943): 545–59.

Kimball, E. Smith. "Characteristics of U.S. Poultry Statistics." *Journal of Farm Economics* 22 (1940): 359–66.

Petersen, William J. "Agriculture and the AAA." *Palimpsest* 17 (August 1936): 255–61.

———. "The Beginnings of Davenport: Then and Now." *Palimpsest* 20 (August 1939): 273–80.

———. "The Beginnings of Dubuque: Then and Now." *Palimpsest* 21 (November 1940): 387–92.

———. "Iowa in 1936: Agriculture and Industry." *Palimpsest* 18 (August 1937): 262–69.

———. "The Political Potpourri." *Palimpsest* 16 (August 1936): 271–79.

———. "Remember Pearl Harbor." *Palimpsest* 23 (February 1942): 33–46.

Peterson, Arthur G. "Governmental Policy Relating to Farm Machinery in World War I." *Agricultural History* 17 (January 1943): 31–40.

Schwartz, Harry. "Hired Farm Labor in World War II." *Journal of Farm Economics* 24 (1942): 826–44.

Smith, Raymond C. "Social Effects of the War and the Defense Program on American Agriculture." *Journal of Farm Economics* 23 (1941): 15–27.

Swisher, J. A. "Remember Our Heroes." *Palimpsest* 23 (June 1942): 189–203.

Thornton, Harrison John. "State of the Union in 1946." *Palimpsest* 27 (January 1946): 1–18.

Books

Alsop, Joseph, and Robert Kintner. *American White Paper: The Story of American Diplomacy and the Second World War.* New York: Stratford, 1940.

Anderson, Sherwood. *Home Town.* New York: Alliance, 1940.

Anthony, Susan B., II. *Out of the Kitchen—Into the War: Women's Winning Role in the Nation's Drama.* New York: Stephen Daye, 1943.

Baker, Laura Nelson. *Wanted: Women in War Industry. The Complete Guide to a War Factory Job.* New York: E. P. Dutton, 1943.

Baker, O. E., Ralph Borsodi, and M. L. Wilson. *Agriculture in Modern Life.* New York: Harper & Brothers, 1939.

Barclay, Hartley W., ed. *How Your Business Can Help Win the War.* New York: Simon & Schuster, 1942.

Bayles, William D. *Caesars in Goose Step.* New York: Harper & Brothers, 1940.

Bourke-White, Margaret. *"Purple Heart Valley": A Combat Chronicle of the War in Italy.* New York: Simon & Schuster, 1944.

Bromfield, Louis. *Pleasant Valley.* Mattituck, NY: Aeonian, 1943.

———. *The World We Live In.* Philadelphia: Blakiston, 1944.

Burke, Helen. *War-Time Kitchen.* London: Hutchinson, 1943.

Campbell, Levin H., Jr. *The Industry Ordnancy Team.* New York: Whittlesey House, 1946.

Carpenter, Allan. *Between Two Rivers: Iowa, Year by Year, 1846–1939.* Mason City, IA: Klipto Loose Leaf, 1940.

Cherne, Leo M. *Your Business Goes to War.* Boston: Houghton Mifflin, 1942.

Cora, Rose, and Bob Brown. *The Country Cookbook.* New York: A. S. Barnes, 1937.

Corey, Paul. *Acres of Antaeus.* New York: Henry Holt, 1946.

———. *Buy an Acre: America's Second Front.* New York: Dial, 1944.

Corson, John J. *Manpower for Victory: Total Mobilization for Total War.* New York: Farrar & Rhinehart, Inc., 1943.

Croy, Homer. *Corn Country.* New York: Duell, Sloan, & Pearce, 1947.

Davis, Forrest, and Ernest K. Lindley. *How War Came: An American*

White Paper; From the Fall of France to Pearl Harbor. New York: Simon & Schuster, 1942.
Dos Passos, John. *State of the Nation.* Boston: Houghton Mifflin, 1944.
Dryer, Sherman H. *Radio in Wartime.* New York: Greenberg, 1942.
Faulkner, Edward H. *Plowman's Folly.* Norman: University of Oklahoma Press, 1943.
Fleming, D. F. *While America Slept: A Contemporary Analysis of World Events from the Fall of France to Pearl Harbor.* New York: Abingdon-Cokesbury, 1944.
Flynn, Edward. *You're the Boss.* New York: Viking, 1947.
Flynn, Elizabeth Gurley. *Women in the War.* New York: Workers Library Publishers, Inc., 1942.
Fowler, Bertram. *Food: A Weapon for Victory.* Boston: Little, Brown, 1942.
Garwood, Darrell. *Artists in Iowa: A Life of Grant Wood.* Westport, CT: Greenwood, 1942.
Gibbs, Philip. *America Speaks.* Garden City, NY: Doubleday, Doran, 1942.
Giles, Nell. *Punch In, Susie! A Woman's War Factory Diary.* New York: Harper & Brothers, 1942.
Given, Meta. *The Modern Family Cook Book.* Chicago: J. G. Ferguson, 1942.
Grafton, Samuel. *An American Diary.* Garden City, NJ: Doubleday, Doran, 1943.
Heath, Ambrose. *Kitchen Front Recipes and Hints: Extracts from the First Seven Months Early Morning Broadcasts.* London: Adam and Charles Black, 1941.
———. *More Kitchen Front Recipes. Further Extracts from the Early Morning Broadcasts with Other Recipes and Hints.* London: Adam and Charles Black, 1941.
Henderson, Harry B., and Herman C. Movis. *War in Our Time.* Garden City, NJ: Doubleday, Doran, 1942.
Hershey, John. *Hiroshima.* New York: Alfred A. Knopf, 1946.
Hinshaw, David. *The Home Front.* New York: G. P. Putnam's Sons, 1943.
Hopkins, John A. *Elements of Farm Management.* New York: Prentice-Hall, 1937.
Hutton, Graham. *Midwest at Noon.* Chicago: University of Chicago, 1946.

Iowa Development Commission. *Iowa . . . Land of Industrial Opportunity.* Des Moines: Iowa Development Commission, 1946.
Iowa's Industrial Survey. *The Book of Iowa.* Des Moines: State of Iowa, 1932.
Iowa State College, Members of the Staff and the Iowa Agricultural Experiment Station. *A Century of Farming in Iowa, 1846–1946.* Ames: Iowa State College Press, 1946.
Kantor, MacKinlay. *Happy Land.* New York: Coward-McCann, 1942.
Lerner, Max. *Public Journal: Marginal Notes on Wartime America.* New York: Viking, 1945.
Lewis, Faye Cashatt, M.D. *Doc's Wife.* New York: Macmillan, 1940.
Lindbergh, Anne Morrow. *The Wave of the Future: A Confession of Faith.* New York: Harcourt, Brace, 1940.
Lydgate, William A., ed. *What Our People Think.* New York: Thomas Y. Crowell, 1944.
Maddox, Gaynor, ed. *Russian Cook Book for American Homes.* New York: Russian War Relief, 1942.
Markham, R. H. *The Wave of the Past.* Chapel Hill, NC: University of North Carolina Press, 1941.
McCune, Wesley. *The Farm Bloc.* Garden City, NJ: Doubleday, Doran, 1943.
McWilliams, Carey. *Ill Fares the Land: Migrants and Migratory Labor in the United States.* Boston: Little, Brown, 1942.
Menefee, Selden. *Assignment U.S.A.* New York: Reynal & Hitchcock, 1943.
Merrill, Francis E. *Social Problems on the Home Front: A Study of War-Time Influences.* New York: Harper & Brothers, 1948.
Merton, Robert K. *Mass Persuasion: The Social Psychology of a War Bond Drive.* With the Assistance of Marjorie Fiske and Alberta Curtis. New York: Harper & Brothers, 1946.
Millis, Walter. *Why Europe Fights.* New York: Morrow, 1940.
Mohair, Annie Laurie, and Doris Benardete, eds. *American Expression on the War and Peace.* New York: American Book, 1943.
Muntz, Otto S. *Iowa: The Future Inland Empire.* Greater Iowa Commission State of Iowa Report. Des Moines: State of Iowa, 1936.
Murphy, Margot [Jane Holt]. *Wartime Meals: How to Plant Them, How to Buy Them, How to Cook Them.* New York: Greenberg, 1942.
Nelson, Daniel. *Farm and Factory: Workers in the Midwest, 1880–1990.*

Bloomington: Indiana University Press, 1995.
Ogburn, William Fielding, ed. *American Society in Wartime.* Charles R. Walgreen Foundation Lectures. Chicago: University of Chicago Press, 1943.
Perkins, Frances. *The Roosevelt I Knew.* New York: Viking, 1946.
Pierce, Anne, ed. *Home Canning for Victory.* New York: M. Barrows, 1942.
Pyle, Ernie. *Brave Men.* New York: Henry Holt, 1944.
——. *Here is Your War.* New York: Henry Holt, 1943.
——. *Last Chapter.* New York: Henry Holt, 1945.
Rae, Barbara. *Cooking without Meat: A Supplementary Kitchen Guide for War-Time Cookery.* New York: M. S. Mill, 1943.
Saunders, Hilary St. George. *Pioneers! O Pioneers!* New York: Macmillan, 1944.
Schmidt, Carl T. *American Farmers in the World Crisis.* New York: Oxford University Press, 1941.
Schultz, Theodore W. *Agriculture in an Unstable Economy.* New York: McGraw-Hill, 1945.
Steele, Evelyn. *Wartime Opportunities for Women.* New York: E. P. Dutton, 1943.
Stegner, Wallace, and the Editors of *Look. One Nation.* Boston: Houghton Mifflin, 1945.
Steinbeck, John. *The Moon Is Down.* New York: Viking, 1942.
Stong, Phil. *Hawkeyes: A Biography of the State of Iowa.* New York: Dodd, Mead, 1940.
——. *One Destiny.* New York: Reynal & Hitchcock, 1942.
Struther, Jan. *Mrs. Miniver.* New York: Harcourt, Brace, 1940.
Swisher, Jacob A. *Iowa—In Times of War.* Iowa City, IA: State Historical Society of Iowa, 1943.
Taylor, Demetria M. *Complete Book of Home Canning.* New York: Greenberg, 1943.
Tolley, Howard R. *The Farmer Citizen at War.* New York: Macmillan, 1943.
Wallace, Henry A. *The American Choice.* New York: Reynal & Hitchcock, 1940.
Wallace, Zela. *On Such a Night.* New York: Henry Harrison, Poetry Publisher, 1940.

West, James. *Plainville, U.S.A.* New York: Columbia University Press, 1945.

White, Marion. *Sweets without Sugar.* New York: M. S. Mill, 1942.

Willkie, Wendell L. *One World.* New York: Simon & Schuster, 1943.

Winn-Smith, Alice B. *Thrifty Cooking for Wartime.* New York: Macmillan, 1942.

Wolfe, Jack. *A Century with Iowa Jewry, 1833–1940.* Des Moines: Iowa Printing & Supply, 1941.

~ *Pamphlets and Government Publications*

American Can Company. *Wartime Recipes from Canned Foods.* Wartime Household Guides and Recipe Book Collection, Department of Special Collections, Parks Library, Iowa State University Archives, Ames, IA.

American Gas Association. *Victory Canning in the Home.* Wartime Household Guides and Recipe Book Collection, Department of Special Collections, Parks Library, Iowa State University Archives, Ames, IA.

Anderson, C. Arnold. "Food Rationing and Morale." *Wartime Farm and Food Policy, No. 4.* Ames: Iowa State College Press, 1943.

Aunt Jenny's Wartime Better Cook Club. *Delicious Desserts Every Day in Spite of Rationing.* Wartime Household Guides and Recipe Book Collection, Department of Special Collections, Parks Library, Iowa State University Archives, Ames, IA.

Baker, Helen. *Women in War Industries.* Princeton, NJ: Princeton University, 1942.

Better Homes Gardening. *Handbook for the Garden: Cultural Information on Vegetables—Flowers—Bulbs—Shrubs—Fruit.* Minneapolis, MN: Northrup King, 1944.

Blair, Gladys, ed. *Meat S-T-R-E-T-C-H-E-R-S. 125 Tested Recipes.* Chicago: The Prairie Press (*Prairie Farmer* Publishing Company), 1943.

Brownlee, O. H. "Putting Dairying on a War Footing." Rev. ed. *Wartime Farm and Food Policy, No. 5.* Ames: Iowa State College Press, 1944.

Bunce, Arthur C. "Using Our Soils for War Production." *Wartime Farm and Food Policy, No. 7.* Ames: Iowa State College Press, 1943.

Burke, Sandra Charvat, and Willia Goudy. *Women in Iowa: 1980 and a Century of Perspective.* Extension Publication, 1980, Iowa State University Archives, Ames, IA.

Duffy-Mott Company. *Real Ideas of Real Housewives on Wartime Living.* New York: Duffy Mott Company, 1942.

Gifford, Marie. *Defense of Health with Economy Meats.* Chicago: Armour, 1942.

A Guide to Burlington, Iowa. Federal Writers Project, WPA, State of Iowa. Des Moines: A Cres-Blackmar Company, 1939.

Harness, Chas. W., Commissioner. *Report of the Bureau of Labor for the Biennial Period Ending June 30, 1940.* Des Moines: State of Iowa, 1940.

Heath, Ambrose. *How to Cook in Wartime.* London: Eyre & Spittiswoode, 1942.

Home Economics Institute. *Health for Victory: How to Pack Lunch Boxes for War Workers.* Mansfield, OH: Westinghouse Electric and Manufacturing Co., 1943.

Home Economics Institute. *Health for Victory Club. Early Summer Home Canning.* Mansfield, OH: Westinghouse Electric and Manufacturing Co., 1943.

Home Economics Institute. *Health for Victory Club. Meal Planning Guide.* Mansfield, OH: Westinghouse Electric and Manufacturing Co., 1942.

Home Economics Institute. *Home Canning Guide.* Mansfield, OH: Westinghouse Electric and Manufacturing Co., 1944.

Home Economics Institute. *Meal Planning Guide.* Mansfield, OH: Westinghouse Electric and Manufacturing Co., 1943.

House and Garden. House and Garden's Wartime Manual for the Home. Greenwich, CT: Conde Nast, 1943. Iowa State University Archives, Ames, IA.

Iowa Centennial, Des Moines County Committee. *Burlington . . . Then and Now.* Burlington, IA: McMullin & Woelhaf, 1946.

Iowa Dairy Industry Commission. *Food for Victory: New Dairy Recipes.* Chicago: National Dairy Council, 1942.

Iowa State College of Agriculture, Ames. Cooperative Extension Work in Agriculture and Home Economics. *Aids in County Extension Program Planning, 1943–1944.*

Iowa State Department of Agriculture. 1940–1946 *Iowa Year Book of Agriculture.* Des Moines: State of Iowa, 1940–1946.

Maytag Company. *Yesterday, Today, and Tomorrow.* Newton, IA: The Maytag Company, 1945.

McKelvey, Thelma. *America in a World at War, No. 22.* Women in War Production. New York: Oxford University Press, 1942.

Moe, Edward O., and Carl C. Taylor. *Culture of a Contemporary Rural Community: Irwin, Iowa.* Rural Life Studies 5. U.S. Department of Agriculture, Bureau of Agricultural Economics, December 1942.

Murray, William G. "Land Boom Controls." *Wartime Farm and Food Policy, No. 9.* Ames: Iowa State College Press, 1943.

National Livestock and Meat Board. *Meat in the Meal for Health Defense.* Chicago: National Livestock and Meat Board, 1942.

National Livestock and Meat Board. *Variety Meats: Recipes for Heart, Liver, Kidney, Sweetbreads, Tongue, Tripe, and Brains.* Chicago: National Livestock and Meat Board, date unknown.

National Livestock and Meat Board. *Wartime Meat Recipe Book: Meat Pointers.* Chicago: National Livestock and Meat Board, date unknown.

Palmer, Albert W., Frank W. McCulloch, and Stoddard Lane. *Social Action: Labor Troubles and the Local Church.* New York: Council for Social Action of the Congregational and Christian Churches, 1939.

Pidgeon, Mary Elizabeth. *Women in the Economy of the United States of America: A Summary Report.* Washington, DC: United States Government Printing Office, 1937.

Rasmussen, Wayne D. *A History of the Emergency Farm Labor Supply Program, 1943–1947.* Agricultural Monograph No. 13. Washington, DC: U.S. Department of Agriculture, September 1951.

Schickele, Rainer. "Manpower in Agriculture." *Wartime Farm and Food Policy, No. 3.* Ames: Iowa State College Press, 1943.

Schultz, Theodore W. "Farm Prices for Food Production." *Wartime Farm and Food Policy, No. 2.* Ames: Iowa State College Press, 1943.

Shaw, L. M., ed. *State of Iowa: Official Register, 1941–1942.* Des Moines: State of Iowa, 1942.

Shepherd, Geoffrey. "Agricultural Prices after the War." *Wartime Farm and Food Policy, No. 11.* Ames: Iowa State College Press, 1945.

Shirer, William L. *An August to Remember: A Historian Remembers the Last Days of World War II and the End of the World That Was.* West Stockbridge, NY: Thornwillow, 1986.

Sims, Grover J. *Meat and Meat Animals in World War II.* Agricultural Monograph No. 9. Washington, DC: United States Department of Agriculture, February 1951.

U.S. Congress. Senate. Committee on Banking and Currency. *Conversion of Small Business Enterprises to War,* Production Hearings, 77th Cong., 2nd sess., 1942, S. 2250. Washington, DC: U.S. Government Printing Office, 1942.

U.S. Office of War Information. *Small Town U.S.A.* Washington, DC: Public Affairs Press, no year stated.

U.S. Office of War Information. *Surplus War Property.* Washington, DC: Public Affairs Press, 1944.

War Production Board. *Converting Industry: Turning a Nation's Production to War.* Washington, DC: Division of Information, 1942.

Women's Interests Section, War Department, Bureau of Public Relations. *The Soldier and His Food.* Washington, DC: U.S. Government Printing Office, 1942.

Women's Interests Section, War Department, Bureau of Public Relations. *The Soldier and His Housekeeping.* Washington, DC: U.S. Government Printing Office, 1942.

Iowa State Planning Board, Business Research Committee. *Social and Economic Statistics: Distribution of Business.* Iowa: Iowa State Planning Board, 1939.

Postwar Sources

~ *Journal Articles*

Alexander, Thomas G. "Utah War Industry during World War II: A Human Impact Analysis." *Utah Historical Quarterly* 51 (Winter 1983): 72–92.

Allen, Susan L. "Preparing Women for the National Crisis: The Role of Oklahoma A and M College." *Chronicles of Oklahoma* 69 (Winter 1992): 392–407.

Anderson, Karen Tucker. "Last Hired, First Fired: Black Women Workers during World War II." *Journal of American History* 69 (June 1982): 82–97.

Andrews, Clarence. "Sheldon, Iowa, during World War II." *Palimpsest 70* (Fall 1989): 146–55.

Ankli, Robert E. "Horses vs. Tractors on the Corn Belt." *Agricultural*

History 54 (January 1980): 134–48.

Aruga, Natsuki. "'An' Finish School': Child Labor during World War II." *Labor History* 29 (Fall 1988): 498–520.

Atherton, Lewis. "The Farm Novel and Agricultural History: A Review." *Agricultural History* 40 (April 1966): 131–40.

Atherton, Lewis. "The Midwestern Country Town—Myth and Reality." *Agricultural History* 26 (July 1952): 73–80.

Barkin, Steve M. "Fighting the Cartoon War. Information Strategies in World War II." *Journal of American Culture* 7 (Spring/Summer 1984): 113–17.

Bernstein, Barton J. "The Postwar Famine and Price Control, 1946." *Agricultural History* 38 (October 1964): 235–40.

Blum, Albert A. "The Farmer, the Army and the Draft." *Agricultural History* 38 (October 1964): 34–42.

Blum, John M. "United Against: American Culture and Society during World War II." In *The Harmon Memorial Lectures in Military History, 1959–1987,* ed. Lt. Col. Harry R. Borowski. Washington, DC: Offices of Air Force History, 1988.

Brcak, Nancy, and John R. Pavia. "Racism in Japanese and U.S. Wartime Propaganda." *Historian* 56 (Summer 1994): 671–84.

Brown, William R. "The American Girl and the Christmas Tree: World War II Soldier Poets Look at What the G.I.s Were Fighting For." *Journal of American Culture* 8 (Summer 1985): 25–30.

Buffum, Hazel P. "Iowa Federation of Women's Clubs—Ideas and Achievements." *Palimpsest* 34 (May 1953): 239–49.

Cavert, William L. "The Technological Revolution in Agriculture, 1910–1955." *Agricultural History* 30 (January 1956): 18–27.

Chase, Edwin Percy. "Forty Years of Main Street." *Iowa Journal of History and Politics* 34, no. 3, 227–61.

Cheever, L. O. "Industries of Iowa: Comments on Eleven Years." *Palimpsest* 43 (March 1967): 93–96.

Clive, Alan. "The Michigan Farmer in World War II." *Michigan History* 60 (1976): 291–314.

———. "Women Workers in World War II: Michigan as a Test Case." *Labor History* 20 (Winter 1979): 44–72.

Corbett, William P. "'They Hired Every Farm in the County': Establishing the Prisoner of War Camp at Tonkawa." *Chronicles of Oklahoma*

69 (Winter 1992): 368–91.

Curtis, Peter H. "A Place of Peace in a World of War: The Scattergood Refugee Hostel, 1939–1943." *Palimpsest* 65 (March/April 1984): 42–52.

Davidson, J. Brownlee. "Influence of Farm Machinery." *Palimpsest* 31 (March 1950): 113–17.

Dembo, Jonathan. "Washington State Labor Politics during World War II, 1942–1945." *Journal of the West* 25 (July 1986): 44–58.

Doenecke, Justus D. "Verne Marshall's Leadership of the No Foreign War Committee, 1940." *Annals of Iowa* 41 (Winter 1973): 1153–72.

Dooley, Patricia. "Gopher Ordnance Works: Condemnation, Construction, and Community Response." *Minnesota History* 49 (Summer 1985): 214–28.

Drache, Hiram. "Midwest Agriculture: Changing with Technology." *Agricultural History* 50 (January 1976): 290–302.

Dyson, Lowell K. "Was Agricultural Distress in the 1930s a Result of Land Speculation during World War I? The Case of Iowa." *Annals of Iowa* 40 (Spring 1971): 577–84.

Fox-Genovese, Elizabeth. "Mixed Messages: Women and the Impact of World War II." *Southern Humanities Review* 27 (Summer 1993): 235–45.

Frank, Miriam, Marilyn Ziebarth, and Connie Field. "Rosie the Riveter: Photo Essay." *Society* 21 (March/April 1984): 75–78.

Franks, Kenny A. "'Goodbye, Dear, I'll Be Back in a Year': The Mobilization of the Oklahoma National Guard for World War II." *Chronicles of Oklahoma* 69 (Winter 1992): 340–66.

Frederick, John T. "Town and City in Iowa Fiction: The Nineteen Forties." *Palimpsest* 35 (February 1954): 85–97.

Gabin, Nancy. "The Hand That Rocks the Cradle Can Build Tractors, Too." *Michigan History Magazine* (March/April 1992): 12–21.

Gordon, Susan L. "Home Front Tennessee: The World War II Experience." *Tennessee Historical Quarterly* 51 (Spring 1992): 3–18.

Hale, Duane K. "American Indians in World War II." *Chronicles of Oklahoma* 69 (Winter 1992): 408–22.

Harrison, Mark. "Resource Mobilization for World War II: The U.S.A., U.S.S.R., and Germany, 1938–1945." *Economic History Review* 41 (May 1988): 171–92.

Hartmann, Susan M. "Prescriptions for Penelope: Literature on Women's Obligations to Returning World War II Veterans." *Women's Studies* 5 (1978): 223–39.

Hartzell, Karl D. "New York State and World War II: Preserving the Record." *New York History* 73 (July 1992): 321–36.

Hearst, Gladys Whitley. "The WAVES at Cedar Falls." *Palimpsest* 28 (December 1947): 367–76.

Heath, Jim F. "Domestic America during World War II: Research Opportunities for Historians." *Journal of American History* 58 (September 1971): 384–414.

Hewitt, William L. "Mexican Workers in Wyoming during World War II: Necessity, Discrimination and Protest." *Annals of Wyoming* 54 (Fall 1982): 20–33.

Hoadley, Ruth L. "Industrial Growth of Iowa." *Iowa Studies in Business,* vol. 2. Bureau of Business Research. Iowa City: State University of Iowa, May 1928.

Honey, Maureen. "The Working-Class Woman and Recruitment Propaganda during World War II: Class Differences in the Portrayal of War Work." *Signs: Journal of Women in Culture and Society* 8 (Summer 1983): 672–87.

Johnson, A. N. "The Impact of Farm Machinery on the Farm Economy." *Agricultural History* 24 (January 1950): 58–62.

Johnson, Keach. "Iowa's Industrial Roots, 1890–1910." *Annals of Iowa* 44 (Winter 1978): 163–81.

Karolevitz, Robert F. "Life on the Home Front: South Dakota in World War II." *South Dakota History* 19 (Fall 1989): 392–423.

Kessler-Harris, Alice. "Rosie the Riveter: Who Was She?" *Labor History* 24 (Spring 1983): 249–53.

Kimeldorf, Howard. "World War II and the Deradicalization of American Labor: The ILWU as a Deviant Case." *Labor History* 33 (Spring 1992): 248–78.

Kirkendall, Richard S. "Harry S Truman: A Missouri Farmer in the Golden Age." *Agricultural History* 48 (October 1974): 467–83.

Kossoudiji, Sherrie A., and Laura J. Dresser. "Working Class Rosies: Women Industrial Workers during World War II." *The Journal of Economic History* 52 (June 1992): 431–45.

Larson, George A. "Nebraska's World War II Bomber Plant: The Glenn L. Martin–Nebraska Company." *Nebraska History* 74 (Spring 1993): 32–43.

Laurie, Clayton D. "Goebbels's Iowan: Frederick W. Kaltenback and Nazi Short-Wave Radio Broadcasts to America, 1939–1945." *Annals of Iowa* 53 (Summer 1994): 219–45.

Leonard, Stephen J. "Denver at War: The Home Front in World War II." *Colorado Heritage,* no. 4 (1987): 30–39.

Lichtenstein, Nelson. "The Making of the Postwar Working Class: Cultural Pluralism and Social Structure in World War II." *Historian* 51 (November 1988): 42–63.

Lobdell, George H. "A Tale of Two Christmases at the Algona Prisoner-of-War Camp." *Palimpsest* 73 (Winter 1992): 171–85.

Lovin, Clifford R. "Farm Women in the Third Reich." *Agricultural History* 60 (Summer 1986): 105–23.

Marshall, Gordon. "Hired Men: Iowa's Unsung Farm Resource." *Palimpsest* 74 (Winter 1993): 146–55.

Mauk, Genevieve Powlison. "The Council Bluffs Story: Kanesville." *Palimpsest* 42 (September 1961): 385–98.

May, George S. "Post-War Road Problems." *Palimpsest* 36 (January 1955): 52–65.

——. "Recent Industrial Development." *Palimpsest* 37 (May 1956): 229–32.

McConaghy, Lorraine. "Wartime Boomtown: Kirland, Washington, a Small Town during World War II." *Pacific Northwest Quarterly* 80 (April 1989): 42–51.

McDaniel, George William. "World War II Comes to Davenport." *Palimpsest* 73 (Summer 1992): 89–96.

Miller, Marc. "Working Women and World War II." *New England Quarterly* 53 (1980): 42–61.

Murray, William G. "Iowa Land Values—War, Technology, Farm Values." *Palimpsest* 48 (October 1967): 481–86.

Nichols, Harry E. "Apple Varieties in Iowa, 1800–1970." *Annals of Iowa* 43 (Fall 1975): 81–102.

Noble, Annette Chambers. "Utah's Rosies: Women in the Utah War Industries during World War II." *Utah Historical Quarterly* 59 (Spring 1991): 123–45.

O'Brien, Patrick G., Thomas D. Isern, and R. Daniel Lumley. "Stalag Sunflower: German Prisoners of War in Kansas." *Kansas Quarterly, A Journal of the Central Plains* 7 (Autumn 1984): 182–98.

Otey, George N. "New Deal for Oklahoma's Children: Federal Day Care Centers, 1933–1946." *Chronicles of Oklahoma* 62 (Fall 1984): 296–311.

Palimpsest Editorial Department. "Iowa Industries: Farm-Centered Industries and Other Industries." *Palimpsest* 37 (May 1956): 233–89.

Palimpsest Editorial Department. "Some Thoughts on Prisoners of War in Iowa, 1943–1946." *Palimpsest* 65 (March/April 1984): 68–80.

Palimpsest Editorial Department. "Two Iowa Soldiers, Two Individual Stories." *Palimpsest* 76 (Winter 1995): 192–93.

Palimpsest Editorial Department. "War, Conflict, or Campaign." *Palimpsest* 53 (April 1972): 185–224.

Pavalko, Eliza K., and Glen H. Elder, Jr. "World War II and Divorce: A Life Course Perspective." *American Journal of Sociology* 95 (March 1990): 1213–34.

Petersen, William J. "Industry in 1840." *Palimpsest* 37 (May 1956): 225–28.

Polenberg, Richard. "The Good War? A Reappraisal of How World War II Affected American Society." *Virginia Magazine of History and Biography* 100 (July 1992): 295–322.

Power, Marilyn. "From Home Production to Wage Labor: Women as a Reserve Army of Labor." *Review of Radical Political Economics* 15 (Spring 1983): 71–91.

Riley, Glenda, and Richard S. Kirkendall. "Henry A. Wallace and the Mystique of the Farm Male, 1921–1933." *Annals of Iowa* 48 (Summer/Fall 1985): 32–55.

Rooker, Oliver E. "Supplying the Civilians: A Photo Essay of World War II Ration Stamps." *Chronicles of Oklahoma* 69 (Winter 1992): 430–41.

Rosen, Jerold A. "Henry A. Wallace and American Liberal Politics, 1945–1948." *Annals of Iowa* 44 (Fall 1978): 462–74.

Ross, Earl D. "Farm Tenancy in Iowa." *Annals of Iowa* 31 (July 1951): 36–40.

Rutland, Robert. "Iowa in 1952: The Web of Life." *Palimpsest* 34 (July 1953): 325–36.

Sage, Leland L. "Rural Iowa in the 1920s and 1930s: Roots of the Farm Depression." *Annals of Iowa* 47 (Fall 1983): 91–103.

Schmidt, Louis B. "The Farm Bureau." *Palimpsest* 31 (April 1950): 148–62.

Schoenbaum, Tamara Holtermann. "Coming of Age under Hitler, Truman, and Stalin." *Palimpsest* 76 (Winter 1995): 182–91.

Schwieder, Dorothy. "Rural Iowa in the 1920s: Conflict and Continuity." *Annals of Iowa* 47 (Fall 1983): 104–15.

Smetak, Jacqueline. "Women on the Home Front: The Iowa WIPEs." *Palimpsest* 76 (Winter 1995): 174–81.

Spitzer, Alan B. "A Historian's Memory of the Second World War." *Palimpsest* 76 (Winter 1995): 162–73.

Swierenga, Robert P. "Theoretical Perspectives on the New Rural History: From Environmentalism to Modernism." *Agricultural History* 56 (July 1982): 495–502.

Throne, Mildred. "Iowa Politics, 1916–1948." *Palimpsest* 33 (October 1952): 334–37.

Tobias, Sheila, and Lisa Anderson. "Whatever Happened to Rosie the Riveter?" *Ms.* 1 (June 1973): 92–97.

Waite, Paul J. "Outstanding Iowa Storms." *Annals of Iowa* 40 (Winter 1970): 194–209.

Warren, Wilson J. "The 'People's Century' in Iowa: Coalition-Building among Farm and Labor Organizations, 1945–1950." *Annals of Iowa* 49 (Summer 1988): 371–93.

Westbrook, Robert. "Horrors—Theirs and Ours: The *Politics* Circle and the Good War." *Radical History Review* 36 (1986): 9–25.

———. "'I Want a Girl, Just Like the Girl That Married Harry James': American Women and the Problem of Political Obligation in World War II." *American Quarterly* 42 (December 1990): 587–611.

Wik, Reynold. "The American Farm Tractor as Father of the Military Tank." *Agricultural History* 54 (January 1980): 126–33.

Zagel, Henrietta. "The Iowa BPW—1919–1970." *Palimpsest* 52 (March 1971): 129–42.

Books, Theses, and Dissertations

Abrahamson, James L. *The American Home Front: Revolutionary War, Civil War, World War I, World War II.* Washington, DC: National Defense University Press, 1983.

Adams, Michael C. C. *The Best War Ever: America and World War II.* Baltimore: John Hopkins University Press, 1994.

Albrecht, Donald, ed. *World War II and the American Dream: How Wartime Building Changed a Nation.* Cambridge: MIT Press, 1995.

Alsop, Joseph. *FDR—1882–1945: A Centenary Remembrance.* New York: Viking, 1982.

Ambrose, Stephen E. *Americans at War.* Jackson: University Press of Mississippi, 1997.

———. *Citizen Soldiers: The U.S. Army from the Normandy Beaches to the Bulge to the Surrender of Germany, June 7, 1944–May 7, 1945.* New York: Simon & Schuster, 1997.

———. *Eisenhower: Soldier and President.* New York: Simon & Schuster, 1991.

———. *The Supreme Commander: The War Years of General Dwight D. Eisenhower.* Garden City, NY: Doubleday, 1970.

Anderson, Karen. *Wartime Women: Sex Roles, Family Relationships, and the Status of Women during World War II.* Westport, CT: Greenwood, 1981.

Andre, Rae. *Homemakers: The Forgotten Workers.* Chicago: University of Chicago Press, 1981.

Andrews, Clarence A. *This Is Iowa: A Cavalcade of the Tall Corn State.* Iowa City: Midwest Heritage, 1982.

Ankrum, Homer R. *Dogfaces Who Smiled Through Tears: The 34th Red Bull Infantry Division.* Lake Mills, IA: Graphic Publishing, 1987.

Arnold, Eleanor, ed. *Voices of American Homemakers.* Bloomington, IN: Indiana University Press, 1985.

Bailey, Ronald H., and the Editors of *Time-Life* Books. *The Home Front: U.S.A.* Alexandria, VA: *Time-Life* Books, 1977.

Baker, M. Joyce. *Images of Women in Film: The War Years, 1941–1945.* Ann Arbor, MI: UMI Research Press, 1978.

Baldwin, Hanson W. *The Crucial Years, 1939–1941: The World at War.* New York: Harper & Row, 1976.

Barker, A. J. *Midway.* New York: Galahad Books, 1981.

———. *Okinawa.* New York: Galahad Books, 1981.

Beard, Charles A. *President Roosevelt and the Coming of War, 1941: A Study in Appearances and Realities.* New Haven: Yale University Press, 1948.

Beck, Earl R. *The European Home Fronts, 1939–1945.* Arlington Heights, IL: Harlan Davidson, 1993.

Beneria, Lourdes, and Catharine R. Stimpson, eds. *Women, Households, and the Economy.* New Brunswick: Rutgers University Press, 1987.

Bennett, Mary. *An Iowa Album: A Photographic History, 1860–1920.* Iowa City: University of Iowa Press, 1990.
Bergman, Marvin, ed. *Iowa History Reader.* Ames: State Historical Society of Iowa in association with the Iowa State University Press, 1996.
Bernstein, Irving. *Turbulent Years: A History of the American Worker, 1933–1941.* Boston: Houghton Mifflin, 1970.
Bied, Dan. *Encore . . . Burlington Revisited.* Burlington, IA: Craftsman, 1976.
Birkby, Evelyn. *Neighboring on the Air: Cooking with the KMA Radio Homemakers.* Iowa City: University of Iowa Press, 1991.
Blum, John Morton. *V Was for Victory: Politics and American Culture during World War II.* New York: Harcourt Brace Jovanovich, 1976.
Braverman, Jordan. *To Hasten the Homecoming: How Americans Fought World War II through the Media.* New York: Madison Books, 1996.
Brinkley, Douglas, ed. *The New York Times Living History: World War II, 1939–1942: The Axis Assault.* New York: Times Books, 2003.
Brooks, Lester. *Behind Japan's Surrender: The Secret Struggle That Ended an Empire.* Stamford, CT: Veritas Books, 1968.
Buchanan, A. Russell. *Black Americans in World War II.* Santa Barbara, CA: Clio Books, 1977.
Buhite, Russel D., and David W. Levy. *FDR's Fireside Chats.* Norman: University of Oklahoma Press, 1992.
Burns, E. Bradford. *Kinship with the Land: Regionalist Thought in Iowa, 1894–1942.* Iowa City: University of Iowa Press, 1996.
Burns, James MacGregor. *Roosevelt: The Lion and the Fox.* New York: Harcourt, Brace, 1956.
——. *Roosevelt: The Soldier of Freedom.* New York: Harcourt Brace Jovanovich, 1970.
Butterfield, Ralph, ed. *Patton's GI Photographers.* Ames: Iowa State University Press, 1992.
Campbell, D'Ann. *Women at War with America: Private Lives in a Patriotic Era.* Cambridge: Harvard University Press, 1984.
Cardozier, V. R. *The Mobilization of the United States in World War II: How the Government, Military and Industry Prepared for War.* Jefferson, NC: McFarland, 1995.
Carr, Lowell Juilliard, and James Edson Stermer. *Willow Run: A Study of Industrialization and Cultural Inadequacy.* New York: Harper, 1952.

Casdorph, Paul. *Let the Good Times Roll: Life at Home in America during World War II.* New York: Paragon House, 1989.
Cavnes, Max Parvin. *The Hoosier Community at War.* Bloomington, IN: Indiana University Press, 1961.
Churchill, Winston S. *Memoirs of the Second World War: An Abridgement of the Six Volumes of "The Second World War."* Boston: Houghton Mifflin, 1991.
Clive, Alan. *State of War: Michigan in World War II.* Ann Arbor: University of Michigan Press, 1979.
Cohen, Stan. *V for Victory: America's Home Front during World War II.* Missoula, MT: Pictorial Histories Publishing, 1991.
Cole, Wayne S. *America First: The Battle against Intervention, 1940–1941.* Madison: University of Wisconsin Press, 1953.
——. *Roosevelt and the Isolationists, 1932–1945.* Lincoln: University of Nebraska Press, 1983.
Collier, Richard. *1940: The World in Flames.* London: Hamish Hamilton, 1979.
——. *The Road to Pearl Harbor: 1941.* New York: Bonanza Books, 1981.
Cowan, Ruth Schwartz. *More Work for Mother: The Ironies of Household Technology from the Open Hearth to the Microwave.* New York: Basic Books, 1983.
Danbom, David B. *The Resisted Revolution: Urban America and the Industrialization of Agriculture, 1900–1930.* Ames: Iowa State University Press, 1979.
Daniels, Jonathan. *The Time between the Wars: Armistice to Pearl Harbor.* Garden City, NY: Doubleday, 1966.
Darling, Jay N. *Ding's Half Century.* Ed. John M. Henry. New York: Duell, Sloan, and Pearce, 1962.
Davis, Kenneth S. *Experience of War: The United States in World War II.* Garden City, NY: Doubleday, 1965.
DeMirgian, Arlo, Jr., and Eve Nelson, eds. *Front Page History of the World Wars as Reported by the New York Times.* New York: Arno, 1976.
Dennis, James M. *Grant Wood: A Study in American Art and Culture.* New York: Viking, 1975.
Derr, Nancy Ruth. *Iowans during World War I: A Study of Change under Stress.* Ph.D. diss., George Washington University, 1979.
Dick, Bernard F. *The Star-Spangled Screen: The American World War II*

Film. Lexington: University Press of Kentucky, 1985.

Diggins, John Patrick. *The Proud Decades: America in War and Peace, 1941–1960.* New York: W. W. Norton, 1988.

Divine, Robert A. *The Reluctant Belligerent: American Entry into World War II.* New York: John Wiley & Sons, 1965.

Dodds, Robert Hungerford. *World War II Construction and Construction Problems at the Navy's Continental Ammunition Depots.* M.S. thesis, Iowa State College, 1946.

Doherty, Thomas. *Projections of War: Hollywood, American Culture, and World War II.* New York: Columbia University Press, 1993.

Doubler, Michael D. *Closing with the Enemy: How GIs Fought the War in Europe, 1944–1945.* Lawrence: University Press of Kansas, 1994.

Dower, John W. *War without Mercy: Race and Power in the Pacific War.* New York: Pantheon Books, 1986.

Duis, Perry R., and Scott LaFrance. *We've Got a Job to Do: Chicagoans and World War II.* Chicago: Chicago Historical Society, 1992.

Elizabeth, Mary. *War Time Recipes.* New York: Frederick A. Stokes, 1918.

Ellis, John. *The Sharp End of War: The Fighting Man in World War II.* London: David & Charles, 1980.

Erenberg, Lewis A., and Susan E. Hirsch. *The War in American Culture: Society and Consciousness during World War II.* Chicago: University of Chicago Press, 1996.

Fink, Deborah. *Agrarian Women: Wives and Mothers in Rural Nebraska, 1880–1940.* Chapel Hill, NC: University of North Carolina Press, 1992.

——. *Open Country, Iowa: Rural Women, Tradition and Change.* New York: State University of New York, 1986.

Fite, Gilbert C. *American Farmers: The New Minority.* Bloomington, IN: Indiana University Press, 1981.

Fleming, Peter. *Operation Sea Lion: The Projected Invasion of England in 1940.* New York: Simon & Schuster, 1957.

Flynn, George. *The Draft, 1940–1973.* Lawrence: University Press of Kansas, 1993.

Fox, Frank W. *Madison Avenue Goes to War: The Strange Military Career of American Advertising, 1941–1945.* Charles E. Merrill Monograph Series in the Humanities and Social Sciences, vol. 4, no. 1. Provo, UT: Brigham Young University, 1975.

Frank, Miriam, Marilyn Ziebarth, and Connie Field. *The Life and Times of Rosie the Riveter: The Story of Three Million Working Women during World War II.* Emeryville, CA: Clarity Educational Productions, 1982.

Freidel, Frank. *Franklin D. Roosevelt: A Rendezvous with Destiny.* Boston: Little, Brown, 1990.

Fromkin, David. *In the Time of the Americans: FDR, Truman, Eisenhower, Marshall, MacArthur—The Generation That Changed America's Role in the World.* New York: Alfred A. Knopf, 1995.

Funk, A. B. *Fred L. Maytag: A Biography.* Cedar Rapids, IA: Torch, 1936.

Fussell, Paul. *Wartime: Understanding and Behavior in the Second World War.* New York: Oxford University Press, 1989.

Fyne, Robert. *The Hollywood Propaganda of World War II.* Lanham, MD: Scarecrow, 1994.

Gabin, Nancy F. *Feminism in the Labor Movement: Women and the United Auto Workers, 1935–1975.* Ithaca, NY: Cornell University Press, 1990.

Gansberg, Judith M. *Stalag U.S.A.: The Remarkable Story of German POWs in America.* New York: Thomas Y. Cromwell, 1977.

Gilbert, James. *Another Chance: Postwar America, 1945–1968.* Philadelphia: Temple University Press, 1981.

Gilbert, Martin. *The Day the War Ended: May 8, 1945—Victory in Europe.* New York: Henry Holt, 1995.

——. *The Second World War: A Complete History.* New York: Henry Holt, 1989.

Gluck, Sherna Berger. *Rosie the Riveter Revisited: Women, the War and Social Change.* Boston: Twayne Publishers, 1987.

Gold, Bela. *Wartime Economic Planning in Agriculture: A Study in the Allocation of Resources.* New York: Columbia University Press, 1949.

Goldhagen, Daniel Jonah. *Hitler's Willing Executioners: Ordinary Germans and the Holocaust.* New York: Alfred A. Knopf, 1996.

Goodwin, Doris Kearns. *No Ordinary Time: Franklin and Eleanor Roosevelt, The Home Front in World War II.* New York: Simon & Schuster, 1994.

Gough, Phyllis Elvira. *Tasks Done by 100 Iowa State College Freshmen Women Living on Farms during 1942 in Iowa and Surrounding States.* M.S. thesis, Iowa State College, 1943.

Graebner, William S. *The Age of Doubt: American Thought and Culture in the 1940s.* Boston: Twayne Publishers, 1991.

Graham, Nan Wood, with John Zug and Julie Jensen McDonald. *My Brother, Grant Wood.* Iowa City: State Historical Society of Iowa, 1993.

Gregory, Chester W. *Women in Defense Work during World War II: An Analysis of the Labor Problem and Women's Rights.* New York: Exposition, 1974.

Gregory, Ross. *America in 1941: A Nation at the Crossroads.* New York: Free Press, 1989.

Gruhzit-Hoyt, Olga. *They Also Served: America Women in World War II.* New York: Birch Lane, 1995.

Hamby, Alonzo L. *Man of the People: A Life of Harry S. Truman.* New York: Oxford University Press, 1995.

Handy, Amy. *War Food: Practical and Economical Methods of Keeping Vegetables, Fruits and Meats.* Boston: Houghton Mifflin, 1917.

Harris, Mark Jonathan, Franklin D. Mitchell, and Steven J. Schechter. *Homefront: America during World War II.* New York: G. P. Putnam's Sons, 1984.

Hartmann, Susan M. *The Home Front and Beyond: American Women in the 1940s.* Boston: Twayne Publishers, 1982.

Hartzell, Karl Drew. *The Empire State at War.* New York: State of New York, 1949.

Hastings, Max. *Victory in Europe: D-Day to V-E Day.* Boston: Little, Brown, 1985.

Heacock, Nan. *Battle Stations! The Homefront World War II.* Ames: Iowa State University Press, 1992.

Heide, Robert, and John Gilman. *Home Front America: Popular Culture of the World War II Era.* San Francisco: Chronicle Books, 1995.

Heinrichs, Waldo. *Threshold of War: Franklin D. Roosevelt and American Entry into World War II.* New York: Oxford University Press, 1988.

Heller, Joseph. *Catch-22.* New York: Simon & Schuster, 1955.

Herridge, Charles. *Pictorial History of World War II.* New York: Hamlyn Publishing, 1975.

Herzstein, Robert Edwin. *Roosevelt and Hitler: Prelude to War.* New York: Paragon House, 1989.

Higonnet, Margaret Randolph, Jane Jensen, Sonya Michel, and Margaret Collins Weitz, eds. *Behind the Lines: Gender and the Two World Wars.* New Haven: Yale University Press, 1987.

Hill, Reuben. *Families under Stress: Adjustment to the Crises of War.* New York: Harper & Brothers, 1949.

Hoehling, A. A. *America's Road to War: 1939–1941.* New York: Abelard-Schuman, 1970.

Hogg, Ian. *Decisive Battles: The Turning Points of World War II.* New York: Gallery Books, 1986.

Holsinger, M. Paul, and Mary Anne Schofield. *Visions of War: World War II in Popular Literature and Culture.* Bowling Green, OH: Bowling Green State University, 1992.

Honey, Maureen. *Creating Rosie the Riveter: Class, Gender, and Propaganda during World War II.* Amherst: University of Massachusetts Press, 1984.

Hoopes, Roy. *Americans Remember the Home Front: An Oral Narrative.* New York: Hawthorn Books, 1977.

Hoover, Robert, and John Hoover. *An American Quality Legend: How Maytag Saved Our Moms, Vexed the Competition, and Presaged America's Quality Revolution.* New York: McGraw-Hill, 1993.

Houlette, William. *Iowa: The Pioneer Heritage.* Des Moines: Wallace-Homestead, 1970.

Huggett, Frank E. *"Goodnight Sweetheart": Songs and Memories of the Second World War.* London: W. H. Allen, 1979.

Iriye, Akira. *Power and Culture: The Japanese-American War, 1941–1945.* Cambridge: Harvard University Press, 1981.

James, D. Clayton, and Anne Sharp Wells. *From Pearl Harbor to V-J Day: The American Armed Forces in World War II.* Chicago: Ivan R. Dee, 1995.

Jonas, Manfred. *Isolationism in America, 1935–1941.* Ithaca, NY: Cornell University Press, 1966.

Jones, Jacqueline. *Labor of Love, Labor of Sorrow: Black Women, Work, and the Family, from Slavery to the Present.* New York: Vintage Books, 1985.

Kee, Robert. *1945: The World We Fought For.* Boston: Little, Brown, 1985.

Keegan, John. *The Second World War.* New York: Penguin Books, 1989.

Kennedy, David M. *Freedom from Fear: The American People in Depression and War, 1929–1945.* New York: Oxford University Press, 1999.

Kennett, Lee. *For the Duration . . . The United States Goes to War, Pearl Harbor–1942.* New York: Charles Scribner's Sons, 1985.

———. *G. I.: The American Soldier in World War II.* New York: Charles Scribner's Sons, 1987.

Kesselman, Amy. *Fleeting Opportunities: Women Shipyard Workers in Portland and Vancouver during World War II and Reconversion.* Albany: State University of New York Press, 1990.

Kessler, Lauren. *Stubborn Twig: Three Generations in the Life of a Japanese-American Family.* New York: Random House, 1993.

Ketchum, Richard M. *The Borrowed Years, 1938–1941: America on the Way to War.* New York: Random House, 1989.

Kimball, Warren F. *Forged in War: Roosevelt, Churchill, and the Second World War.* New York: Morrow, 1997.

———. *The Juggler: Franklin Roosevelt as Wartime Statesman.* Princeton, NJ: Princeton University Press, 1991.

Kingaman, William K. *1941: Our Lives in a World on the Edge.* New York: Harper & Row, 1988.

Kurzman, Dan. *Left to Die: The Tragedy of the* U.S.S. Juneau. New York: Pocket Books, 1994.

Kyvig, David E., and Myron A. Marty. *Nearby History: Exploring the Past around You.* Nashville: American Association for State and Local History, 1982.

Larrabee, Eric. *Commander in Chief: Franklin Delano Roosevelt, His Lieutenants, and Their War.* New York: Simon & Schuster, 1987.

Larson, T. A. *Wyoming's War Years, 1941–1945.* Laramie: University of Wyoming Press, 1954.

Lee, Harold. *Roswell Garst—A Biography.* Ames: Iowa State University Press, 1984.

Lee, Robert Edson. *To the War.* New York: Alfred A. Knopf, 1968.

Lemert, Ann Arnold. *First You Take a Pick and Shovel—The Story of the Mason Companies.* Lexington, KY: John Bradford, 1979.

Lendt, David L. *The Life of Jay Norwood Darling.* Ames: Iowa State University Press, 1979.

Leuchtenburg, William E. *Franklin D. Roosevelt and the New Deal.* New York: Harper & Row, 1963.

———. *The Perils of Prosperity, 1914–1932.* Chicago: University of Chicago Press, 1958.

Lichtenstein, Nelson. *Labor's War at Home: The CIO in World War II.* Cambridge, MA: Cambridge University Press, 1982.

Lifton, Robert Jay, and Greg Mitchell. *Hiroshima in America: Fifty Years of Denial.* New York: G. P. Putnam's Sons, 1995.

Lindbergh, Anne Morrow. *War Within and Without: Diaries and Letters of Anne Morrow Lindbergh, 1939–1944.* New York: Harcourt Brace Jovanovich, 1980.

Linderman, Gerald F. *The World within War: America's Combat Experience in World War II.* New York: Free Press, 1997.

Lingeman, Richard R. *Don't You Know There's a War On? The American Home Front, 1941–1945.* New York: G. P. Putnam's Songs, 1970.

Lipstadt, Deborah E. *Beyond Belief: The American Press and the Coming of the Holocaust, 1933–1945.* New York: Free Press, 1986.

Litoff, Judy Barrett, and David C. Smith, eds. *American Women in a World at War: Contemporary Accounts from World War II.* Wilmington, DE: Scholarly Resources, 1997.

——, eds. *Since You Went Away: World War II Letters from American Women on the Home Front.* New York: Oxford University Press, 1991.

Longmate, Norman, ed. *The Home Front: An Anthology of Personal Experience, 1938–1945.* London: Chatto & Windus, 1981.

Lord, Russell. *The Wallaces of Iowa.* Boston: Houghton Mifflin, 1947.

Macdonald, Dwight. *Henry Wallace: The Man and the Myth.* New York: Vanguard, 1982.

Madison County Genealogical Society. *Madison County, Iowa.* Dallas, TX: Taylor Publishing, 1984.

Madson, John. *Where the Sky Began: Land of the Tallgrass Prairie.* Ames: Iowa State University Press, 1982.

Malos, Ellen, ed. *The Politics of Housework.* London: Allison & Busby Limited, 1980.

Maney, Patrick J. *The Roosevelt Presence: A Biography of Franklin Delano Roosevelt.* New York: Twayne Publishers, 1992.

Margolin, Victor, ed. *Propaganda: The Art of Persuasion, World War II.* New York: Chelsea House Publishers, 1976.

Markowitz, Norman D. *The Rise and Fall of the People's Century: Henry A. Wallace and American Liberalism, 1941–1948.* New York: Free Press, 1973.

Matusow, Allen J. *Farm Policies and Politics in the Truman Years.* Cambridge: Harvard University Press, 1967.

McCullough, David G., ed. *The American Heritage Picture History of World War II.* New York: Crown Publishers, 1966.

McDonald, Julie. *Ruth Buxton Sayre: First Lady of the Farm.* Ames: Iowa State University Press, 1980.

McJimsey, George. *Harry Hopkins: Ally of the Poor and Defender of Democracy.* Cambridge: Harvard University Press, 1987.

Milkman, Ruth. *Gender at Work: The Dynamics of Job Segregation by Sex during World War II.* Chicago: University of Illinois Press, 1987.

Miller, Lee G. *An Ernie Pyle Album: Indiana to Ie Shima.* New York: William Sloane Associates, 1946.

——. *The Story of Ernie Pyle.* New York: Viking, 1950.

Miller, Marc Scott. *The Irony of Victory: World War II and Lowell, Massachusetts.* Urbana: University of Illinois Press, 1988.

Miller, Sally M., and Daniel A. Cornford, eds. *American Labor in the Era of World War II.* Westport, CT: Greenwood, 1995.

Minns, Rayness. *Bombers and Mash: The Domestic Front, 1939–1945.* London: Virago Limited, 1980.

Mitchell, Allan, ed. *The Nazi Revolution.* Lexington, MA: Heath, 1990.

Morain, Thomas J., ed. *Family Reunion: Essays on Iowa.* Ames: Iowa State University Press, 1995.

Moskin, J. Robert. *Mr. Truman's War: The Final Victories of World War II and the Birth of the Postwar World.* New York: Random House, 1996.

Nash, Gerald D. *The Crucial Era: The Great Depression and World War II, 1929–1945.* New York: St. Martin's, 1992.

Noakes, Jeremy, ed. *The Civilian in War: The Home Front in Europe, Japan, and the USA in World War II.* Exeter, UK: University of Exeter Press, 1992.

Novick, David, Melvin Anshen, and W. C. Truppner. *Wartime Production Controls.* New York: Columbia University Press, 1949.

Oakley, Ann. *The Sociology of Housework.* Bath, UK: Pitman, 1974.

O'Brien, Kenneth Paul, and Lynn Hudson Parsons, eds. *The Home-Front War: World War II and American Society.* Westport, CT: Greenwood, 1995.

O'Neill, William L. *A Democracy at War: America's Fight at Home and Abroad in World War II.* Cambridge, MA: Harvard University Press, 1993.

Overy, Richard. *The Road to War.* With Andrew Wheatcroft. London: BBC Books, 1989.

——. *Why the Allies Won.* New York: W. W. Norton, 1997.

Parker, Matthew. *Monte Cassino: The Hardest-Fought Battle of World War II.* New York: Doubleday, 2004.

Parrish, Thomas. *Roosevelt and Marshall: Partners in Politics and War.* New York: William Morrow, 1989.

Perret, Geoffrey. *A Country Made by War: From the Revolution to Vietnam—The Story of America's Rise to Power.* New York: Random House, 1989.

——. *Days of Sadness, Years of Triumph: The American People, 1939–1945.* New York: Coward, McCann & Geoghegan, 1973.

——. *Old Soldiers Never Die: The Life of Douglas MacArthur.* New York: Random House, 1996.

——. *There's a War to Be Won: The United States Army in World War II.* New York: Random House, 1991.

Phillips, Cabell. *The 1940s: Decade of Triumph and Trouble.* New York: Macmillan, 1975.

Plante, Ellen M. *The American Kitchen, 1700 to the Present: From Hearth to Highrise.* New York: Facts on File, 1995.

Polan, Dana. *Power and Paranoia: History, Narrative, and the American Cinema, 1940–1950.* New York: Columbia University Press, 1986.

Polenberg, Richard, ed. *America at War: The Home Front, 1941–1945.* Englewood Cliffs, NJ: Prentice-Hall, 1968.

——. *One Nation Divisible: Class, Race, and Ethnicity in the United States since 1938.* New York: Viking, 1980.

——. *War and Society: The United States, 1941–1945.* Philadelphia: J. B. Lippincott, 1972.

Ponting, Clive. *1940: Myth and Reality.* Chicago: Ivan R. Dee, 1991.

Puckett, Susan. *A Cook's Tour of Iowa.* Iowa City: University of Iowa Press, 1990.

Rhodes, Richard. *The Making of the Atomic Bomb.* New York: Simon & Schuster, 1986.

Rifkind, Carole. *Main Street: The Face of Urban America.* New York: Harper & Row, 1977.

Roll, David L., and Keith D. McFarland. *Louis Johnson and the Arming of America: The Roosevelt and Truman Years.* Indianapolis: Indiana University Press, 2005.

Rose, Mary Swartz. *Everday Foods in War.* New York: Macmillan, 1918.

Ross, Earle D. *Iowa Agriculture: An Historical Survey.* Ames: Iowa State College Press, 1951.

Rupp, Leila J. *Mobilizing Women for War: German and American Propaganda, 1939–1945.* Princeton, NJ: Princeton University Press, 1978.

Sage, Leland L. *A History of Iowa.* Ames: Iowa State University Press, 1974.

Satterfield, Archie. *The Home Front: An Oral History of the War Years in America, 1941–1945.* New York: Playboy Press, 1981.

Satterfield, John R. *We Band of Brothers: The Sullivans and World War II.* Parkersburg, IA: Mid-Prairie Books, 1995.

Schapsmeier, Edward L., and Frederick H. Schapsmeier. *Henry A. Wallace of Iowa: The Agrarian Years, 1910–1940.* Ames: Iowa State University Press, 1968.

Schwieder, Dorothy. *Iowa—The Middle Land.* Ames: Iowa State University Press, 1996.

———. *Seventy-five Years of Service: Cooperative Extension in Iowa.* Ames: Iowa State University Press, 1993.

Sciancalepore, Donna Marie. *The Contribution of Working Women of Waterloo during World War II.* M.A. thesis, University of Northern Iowa, 1990.

Seidman, Joel. *American Labor from Defense to Reconversion.* Chicago: University of Chicago Press, 1953.

Sherman, William L., ed. *Iowa's Country Schools: Landmarks of Learning.* Parkersburg, IA: Iowa State Education Association and Mid-Prairie Books, 1998.

Shindler, Colin. *Hollywood Goes to War: Films and American Society, 1939–1952.* London: Routledge & Kegan Paul, 1979.

Shirer, William L. *The Rise and Fall of the Third Reich: A History of Nazi Germany.* New York: Simon & Shuster, 1959.

Simpson, Elizabath, ed. *The Spoils of War. World War II and Its Aftermath: The Loss, Reappearance, and Recovery of Cultural Property.* New York: Harry N. Abrams, 1997.

Skahill, Jim. *Way Back When! 1924–1944. Hundreds of Characters Stumbling through the Great Depression.* Privately printed, 1991. Iowa Authors Collection, University of Iowa Special Collections, University of Iowa Libraries.

Smith, Bruce C. *The War Comes to Plum Street.* Indianapolis: Indiana University Press, 2005.

Smith, C. Calvin. *War and Wartime Changes: The Transformation of Arkansas, 1940–1945.* Fayetteville: University of Arkansas Press, 1986.

Stadtfeld, Curtis K. *From the Land and Back.* New York: Charles Scribner's Sons, 1972.

Steinbeck, John. *Once There Was a War.* New York: Viking, 1958.

Stock, Catherine McNicol. *Main Street in Crisis: The Great Depression and the Old Middle Class on the Northern Plains.* Chapel Hill, NC: University of North Carolina Press, 1992.

Stong, Phil. *State Fair.* New York: Literary Guild, 1932.

Stout, Wesley W. *Mobilized.* Detroit, MI: Chrysler Corporation, 1949.

Strasser, Susan. *Never Done: A History of American Housework.* New York: Pantheon Books, 1982.

Stromquist, Shelton. *Solidarity and Survival: An Oral History of Iowa Labor in the Twentieth Century.* Iowa City: University of Iowa Press, 1993.

Takaki, Ronald. *Hiroshima: Why America Dropped the Atomic Bomb.* Boston: Little, Brown, 1995.

Terkel, Studs. *"The Good War": An Oral History of World War II.* New York: New Press, 1984.

Thomas, Mary Martha. *Riveting and Rationing in Dixie: Alabama Women and the Second World War.* Tuscaloosa: University of Alabama Press, 1987.

Thomson, Harry C., and Lida Mayo. *The Ordnance Department: Procurement and Supply.* Washington, DC: Office of the Chief of Military History, Department of the Army, 1960.

Titus, James, ed. *The Home Front and War in the Twentieth Century: The American Experience in Comparative Perspective.* Proceedings of the Tenth Military History Symposium, United States Air Force Academy, October 20–22, 1982. Washington, DC: U.S. Government Printing Office, 1982.

Tobin, James. *Ernie Pyle's War: America's Eyewitness to World War II.* New York: Free Press, 1997.

Tucker, David M. *Kitchen Gardening in America: A History.* Ames: Iowa State University Press, 1993.

Tuttle, William M., Jr. *"Daddy's Gone to War": The Second World War in the Lives of America's Children.* New York: Oxford University Press, 1993.

Verness, Lucile Driftmier. *The Story of an American Family.* Shenandoah, IA: Driftmier Publishing Co., 1950.

Voss, Frederick S. *Reporting the War: The Journalistic Coverage of World War II.* Washington, DC: Smithsonian Institution Press for the National Portrait Gallery, 1994.

Wall, Joseph Frazier. *Iowa: A Bicentennial History.* New York: W. W. Norton, 1978.

Waller, George M., ed. *Pearl Harbor: Roosevelt and the Coming of the War.* Boston: Heath, 1953.

Walton, Francis. *Miracle of World War II: How American Industry Made Victory Possible.* New York: Macmillan, 1956.

Watters, Mary. *Illinois in the Second World War: Operation Home Front.* Vol. 1. Springfield: Illinois State Historical Library, 1951.

Weatherford, Doris. *American Women and World War II.* New York: Facts on File, 1990.

Whitney, Nathaniel R. *The Sale of War Bonds in Iowa.* Iowa City: State Historical Society of Iowa, 1923.

Wilcox, Walter W. *The Farmer in the Second World War.* Ames: Iowa State College Press, 1947.

Willis, Donald J. *The Incredible Year.* Ames: Iowa State University Press, 1988.

Willmott, H. P. *Pearl Harbor.* New York: Galahad Books, 1981.

Winfield, Betty Houchin. *FDR and the News Media.* Urbana: University of Illinois Press, 1990.

Winkler, Allan M. *Home Front U.S.A.* Arlington Heights, IL: H. Davidson, 1986.

——. *The Politics of Propaganda: The Office of War Information, 1942–1945.* New Haven: Yale University Press, 1978.

Wise, Nancy Baker, and Christy Wise. *A Mouthful of Rivets: Women at Work in World War II.* San Francisco: Jossey-Bass, 1994.

Wright, Gordon. *The Ordeal of Total War, 1939–1945.* New York: Harper & Row, 1968.

Wright, Mike. *What They Didn't Teach You about World War II.* Novata, CA: Presidio, 1998.

Wyman, David S. *Paper Walls: America and the Refugee Crisis, 1938–1941.* Amherst: University of Massachusetts Press, 1968.

Wynn, Neil A. *The Afro-American and the Second World War.* New York: Holmes & Meier, 1976.

Zieger, Robert H. *American Workers, American Unions, 1920–1985.* Baltimore: Johns Hopkins University Press, 1986.

——. *John L. Lewis: Labor Leader.* Boston: Twayne Publishers, 1988.

Zielinkski, John M. *Unknown Iowa: Farm Security Photos, 1936–1941.* Kalona, IA: Photo-Art Gallery Publications, 1977.

Zwicky, John F. *A State at War: The Home Front in Illinois during the Second World War.* Ph.D. diss., Loyola University Chicago, 1989.

Index

About the Author

Dr. Lisa Payne Ossian is professor of history at Des Moines Area Community College in central Iowa. She has had three books published by the University of Missouri Press: *The Home Fronts of Iowa, 1939–1945*; *The Forgotten Generation: American Children and World War II*; and *The Depression Dilemmas of Rural Iowa, 1929–1933.*